EXAKTA CAMERAS

1933-1978

Clément Aguila
&
Michel Rouah

HOVE
COLLECTORS
BOOKS

First Edition 1987
Reprinted 1989
Reprinted 2003

Published by
HOVE COLLECTORS BOOKS
30, The Industrial Estate,
Henfield Road,
Small Dole,
West Sussex, BN5-9XR. U.K.

info@hovebooks.com
Fax: 01273-494992

ISBN 0-906447-38-0

Printed in China by Midas Printing International Ltd
on behalf of Compass Press Ltd.

CONTENTS

ACKNOWLEDGEMENTS

We would like to thank all the following people for their help and painstaking work in collecting the literature and compiling the material:
M. Cipiere, "Photo Cipiere", Paris; Jacques Dalbera, Paris; Alain Escurignan, Anglet; Jean-Pierre & Dominique Francesch, Paris; Guy Lagache, Loos; Peter Lanczak, Leverkusen, West Germany; M. Latour, "Photo Verdeau", Paris; M. Laurent, "Grenelle Photo", Paris; Colette Michel, "Forum Cine Foto", Nice; Walter de Vita, Cannes and Jean-Pierre Salanick, Colombes, for translating the German literature.

PREFACE

To Jean-Francois, for the kindling of a passion.

In 1960 I was 19. That very same year a good friend lent me for a few days an Exakta Varex II which he had just purchased. We had already developed a passionate interest in astronomy and photography during the previous few years. The instrument he had just entrusted to me quite amazed me. Up to that time I had never had the opportunity to look through the reflex viewfinder of such a camera. I soon realised that this model was just part of a system and it was rather like discovering a new world!

I was not a very wealthy student and my limited means enabled me to buy only a distant equivalent a few months later. At that stage I was certainly in a position to experiment with a reflex camera of the modular type, but right from the start I experienced frustration. I soon realized that to my mind nothing would match the prestigious Exakta Varex, and I started entertaining hopes that I might acquire one as soon as my financial situation would allow.

I was not able to treat myself to a replica of the model my friend had lent me until the Autumn of 1968. Of course I was delighted with it.

Soon afterwards, on the occasion of a visit to the workshop of a Parisian gilder, I discovered a twin brother of my "Varex IIa", very conspicuous and obviously in working order, together with another, smaller model which I had not seen before. It proved to be an "Exa" and its owner explained that this model very cleverly completed the the range which then catered near enough for any contingency. Although the Exa was a little more modest, the body could be used as a film magazine with Exakta equipment, a convenience quite familiar to Hasselblad users. This new discovery enabled me to look forward to new and interesting applications. A few days later I saw an example of this model on the Boulevard Beaumarchais and I immediately acquired it.

From then on my photographic results, the convenient handling of the cameras, and my love for the aesthetic qualitie of the equipment gradually encouraged me to explore further into the field.

The years went by and the items I acquired soon became a collection. Except among my close family and friends I felt a certain embarrassment in not following the current trend, which was to acquire the latest model of everything. This meant that my Exaktas and Exas would only leave the shelf to be put in a bag and come out surreptitiously to take the odd snap. Nonetheless those snaps were of excellent quality.

In 1980 a particularly significant event occured in my barely conscious moves to become a reluctant collector. One of my Exaktas, the RTL 1000, happened to be on a shelf in the study where I work. A colleague, who had just came in to discuss a work situation, suddenly displayed a very keen interest in my RTL 1000. He wanted to buy it, quoting the fact that he already owned three other Exakta's, including a whole set of suitable lenses, but also that he was having problems with two of them. Rather than part with my RTL 1000, I offered to repair his equipment. Another reason for my passion is that an Exakta is rarely totally defunct. Although nowadays surpassed and long since obsolete, the technology used in these cameras is so sound and well conceived that, unless its intricate components have been damaged with bad treatment, the skilled and patient technician can very often restore their strength and vigor.

At the time I only had a vague idea of what being a genuine collector of Exaktas could imply. In the light of past correspondence, and through advertising for particular items or bits of information, I had the opportunity to discover a network of collectors which I never suspected existed. Clement Aguila and Michel Rouah became my friends and I found them to be fine collectors of Ihagee equipment, eager to retrace the history of a model through the evolution of its technology. We have also made many foreign friends, too numerous to mention, who are similarly possessed by the same passion as us, and who have never hesitated to share any information they had on the subjects we were interested in.

The idea of writing about Ihagee, and more particularly about the Exakta, had occured to more than one collector throughout the world; articles and monographs on the subject exist in all languages, or at least most of them. This proves that the universe of Exakta enthusiasts is quite wide and for us that is very conforting. But one thing that is certain is that every document that is written adds something new to our previous knowledge. When it comes to Exaktas, and furthermore Ihagee, nobody knows everything.

So why write a preface for this book, and why this book? First of all I would like to thank Clement Aguila and Michel Rouah for the great honour they have given me in asking me to perform this task. To my knowledge no one before them has accomplished such an enterprising task on the subject so thoroughly and in such a documented way. Without wanting to minimise the respective merits of other authors, who have brilliantly written on the Leica, the Nikon, or closer to us, the Olympus, I would like to point out to the reader that writing about a "sleeping" model, such as Exakta, takes a lot of judgement and effort! It is to my mind one of the merits of this work and I wish to express here my admiration for the authors and their collaborators.

J.P. Salanick.

FOREWORD

There are many questions posed by the Dresden reflex, the Ihagee Exakta, for its collectors and enthusiasts. In France the late Bernard Vial through his many articles was the first to attempt to answer some of these questions. His enthusiasm and his analytical and inquisitive mind caused many amateurs to become infected with the collecting virus. In 1975 an English group, formed round Neil Wright, edited a 30 page monograph. In America in 1977 Norlin Rober published a more comprehensive essay on the 35mm Exakta and Exa cameras, concentrating mainly on the lenses and accessories. An important publication is currently being prepared by a mixed international team: "Ihagee, Historisch Gesellschaft". We hope for a fruitful outcome from this dedicated study and also that it will finally enlighten us upon the history of the Ihagee company.

However, one thing is certain for us all: we will never know for sure the full history of the Ihagee Exakta from Dresden. The main reasons are the destruction of the Dresden factories in February 1945 and the difficulty in obtaining the slightest information from the Ihagee management in the DDR for the period from 1948 to 1970. As Exakta admirers you won't have the same luck as Leica and Contax followers who have no difficulty in finding exhaustive documentation relating to all the different products. But we hope that this book will help you get to know better an instrument which was revolutionary, which evolved, and which at its zenith was the universal reflex.

This attempt is the result of lengthy research work into documents and observation and systematic logging of cameras we have handled. But it is still insufficient and often only approximate. We look forward to further assistance from you the reader to improve it with your comments and any information you may find suitable to put forward. We thank you in advance.

Chapter 1
Historical Background

Dresden was the primary photographic centre of Germany at the beginning of the century and it holds a considerable fascination for the imagination of camera collectors. Numerous companies, some of world importance and some more modest, were established there, such as: Ernemann, Wünsche, Hüttig, Goltz & Breutmann, Ica, Kochmann, Loeber, Zeiss, Balda, Welta, Certo, Zeh, and many others.

The Ihagee company was founded by Johan Steenbergen whose family ran a wholesale camera business in The Hague, in Holland. Johan had been born at Meppel on 7th December, 1886. He chose Dresden as the site for his venture, no doubt because he knew he would find the skilled technicians he would need there. The works of Industrie und Handels Gesellschaft m.b.h., as the company was called, were established at Marcolini Strasse 8. The trade name "Ihagee" was adopted, being the phonet rendering of IHG, the initial letters of the company's name. In 1919 it changed its name to "Ihagee Kamerawerk Steenbergen & Co". The trade mark was a moon crescent from which a rising sun emerged, and this is found on all Ihagee cameras up to the end of the thirties.

It was in April 1912 that the Marcolini Strasse works started manufacturing their first photographic camera, a hand camera called the "Photorex". Many cameras of different types followed, and indeed an account of all the company's products up to the introduction of the Exakta would need a book to itself.

Some of these cameras were masterpieces in terms of ingenuity, and this was particularly true in the case of the reflex cameras. The Patent-Klappreflex (1924 to 1936) made in 6.5x9, 9x12 and 10x15cm sizes, folded into a remarkably small volume so that it formed an extremely compact package for carrying. The Nacht Reflex ("Night Reflex", 1929 to 1935) on the other hand had a rigid cubic body and was made for the small size 4.5x6 or 6.5x9cm plates, but was fitted with very fast f/2 or f/1.5 lenses in the manner of the Ermanox. The Parvola, an all-metal bodied camera for rollfilm in 4x6.5 and 3x4cm sizes had a double helical focusing mount instead of bellows. One can see in these three cameras the strands that came together in the Exakta.

The EXAKTA

It was in February 1933, at the Leipzig fair, that the first Exakta Vest-Pocket models were presented, the production of which had started in 1932. The new era of the modern single lens reflex was beginning. This camera, with a 45° mirror and collapsible viewfinder, and using 127 type film which was then widely used, enjoyed an immediate success, although it was to be criticised by the unconvinced adherents of the Leica and Contax.

Its trapezoid shape provided practical and easy handling. Its small size still causes surprise; it had the dimensions and weight of the 35mm cameras of the sixties. It is indeed the ancestor of the modern single lens reflex: nowadays 50 years later, it still does not seem too old fashioned.

Production expanded very rapidly and numerous variants of this first model completed the range. The engineers from the firm exercised amazing ingenuity and Ihagee produced the following world firsts and major contributions to the evolution of modern photography with the Exakta:

1933 - First modern single lens reflex for rollfilm.
1933 - First focal plane shutter with a range of 12 seconds to 1/1000 second, with delayed speeds of up to 6 seconds. This shutter remained unrivalled until 1972-75.
1934 - First to use a wind-on lever, which was to be used 10 years later by other manufacturers.
1935 - First camera to have built-in flash sockets connected to contacts activated by the shutter (Vacublitz flash). This system enabled the use of one or several reflectors. Synchronisation on all speeds up to 1/1000 second (depending on the type of bulb).
1936 - First reflex in the world to use the small 35mm format, the Kine Exakta.

From the start numerous accessories and lenses were provided for the early Exakta models. The well chosen name "Exakta" was evocative of the technical precision and very soon researchers, biologists, naturalists, and botanists started using it for close-up photography because it avoided all the complex accessories and restrictions of the concurrent Contax and Leica cameras.

However the lack of initiative and commercial drive of the firm is regrettable. They never gave the advertising support, so the Exakta lacked the potential of the giants of the time, the Contax, Leica and Rolleiflex. Nonetheless, with Exakta, Ihagee became the fourth largest manufacturer in the German photographic industry, which at the time held the lead for precision cameras.

In 1936 the Kine Exakta, the first 35mm reflex in the world, revolutionised the small format and embarked on its career, after a few modifications, of more than thirty years. The Kine Exakta adopted all the technical features of the VP Exakta. It had the same trapezoid shape, shutter, viewfinder, interchangeable lenses. 1936 was also the year of the Berlin Olympic Games when the benefits of using the cameras with long focus lenses was demonstrated. Many of the famous optical manufacturers made long focal length lenses for mounting on the Exakta.

We shall explore in more detail in the book all the stages of the different models and their variants, and also their accessories and lenses.

Ihagee also manufactured two 6x6cm models, which were both short lived. The first, in 1939, had a more rounded shape than the VP Exakta. It had the same characteristics but with a wind-on lever system situated underneath the body. Its production was soon halted because of the war, but it was to have an impact on the history of photography because numerous 6x6 post-war models were inspired by it: for example, the Praktisix, Pentacon-Six and Pentax 6x6. The second, the Exakta 66 made from 1952 to 1955, was a superb camera featuring interchangeable lenses, viewfinders, focusing screens and film backs. It also saw its production halted, but for obscure commercial reasons because Pentacon preferred to promote its own future 6x6 formats. This original camera was designed in a vertical configuration with a vertical direction for the film transport and a winding system using an automatic positioning key. It also inspired other manufacturers who remembered the originality of the ideas and a few years later it was to lead to a descendant known as the Kowa Six which was influenced by the Exakta 66.

As the war approached the Ihagee factories slowed down their production of the VP models to concentrate on the Kine Exakta. At that time, at the peak of their glory, Ihagee had no less than five factories in Dresden and its vicinity. As soon as Germany was at war production slowed down considerably and only the Kine was still manufactured. In 1940 Ihagee was confiscated by the Hitler regime who didn't approve of their management.

In February 1945 the main Schandauer Strasse factory was annihilated by Allied bombing. After the bombs and the fire, the looting reduced years of work to nothing. Nothing was left of the archives, documents or publicity material; so now identification of the different series and numbers of models produced is very difficult. An exhaustive list, comprising all the models and their variants and all the accessories, seems impossible to establish. Furthermore, the lack of cooperation on behalf of the Ihagee management after the war was very disapointing. Repeated requests were made for information concerning the different models they had manufactured, but they would only return a leaflet on their latest model.

Exakta collectors will never be able to experience the joy of having access to fabulous collections in the same way Leica authors did. When the Red Army arrived the Blasewitser Strasse factory was evacuated in a rush and Ihagee's future seemed rather uncertain. Some of the premises which were partially spared and rebuilt after enormous difficulties, at No 43 of the same street, enabled a team of former engineers and workers to progressively restart producing the Kine Exakta. Restoration of the equipment and the tooling seemed an impossible task. However the capability and tenacity of the team enabled the recovery to take place which was necessary to salvage the trademark.

Ihagee became the only photographic camera manufacturer to benefit from the status of being a private commercial Dutch company in East Germany. The new leaders of the country realised the interest and substantial revenue that the export sales of the Kine Exakta would bring. At the same time the other firms, Zeiss Jena, Filmosto, Altissa, Waurich & Weber, Guthe & Thorsch, and many others, united together and merged under the sponsorship of VEB Pentacon.

Ihagee Exakta continued to produce different reflex models, all derived from the famous Kine Exakta. These were the Kine Exakta II, the Varex and the VX and their universal system, the Varex IIa, IIb and the VX 1000. Never had so many accessories and lenses been made for the same camera. Everything was catered for, including macro, micro, endoscopy, stereo, medical, astronomy, industry, etc...

Simplified models, but astounding because of their size, sturdiness and ability to integrate with the universal system, were launched in 1950. They were the Exa series of Exa, Exa I, Exa II and Exa 500.

THE DECLINE

By 1968 the Exakta models, despite numerous technical modifications, were experiencing difficulty in matching the Japanese competition and their sales had decreased. In order to retain sales, the company reduced prices considerably.

Meanwhile for several years the Steenbergen heirs and the shareholders had been undertaking numerous legal actions to recover the name of the firm. In 1959 they formed Ihagee Kamerawerk AG in Frankfurt, West Germany. Then in 1962 they formed Ihagee-Exakta Photo AG in Munich and decided to make the Exakta Real which was to have been launched in 1963, but only appeared in 1966 after the company had transferred once again, this time to Berlin.

The inherent difficulties of the firm in East Germany, the drop in export sales and the legal proceedings eventually enabled the inheritors to recover the brand names of Ihagee and Exakta and manufacture of "western" Exaktas was started in Japan, through Cosina and Petri, of the Exakta Twin TL, Exakta TL 500, TL 1000, FE 2000, Exakta EDX 3, EDX 2.

In the meantime the fabulous history of the Ihagee Exakta in Dresden was drawing to its end and models derived from the 1933 camera were dying out. It had survived 35 years with just a few modifications. Cameras will still be found marketed under the name of Elbaflex VX 1000, VX 500, VX 100, VX 200, and sold in Eastern Europe; these were the Exakta 1000 and 500 and the Exas, but the name Exakta had been suppressed and VEB Pentacon was thus able to liquidate its stock of cameras and spare parts. A little later still, Pentacon was to market the Praktica VLC. It had a few details differing from the Exakta RTL 1000, but this camera no longer had anything in common with the famous Kine Exakta. The Ihagee factory which had so proudly carried the name Exakta was now absorbed into the VEB Pentacon group.

So ended the history of a fabulous camera, the Exakta, of which all the models were derived from the model B Vest-Pocket of 1933 and which became in the sixties, with its system, the universal reflex.

THE LATER EXAKTA CAMERAS

For information we list below the Exakta cameras introduced since 1978:-

1979 Exakta EDX-3, automatic reflex with Exakta bayonet
1980 Exakta EDX-2, automatic reflex with Exakta bayonet
1983 Exakta HS-3, automatic reflex with K bayonet
1983 Exakta HS-2, semi-auto reflex with K bayonet
1983 Exakta HS-1, semi-auto reflex with K bayonet
1984 Exakta Autofocus, with fixed lens
1984 Exakta 66, introduced at Photokina

SCARCITY INDEX

We have decided not to put the different cameras into a price table because we are horrified by the extravagant rating of some of them and the consequent bidding that has resulted.

We prefer to present a scarcity index which will enable the reader or the collector to know the different models better, and thus be in a better position to know on which aspects to direct his efforts. We took into account the different criteria which determine their scarcity. One is the quantity manufactured for each model, which with Ihagee is often mysterious and only known approximately. Another is the date when it was made and the effect of the war which accounted for the disappearance of numerous cameras. Finally there is the experience acquired through years of searching for this equipment.

The most difficult period for this evaluation remains of course from 1933 to 1939 when Ihagee produced more than twenty different models of the VP Exakta, the Kine Exakta and the Exakta 66. The serial numbers for these ranged from 400,000 to 600,000 without its being possible to establish even approximately how many of each model or variant were made.

For each camera and for each variant we indicate the degree of rarity by the number of stars, thus:

★	Very common	★	Very common
★★	Common	★★	Common
★★★	Less common	★★★	Less common
★★★★	Quite rare	★★★★	Quite rare
★★★★★	Rare	★★★★★	Rare

This is the significance of the stars and our system cannot be compared with any other scarcity index for other makes of cameras. It only applies to Exakta models in relation to each other.

Chapter 2
The 4×6.5cm VP Exakta

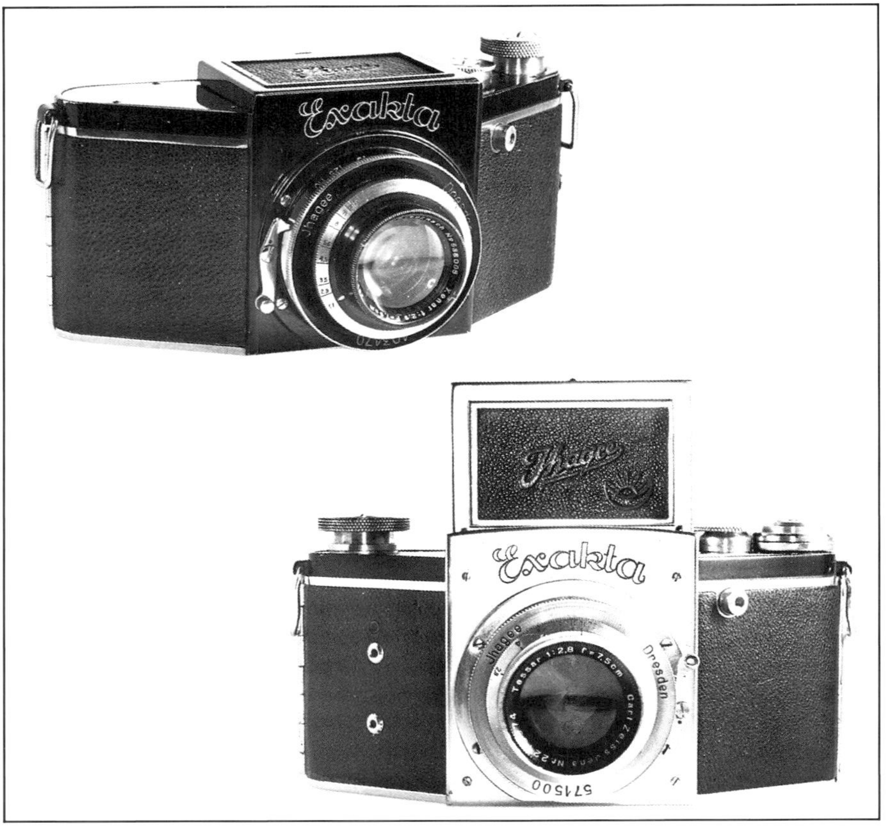

Model A Version 1 1933 ★★★★

This was the first Exakta, known as the VP because of its 4x6.5cm format on 127 film which had been made popular by the Vest Pocket Kodak. It was also the first single lens reflex of an entirely new, compact form which is now so familiar in today's 35mm S.L.R. cameras. Its trapezoid shape became the hall-mark of all Exakta cameras. The body was a monobloc casting in light alloy. The dimensions were 15x6.5x5cm and the weight 750g with lens. The finish was in black paint, with the body covered in black leather and with nickel plated controls and focussing mount. It had a hinged back with red window and two rings on each side of the body for fitting a strap.

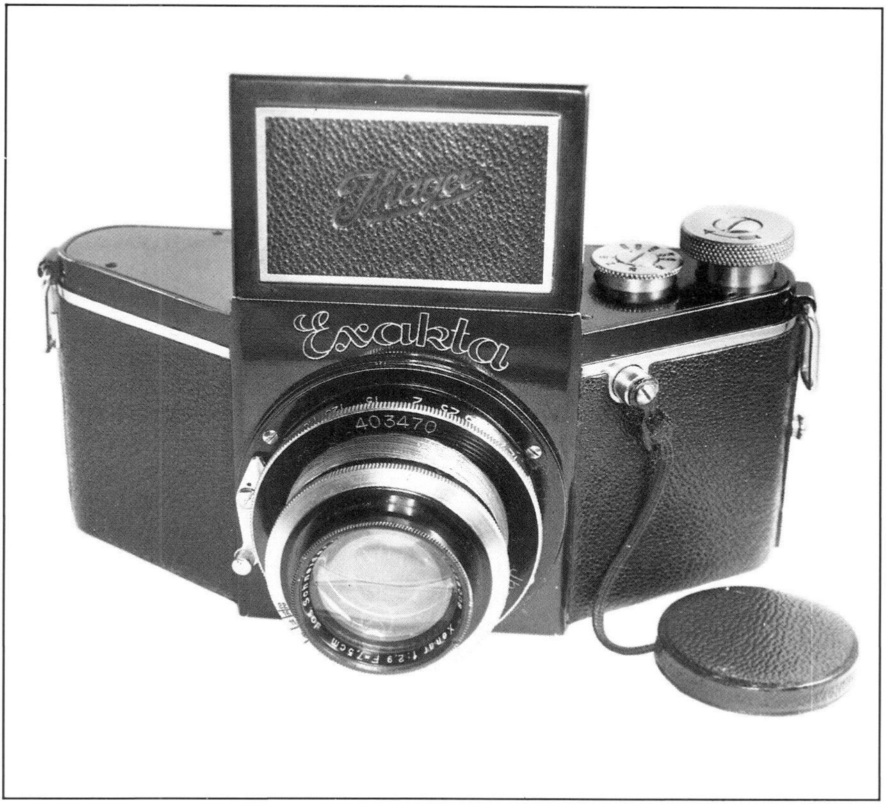

Exakta Model A, 1st Version, No.403470

The shutter was a focal plane type with horizontally running cloth blinds. Speeds were 1/25, 1/50, 1/100, 1/200, 1/300, 1/600, 1/1000 second and B & T, the latter being marked "Z". Film transport and shutter tensioning were by a single milled knob 22mm in diameter. Some models are found with a 26mm diameter knob, but they may have been modified afterwards. The release knob was situated on the front left of the body. The focusing screen, which showed the image inverted left to right, was shielded by a collapsible hood with a hinged magnifier which could be swung into position to enlarge part of the field approximately 4x for more precise focusing. The inner panel of the front side of this hood could be folded in so that the outer metal frame provided a frame finder (position 1 in diagram). This hinged panel was polished on the inside and it could be set at 45° to act as a mirror to reflect part of the screen image so that it could be viewed at eye level, although the camera had to be held some distance from the eye in order to see the image clearly.(position 2). For this application the small rear frame was folded over into the inside. The image was seen upside down and appeared on a screen surface of 36x56mm, slightly smaller than the real format of the picture,

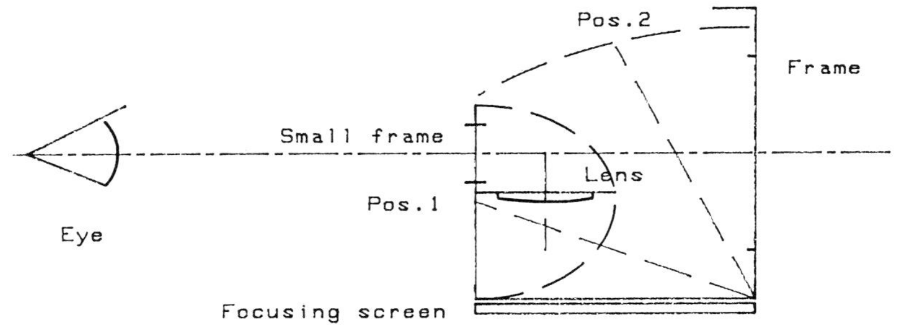

DIAGRAM OF VIEWFINDER

which was 40x62mm. The viewfinder hood folded over in four movements for closing.

The reflex mirror was lowered to the 45° position when the shutter was cocked, but remained flat against the top of the viewfinder after the shutter was released. Ihagee maintained this system for a very long time, although it has to be admitted that it did limit the mechanical vibrations and made the action particularly silent.

The lens was mounted on a helical screw mount. The focussing range was from 0.9m to infinity and the mechanism was a component part of the camera body rather than of the lens. A locking lever for the infinity position was situated on the user's right. When the camera was not in use the lens could be screwed right back into the body thus reducing the overall thickness of the camera from 9cm with the lens was in its infinity position to 75mm when it was retracted. On the earlier models there was no locking device to prevent shutter release without the lens being in its operational position. The lens was removable but not interchangeable with other, later lenses. This was because the thread diameter on the early models was 39.5mm with 0.5mm pitch, whereas on the later models it was 39.8mm with 0.75mm pitch steps. As far as we know, the interchangeable lenses (wide angle and telephoto) were only ever supplied with the bigger diameter thread.

The following lens options were available:

Ihagee Exaktar	75mm f/3.5
Meyer Primotar	75mm f/3.5
Schneider Xenar	75mm f/2.9
Zeiss Tessar	75mm f/3.5
Zeiss Tessar	75mm f/2.8

Note that on all the Exakta 4x6.5 models the focusing scales of the lenses were graduated in metres in feet.

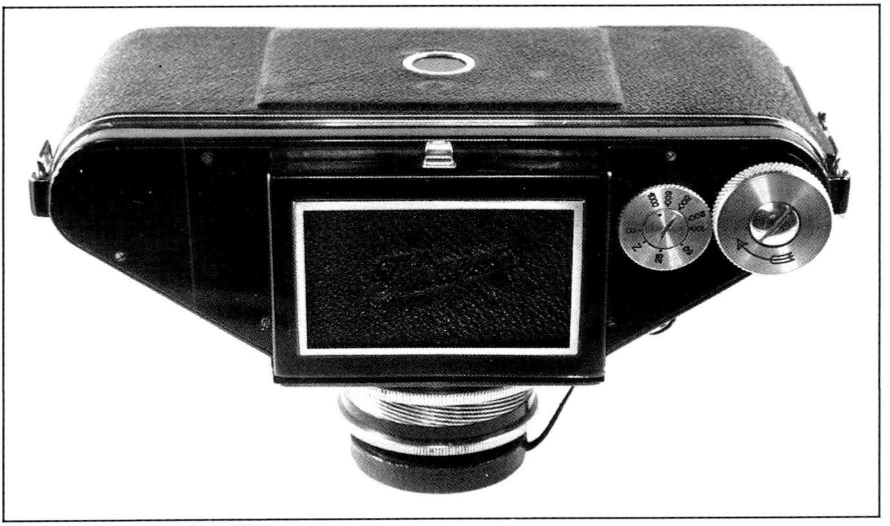

Model A, 1st Version, No.403470

EXAKTA A Version 2 1933 ★★★

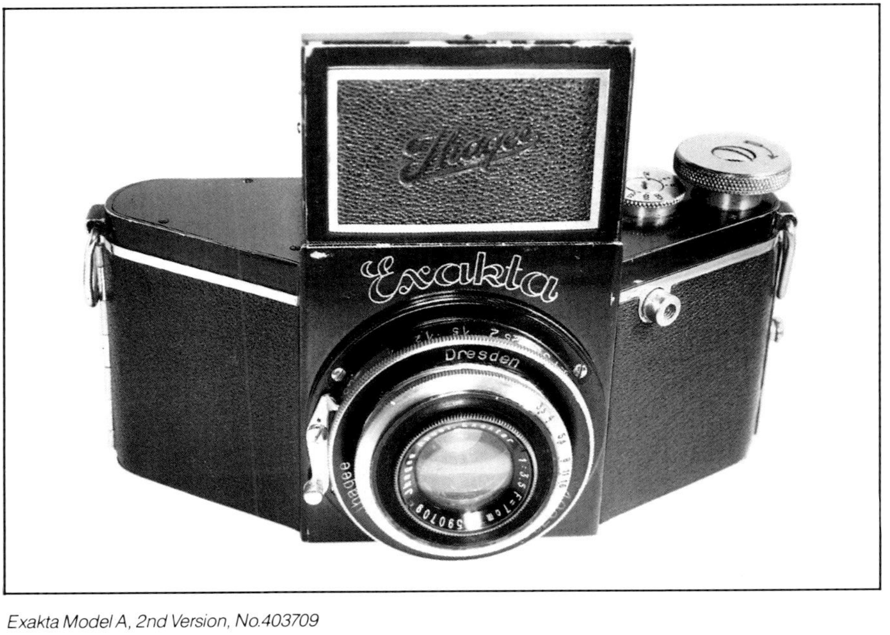

Exakta Model A, 2nd Version, No.403709

At the end of 1933 a few modifications appeared on model A. The diameter of the thread for the lens was changed to 39.8mm with 0.75 pitch. Also at this stage a safety mechanism was incorporated which prevented shutter release unless the lens was screwed out to the infinity position. These modifications were internal. The exterior detail which identifies this version is the diameter of the wind-on knob, which was increased to 26mm.

The same types of lenses were available as for the first version, but with the new mount.

EXAKTA A Version 3 1934 ★★★★★

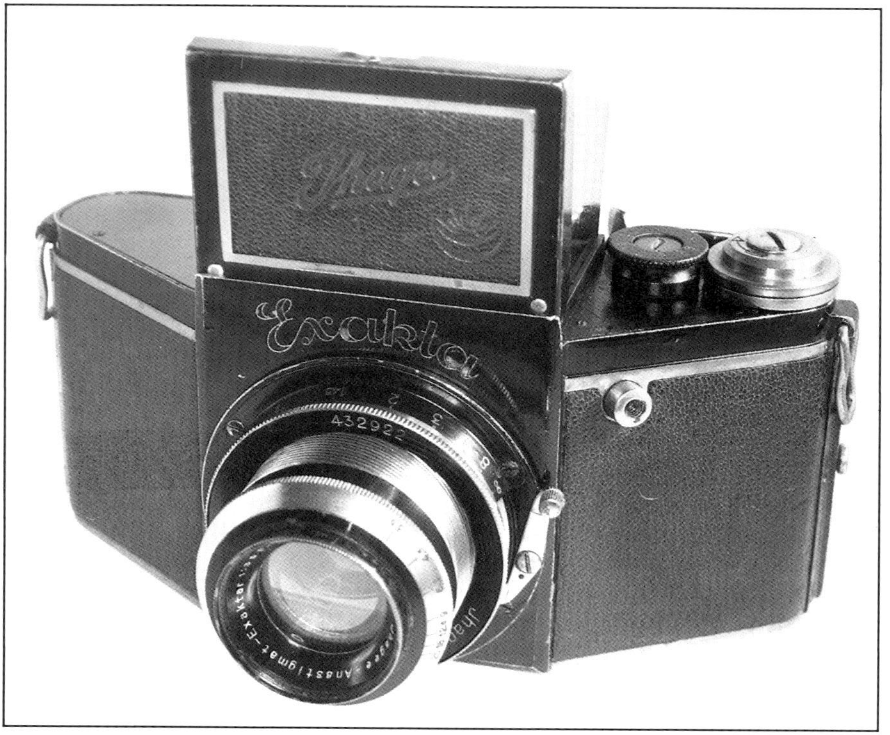

Exakta Model A, 3rd Version, No.432922

This camera had the same general characteristics as the original 1933 version, but with the following modifications:-

- The wind-on knob was replaced by a lever which required several throws.
- The locking lever for the infinity focusing position of the lens mount was now on the user's left-hand side of the lens assembly.

- The shutter speed range remained unchanged, but the speed selection barrel was black with white numbers instead being nickel plated. - A spring-loaded sliding cover protected the red window from light.
- The Ihagee company trade mark, a moon crescent in a rising sun, which did not figure on the earlier versions, was embossed on the hood cover.

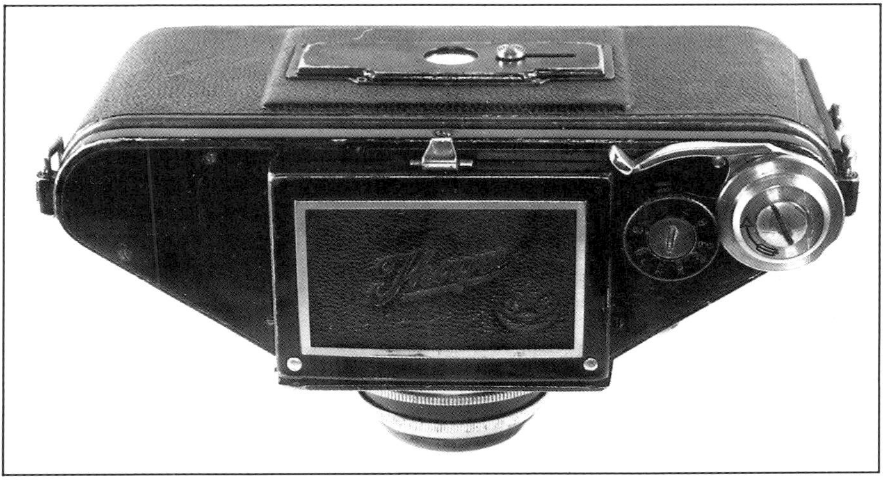

Model A, 3rd Version, No.432922. This view shows the wind-on lever, the shutter speed selection dial and the masking slide for the red window.

EXAKTA A Version 4 1935 ★★★

This was identical to the third version, but with the addition of a Vacublitz socket (2 or 3 pin). Exakta models with flash synchronisation started appearing in 1935, but it did not feature on the Model A in the Ihagee catalogue until 1939. It is possible to find Model A cameras fitted with a Vacublitz socket and bearing serial numbers that would indicate a date earlier than 1939, but these examples would have been modified after purchase. The Vacublitz socket will be described later.

EXAKTA A, Chrome Version 5 1939 ★★★★

This model was listed in the 1939 Ihagee catalogue. In contrast to the earlier models, the two top plates, the viewfinder and the front trade mark plate were finished in matt chrome. The shutter remained unchanged, and the camera had a wind-on lever and a three pin Vacublitz socket.

Here are the catalogue reference numbers, depending on which lens was fitted:

Ihagee Exaktar	75mm f/3.5	A 8150 BR
Meyer Primotar	75mm f/3.5	A 8150 PR
Schneider Xenar	75mm f/2.8	A 8150 AX
Meyer Makro-Plasmat	75mm f/2.7	A 8150 MP
Zeiss Tessar	75mm f/3.5	A 8150 Q
Zeiss Tessar	75mm f/2.8	A 8150 E

EXAKTA B Version 1 1933 ★★★★

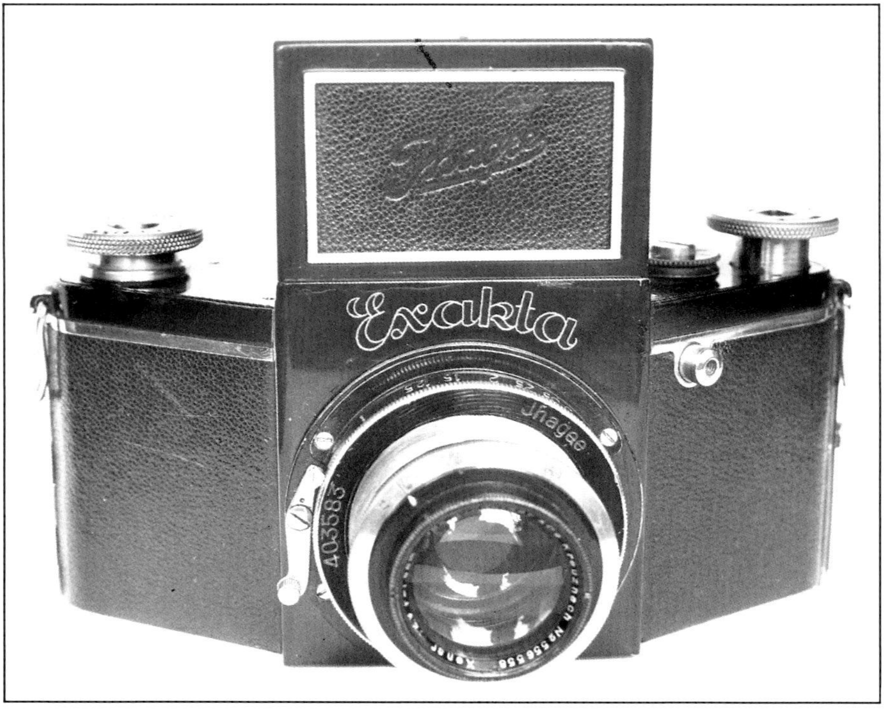

Exakta Model B, 1st Version, No. 403583. Collection J.P. Salanick.

This camera was similar to the 1933 Model A, 1st version, except for the shutter which had an additional mechanism operated by a knob situated on the other side of the top-plate from the shutter speed dial. This gave a range of slow speeds: $^1/_{10}$, $^1/_2$, 1, 2, 3, 4, 5, 6, 9, 10, 12 seconds; as well as a range of delayed speeds: $^1/_{10}$, $^1/_2$, 1, 2, 3, 4, 6 seconds. It was this type of shutter, with its 12 seconds to $^1/_{1000}$ second speed range, which was to be used on all subsequent Exakta cameras, including the 24x36mm and 6x6 models which were to appear later on.

The lenses offered were the same as for Model A (1st version), because the mount diameter was 39.5mm at 0.5mm pitch. However, the release safety mechanism, first introduced with Model A, 2nd version, was fitted to Model B cameras from the start.

EXAKTA B Version 2 1934 ★★★

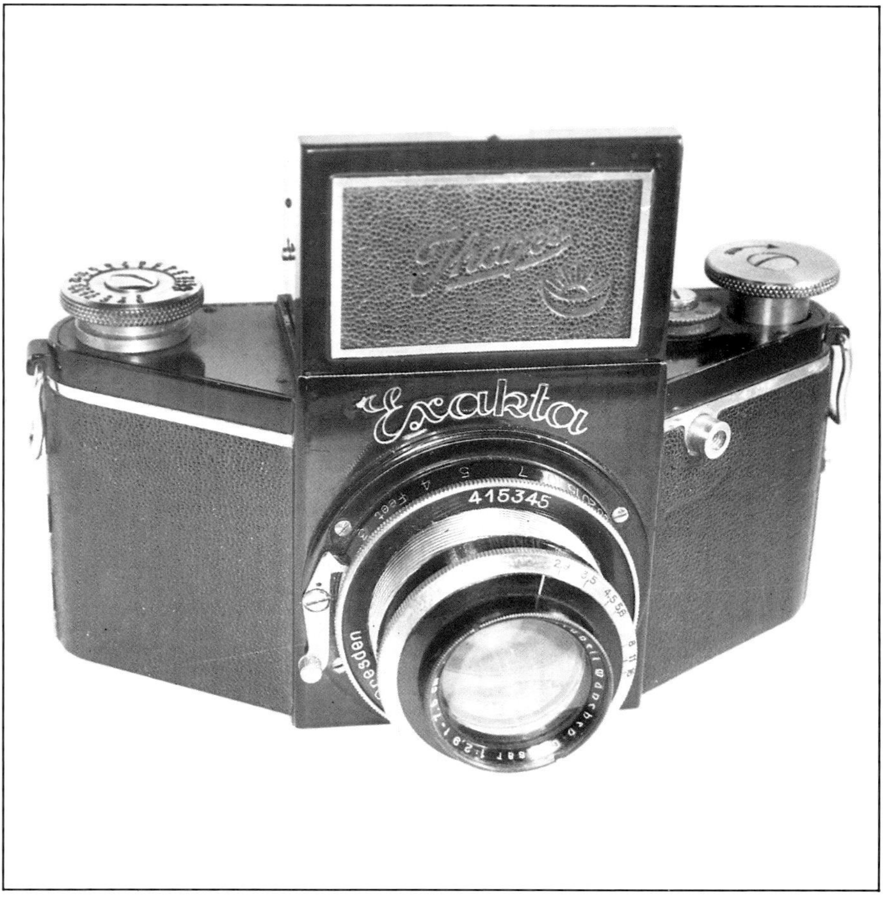

Exakta Model B, 2nd Version, No. 415345.

Identical to Model B, 1st version, as far as its mechanical characteristics were concerned, this model differed only by the presence of the Ihagee emblem on the viewfinder cover (moon crescent in rising sun).

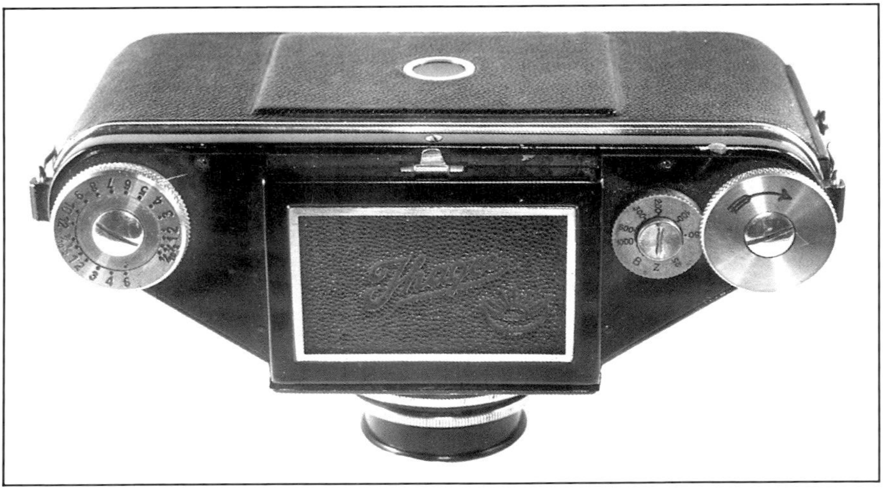

Exakta B, 2nd Version, No. 413345. In this picture can be seen, from left to right: the wind-on knob, the shutter speed dial with range from 1/25 to 1/1000 second plus B & T, viewfinder cover with the Ihagee emblem, and slow and delayed speeds dial. The back of the body does not have a cover to the red window.

EXAKTA B Version 3 1934 ★★★

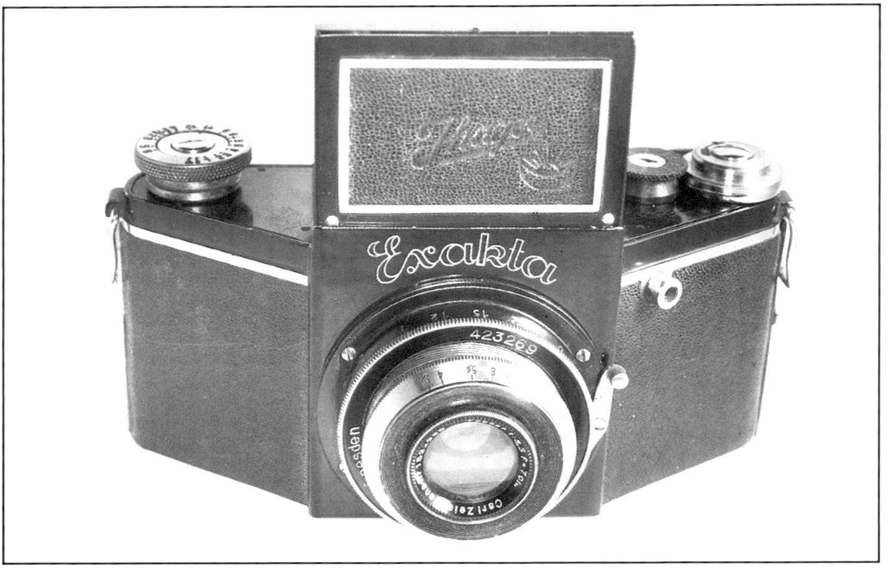

Exakta Model B, 3rd Version, No. 423269.

The important modifications on this model, with respect to the first two versions were:-

- Protective cover for red window.
- Lens thread with 0.75mm pitch.
- Wind-on knob replaced by a lever.
- Locking lever on infinity position on the left from the user's point of view.

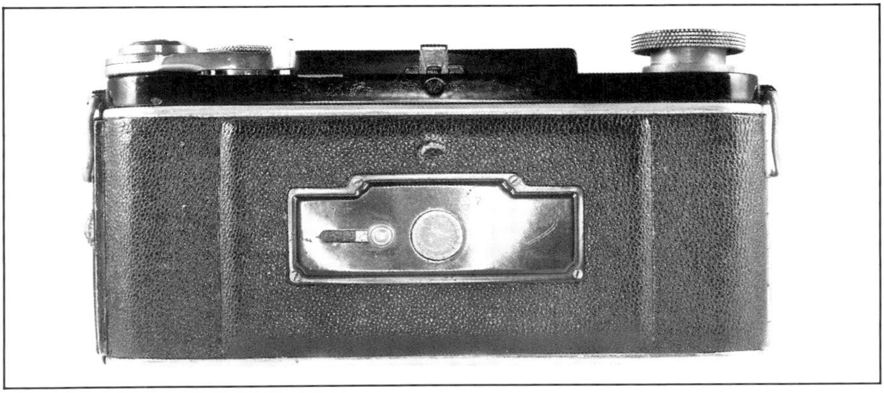

On this rear view one can see the wind-on lever and the sliding cover for the red window. This was kept closed by a spring and to read the frame number it was necessary to slide back the little milled button on the left.

EXAKTA B Version 4 1935 ★★★

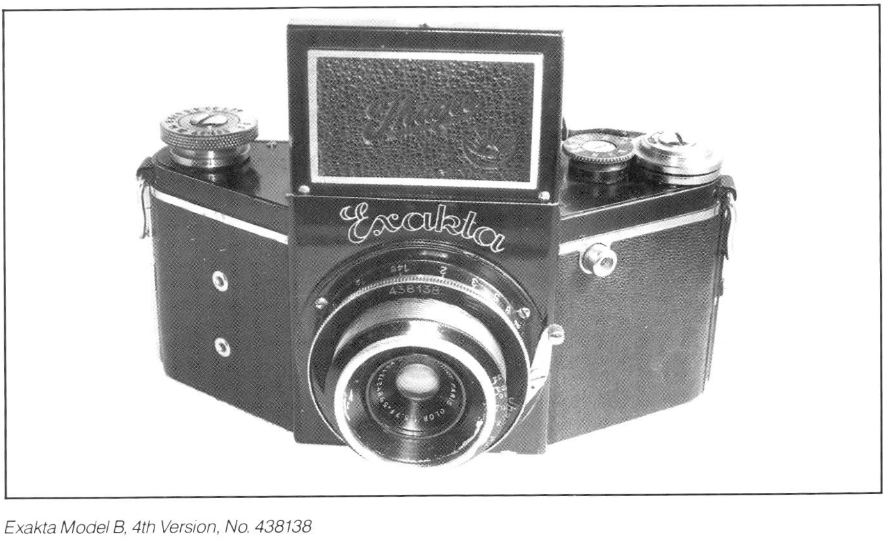

Exakta Model B, 4th Version, No. 438138

The only modification on this camera, compared with the 3rd version, was the addition of a Vacublitz synchronisation connector. It was a two-pin socket which would take either the flash gun or an extension lead. This socket appeared in 1935, at approximately No.435000, on most of the V.P. Exakta models. Bodies with earlier numbers can be found fitted with it, but they would have been modified after 1935.

EXAKTA B Version 5 1937 ★★

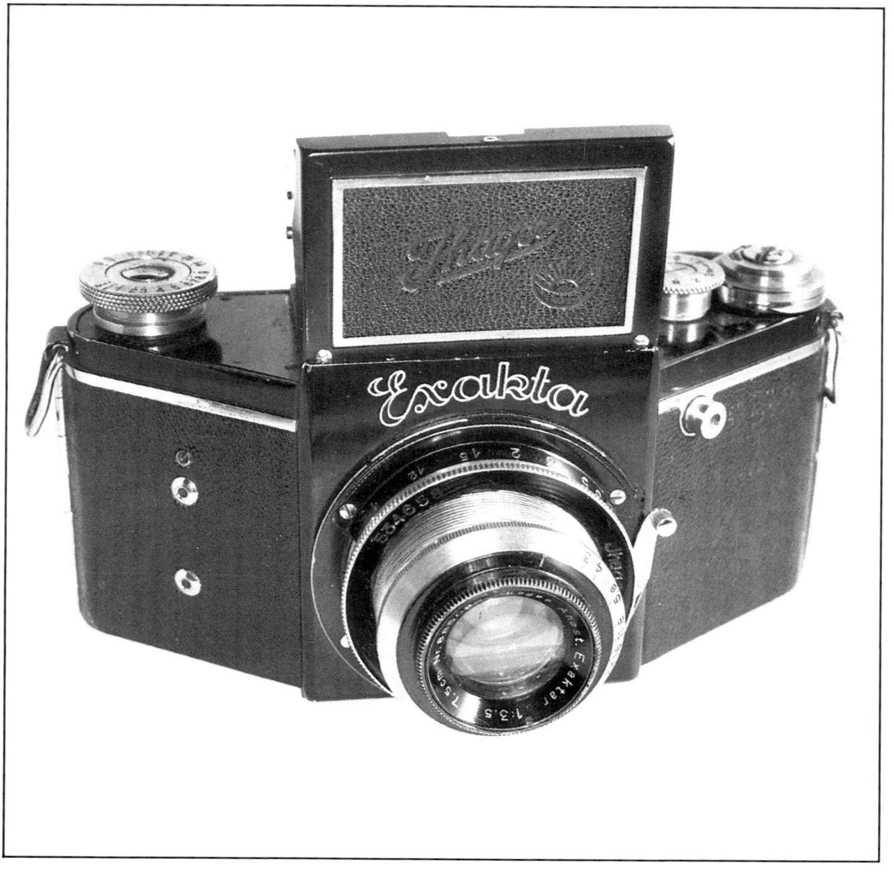

Exakta Model B, 5th Version, No. 534658

This was a modification of the previous version with a third fixing socket for the flashgun. This third socket was threaded; it was not an electrical connection but an improved fixing for the flashgun. Versions 4 and 5 of the Exakta Model B are the most common because they were in production from 1935 to 1938.

EXAKTA B, Chrome Version 6 1938 ★★★★

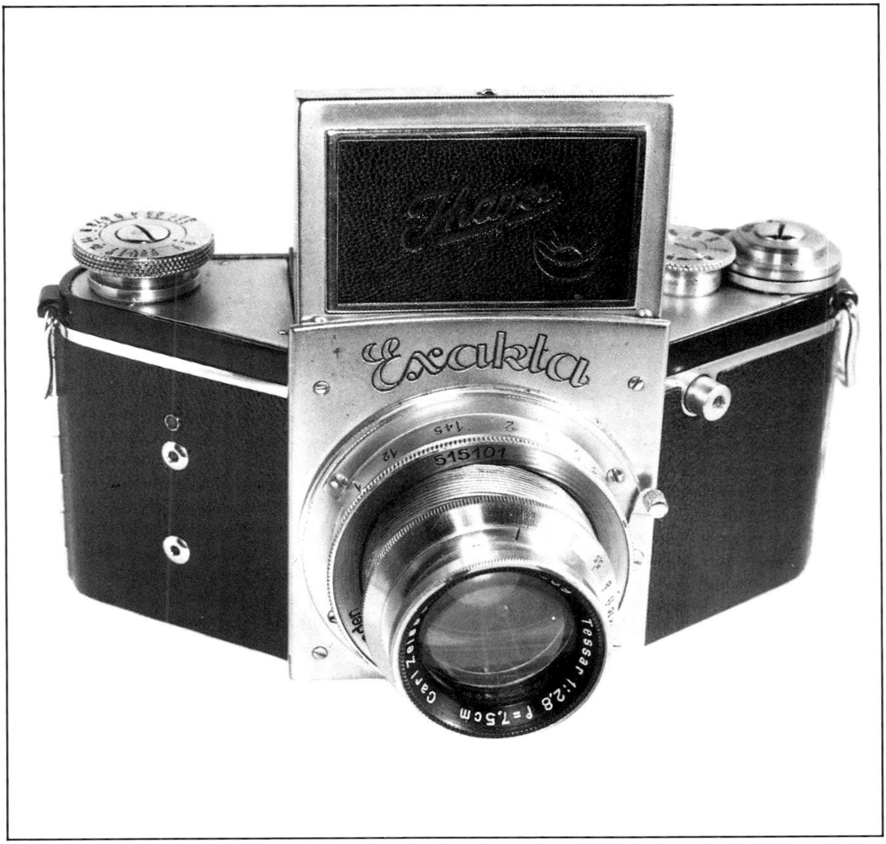

Exakta Model B Chrome, No. 515101

At the end of 1937 the chrome version of the Exakta Model B first appeared. There were no mechanical differences over the previous version, but the outer aspect of the camera had been changed a great deal. The top plates and the frame of the viewfinder hood were in matt chrome, as well as the front name plate which was attached to the body by four chrome screws. The milled shutter speed dials, the wind-on lever and the lens infinity locking lever were in bright chrome.

The Exakta is probably the only camera in the world to have had two spellings of its name: "Exakta" with a "k" or "Exacta" with a "c". Some authors thought that the "c" spelling was for the Latin countries, since in the French publicity material the name Exacta was nearly always spelt with a "c". But numerous Exactas with a "c" were sold on the American market, in particular the Kine Exakta. It is very difficult to know the the exact origin of these two spellings.

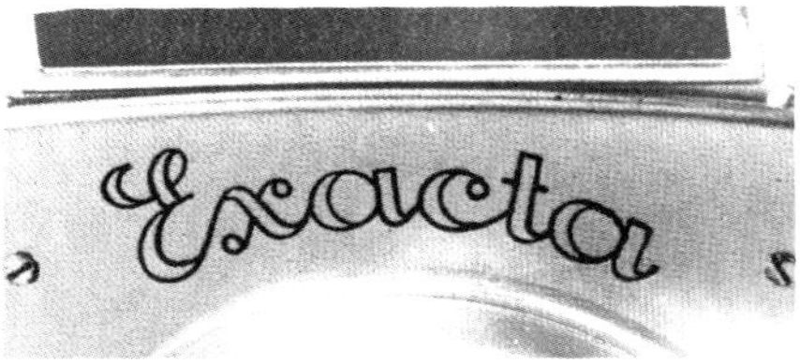

Detail of the front of a chrome Exakta B with "C" spelling.

EXAKTA B Version 7 1938 ★★★

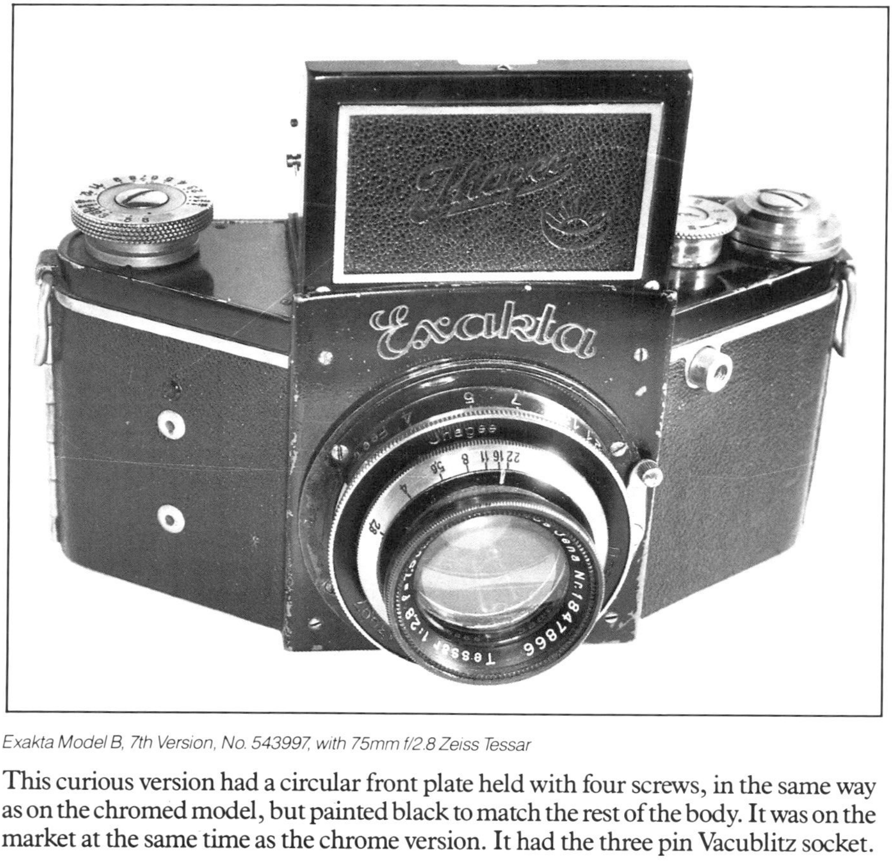

Exakta Model B, 7th Version, No. 543997, with 75mm f/2.8 Zeiss Tessar

This curious version had a circular front plate held with four screws, in the same way as on the chromed model, but painted black to match the rest of the body. It was on the market at the same time as the chrome version. It had the three pin Vacublitz socket.

The Night EXAKTA

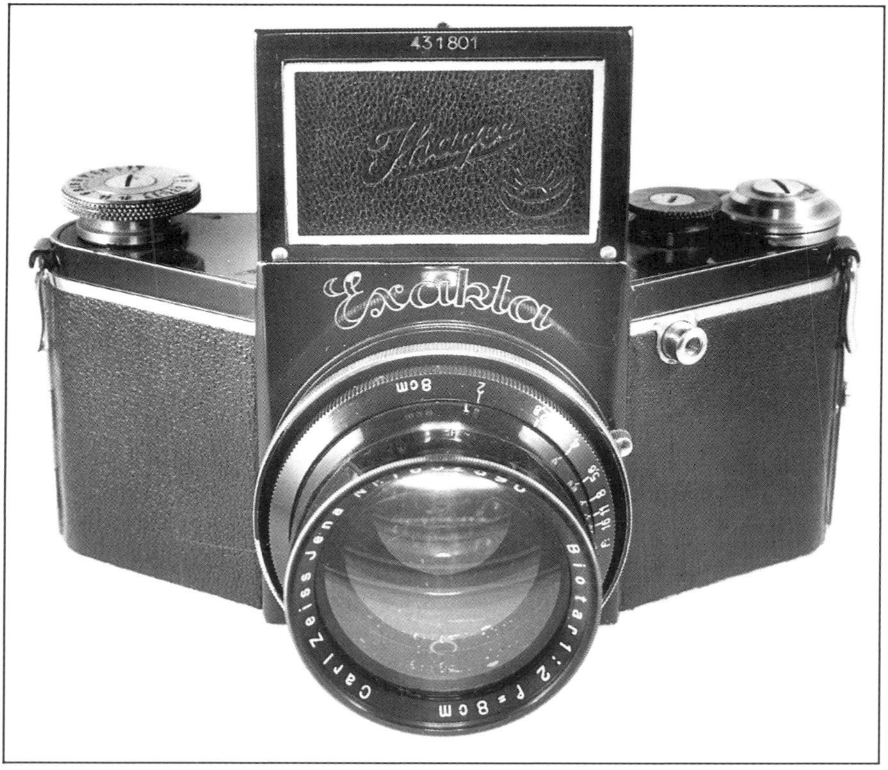

Night Exakta, No. 431801, with 8cm f/2 Zeiss Biotar (1st version)

The name Night Exakta was given to this model to indicate that it was intended for use in very low light, thanks to its wide aperture lens. Three famous German lens makers, Zeiss, Schneider and Meyer, designed special lenses for it. In England Dallmeyer also produced a lens for the Night Exakta with an aperture of f/1.9.

The body of the Night Exakta was identical to that of Models A and B, but the milled ring of the helical screw mount had a bigger diameter. It could accomodate wide aperture lenses, which were heavier, and thus made their handling easier. The camera serial number was no longer engraved on the flange of the helical screw, but on the upper part of the hood. This detail makes it possible to distinguish at a glance between the "Night Exakta" and the standard models. However, it seems that on the first 1934 models the milled ring was of the normal diameter and was engraved with the serial number. We know one specimen of this type, No. 423008, fitted with a Meyer Primoplan 8cm f/1.9 lens.

The Night Exakta existed in Model B form with slow speeds or in Model A form without slow speeds, but it is much less common in Model A form. The Night Exakta had a particuliarly high retail price and represented the top of the Exakta range. In 1939 a Night Exakta with a f/2 Zeiss Biotar lens cost 50.

The following lenses were available for the Night Exakta:-

Meyer Primoplan	8cm	f/1.9	5 elements
Schneider Xenon	8cm	f/2	6 elements
Zeiss Biotar	8cm	f/2	6 elements
Dallmeyer Super-Six	3in	f/1.9	6 elements

Night EXAKTA Version 1 1934 ★★★★

This had a black body, without Vacublitz socket, fitted with one of the above lenses. The shutter speed range was from 12 to 1/1000 seconds plus B & T with delay on all the speeds up to 6 seconds. The Vacublitz socket was fitted from 1935 onwards.

Night EXAKTA (Type A) Version 2 1934 ★★★★

This was identical to the previous model, except that it did not have the delay and slow speeds. It was fitted with a Vacublitz socket from 1935 onwards.

Night EXAKTA Chrome Version 3 1937 ★★★★

It was in 1937 that chrome versions of many Exakta models started to appear and the Night model also benefited from this improvement. The two top plates, the viewfinder frame and the front trade mark plate were matt chrome and the knobs and control levers were bright chrome. The name plate was a metal stamping, curved at the top, which was folded over onto the body. The shutter speed range was identical to that of the previous models. Some Night Exaktas are encountered where the serial number is nowhere to be found. These could be models which were modified in the factory to accomodate wide-aperture lenses. In such cases the original milled ring which carried the serial number would have been changed.

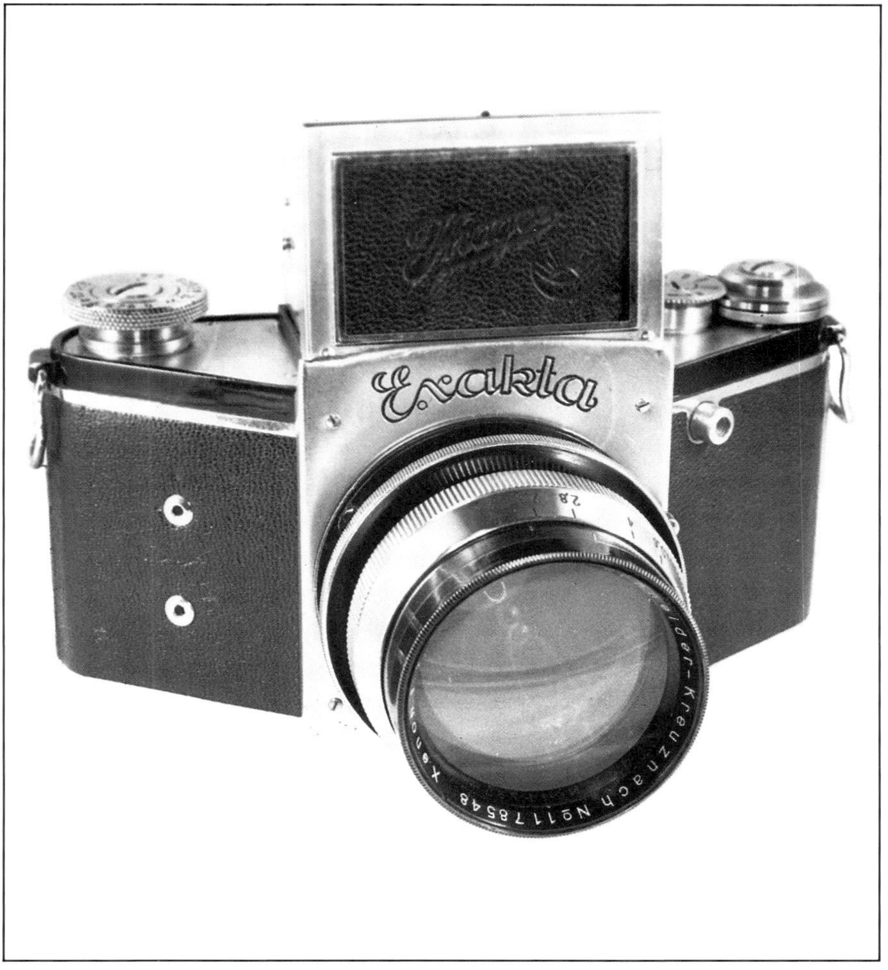

Night Exakta, 3rd Version, without serial number and fitted with 8cm f/2 Schneider Xenon.

Night EXAKTA
Chrome Version 4 1937 ★★★★★

This camera appeared in the 1939 Ihagee catalogue. It was built on the same lines as an Exakta Model A. The finish was chrome, the shutter speed range was from 1/25 to 1/1000 second plus B & T and it had a cocking lever and Vacublitz socket. This model is not very common.

EXAKTA MODEL C, FOR PLATES AND FILMS

In the thirties the glass plate was still used by amateurs, but especially by professionals. One only needs to look through the magazines of the time to realise that the choice of emulsions on plates was much wider than that on film, which was probably the reason for their continuing popularity. The Ihagee company soon offered an Exakta model with a dual purpose back. An opening in the central part received the dark slides for 4.5x6cm plates. These plate holders were positioned 5.5mm to the rear of the film plane, which meant that the lens had to have a mount that was suitable for use with films or plates.

For use with film a 5.5mm ring was interposed between the the lens and the helical screw mount. This ring carried the serial number of the camera. Reflex viewfinding was available as normal.

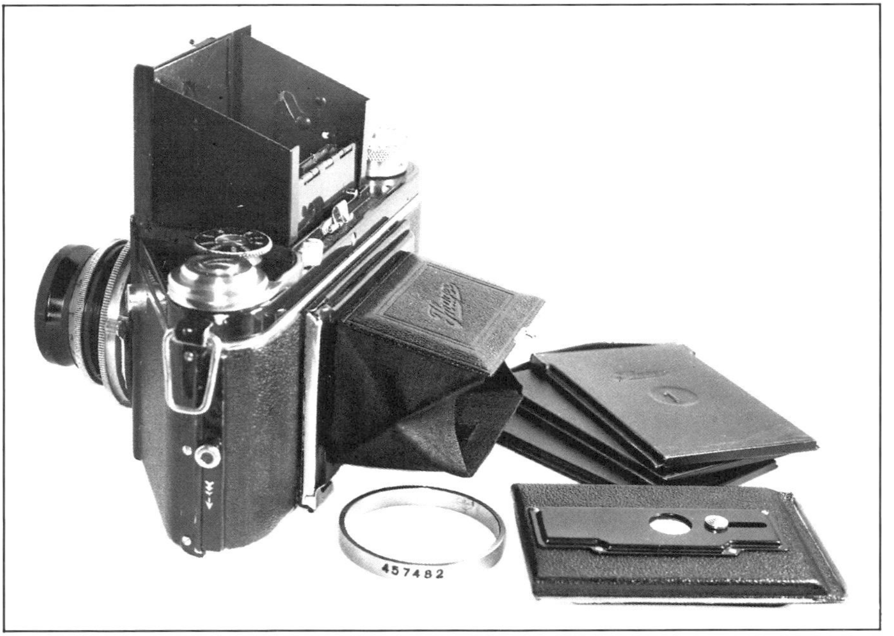

Exakta Model C. This picture shows a model C with all its accessories: the intermediate ring engraved with the body serial number, the ground glass focusing screen with its hood in position on the back, three 4.5x6cm dark slides, and the removable back with pressure plate for using size 127 film.

When using plates the lens had to be mounted directly on the helical mount and viewing and focusing had to be done on the groud-glass screen at the back, in the same way as with most plate cameras of the time. The screen was then replaced by one of the dark slides loaded with a plate. Reflex viewfinding was possible if the framing and focusing were first done with the intermediate ring in place. The lens and ring then had to be removed and the lens replaced without the ring. This dual purpose camera was not intended for impatient photographers!

The following lenses were available for the Exakta Model C:-

Ihagee Exaktar	75mm f/3.5
Zeiss Tessar	75mm f/3.5
Zeiss Tessar	75mm f/2.8

In 1936 the French importer's catalogue (Telos) pointed out that only the Model B could be supplied with this type of back, for an extra 200 Francs approximately. Some retail catalogues from 1936 and 1937 indicated that the Night Exakta fitted with the Zeiss Biotar lens could also be supplied with the dual purpose back. We only present two versions here because the dual option Night model has never been encountered by the authors.

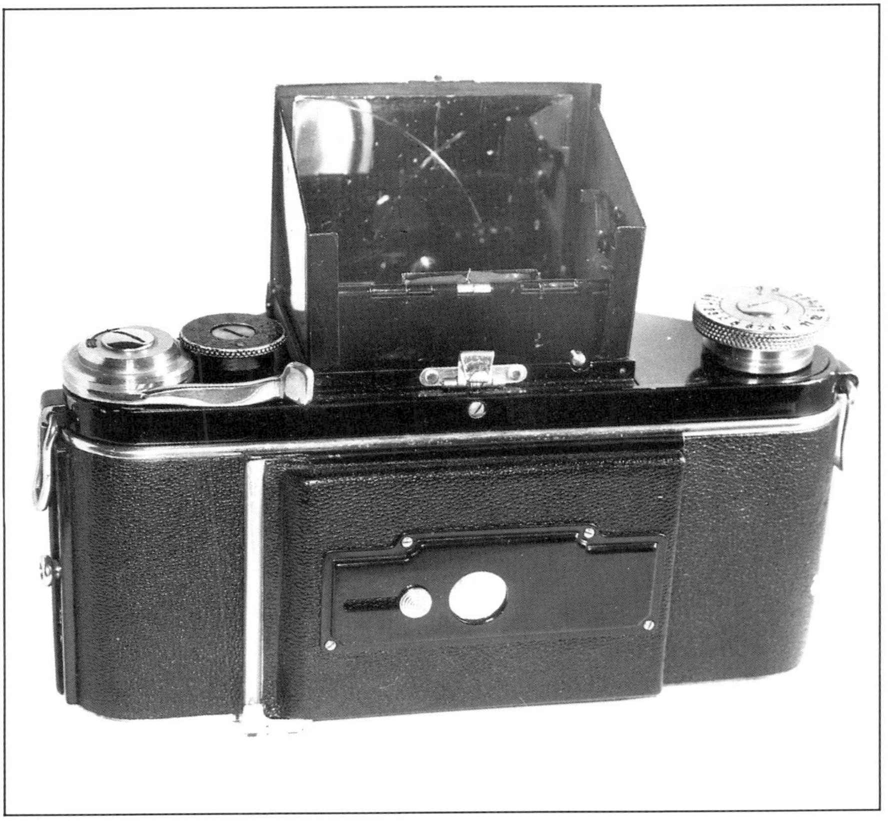

Exakta Model C, No. 457482, seen from the rear. The back with film pressure plate has been put back into place. One can see the cover for the red window.

EXAKTA C Version 1 1935 ★★★

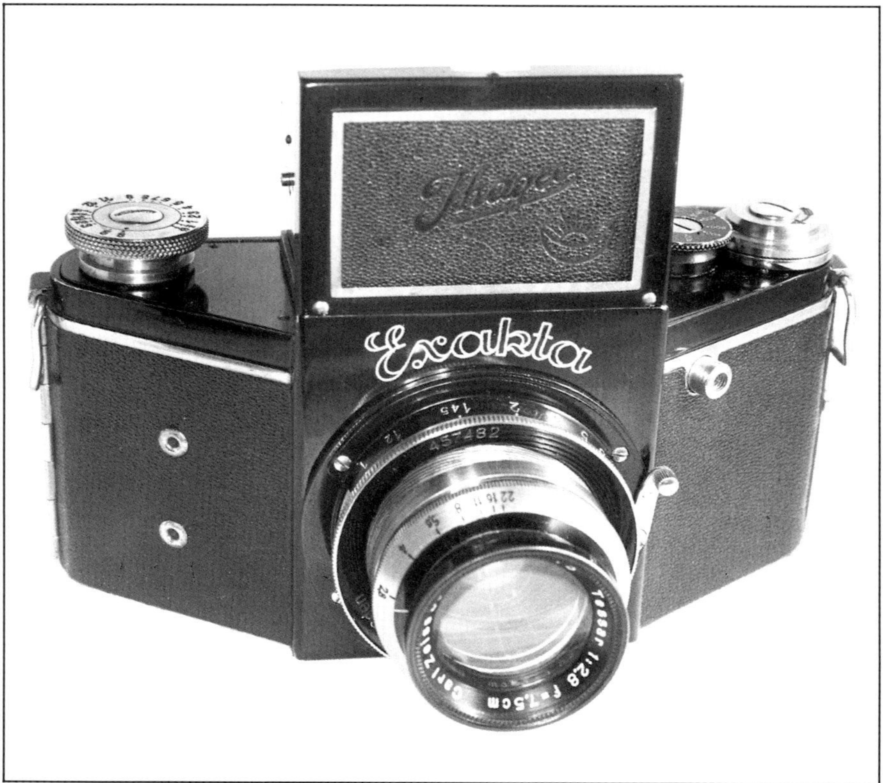

Exakta Model C, 1st Version, No. 457482

This had a black body indentical to that of Model B. The shutter speed range was from 12 seconds to 1/1000 second plus B & T with delay on all the speeds up to 6 seconds. Two pin Vacublitz socket. The camera used size 127 rollfilm and 4.5x6cm plates in single dark slides. It was supplied with ground glass screen, three 4.5x6cm dark slides and numbered intermediate ring.

EXAKTA C Version 2 1937 ★★★★

The chrome version was identical in finish to the Model B chrome, with the same shutter speed range, and three pin Vacublitz socket. It was supplied with ground glass screen, three 4.5x6cm dark slides and numbered ring.

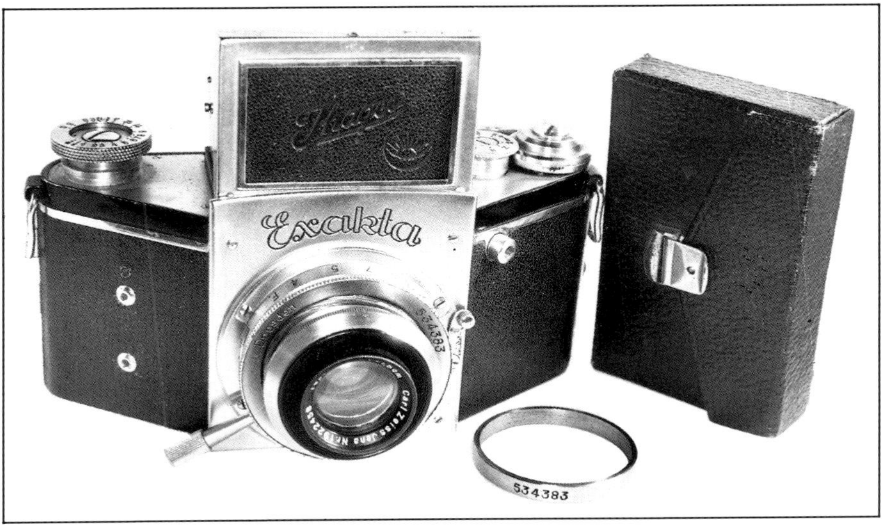

Exakta Model C, 2nd Version, No. 534383. The leather case shown in this picture contains the ground glass screen and the three 4.5x6cm dark slides.

EXAKTA C Chrome (Type A) Version 3 1939 ★★★★★

This chrome model appeared in the 1939 Ihagee catalogue. The shutter speed range was limited to speeds from 1/25 to 1/1000 seconds plus B & T. It had the wind-on lever and Vacublitz socket. It was always supplied with a ground glass screen, three 4.5x6cm dark slides and numbered intermediate ring.

The customer had the choice between the following lenses:-

Ihagee Exaktar	75mm f/3.5
Schneider Xenar	75mm f/2.8
Meyer Primotar	75mm f/3.5
Zeiss Tessar	75mm f/3.5
Zeiss Tessar	75mm f/2.8

EXAKTA Junior

With all its refinements the Exakta was an expensive camera. In 1937 an Exakta Model B with a Carl Zeiss Tessar 75mm f/2.8 lens was sold for the same price as a Leica

II. Ihagee decided to make the Exakta more accessible by simplifying its construction and creating a model which would be complementary to the range.

The shutter was simplified, with a speed range identical to that of Model A, and so was the focussing system by omission of the helical screw. The lens was a simple three-element design with front cell focusing and was no longer interchangeable. The Junior was nonetheless of excellent quality and did not downgrade the range. The lens was a 7.5cm, f/4.5 Ihagee Anastigmat, although in France at the time the importer was fitting a Boyer Topaz lens.

Despite the maker's efforts to widen the market for the Exakta by producing the simplified Junior, the model was never a commercial success, as is often the case with simplified models of a top grade camera.

The body of the camera was identical to that of Model A; so was the viewfinder and the shutter mechanism. The shutter offered the following range of speeds: 1/25, 1/50, 1/100, 1/200, 1/300, 1/400 and 1/500 second plus B & T. The essential difference was in the the lens mount, no longer a helical screw as with Model A, but a telescopic tube which collapsed entirely into the body of the camera when not in use. A safety device prevented the shutter from opening if the lens mount was not drawn out and locked in the infinity position. As already mentioned, focussing was by moving the front element only. The diameter of the lens thread was identical to that of Model A, but interchangability with those models was not possible because the focal length of the Junior lens was not the same.

We know of three versions of the Exakta Junior.

EXAKTA
Junior Version 1 1936 ★★★★

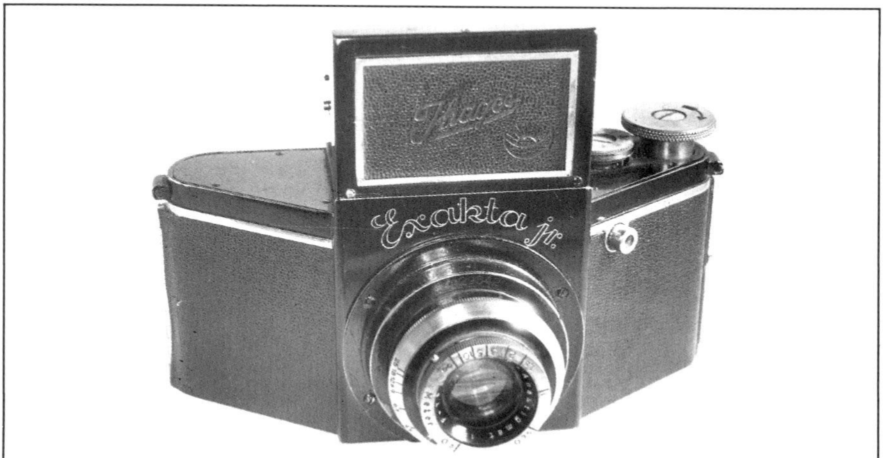

Exakta Junior, 1st Version, No. 429642.

With black body and leather covering, this camera had a milled knob for shutter setting, whereas the Exakta Model A of the same year was fitted with a lever. There was no Vacublitz socket. Shutter speeds were from 1/25 to 1/500 second plus B & T. Ihagee Anastigmat lens 75m f/4.5.

EXAKTA Junior Version 2 1937 ★★★★

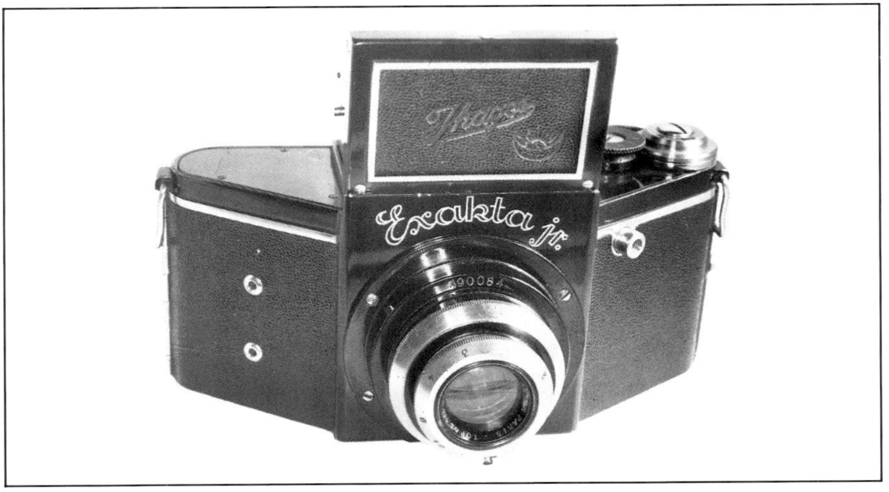

Exakta Junior, 2nd Version, No. 490084, with 75mm f/3.5 Topaz Boyer lens.

The following year the wind-on knob was replaced by a lever, as on Model A. The Vacublitz socket appeared on this version, but the contemporary catalogues indicated that it could be supplied without, according to the customer's requirements. The shutter speed range and other characteristics were identical to the first version. Ihagee Anastigmat lens 75mm f/4.5 or Topaz Boyer 75mm f/3.5.

EXAKTA Junior Chrome Version 3 1938 ★★★★★

This was the period when most manufacturers changed the presentation of their cameras. From the familiar black lacquer they changed to matt or bright chrome. The Exakta Junior also benefitted from this improvement. The two top-plates, the viewfinder frame and the front trade mark plate were finished in matt chrome. The control knobs and levers were in bright chrome. The optical and mechanical characteristics were the same as for the other versions. A Vacublitz socket was fitted. The chrome version of this camera is not very common.

CONCLUSION

Here ends our study of the different VP Exakta models. We cannot claim to have covered all the different variants, since the Exakta subject is so complex, but only the ones we are sufficiently familiar with. From the collector's point of view there were five main models, each having numerous versions. Briefly these were:-

Model A:	5 versions
Model B:	7 versions
Night model:	4 versions
Model C, plate model:	3 versions
Junior model:	versions

This makes a total of 22 different cameras. The VP Exakta was made from 1933 to 1939. The tooling was destroyed during the war and the Ihagee firm did not recommence manufacture of the camera afterwards.

In the next chapter we shall describe the lenses for the VP Exakta, as well as the accessories for macrophotography, flash, etc...

Chapter 3

The Lenses and Accessories of the VP EXAKTA

The table lists the lenses which were generally supplied with the VP Exakta, or offered for it by other makers. They are arranged in order of increasing focal length and increasing aperture. There were other firms also who manufactured lenses for the VP Exakta, or offered their lenses with an Exakta mount, but we do not have the information on their characteristics. Such firms were: Friedrich, Coronar, Hermagis, Eidoscope, Ludwig, Victar, Rodenstock, Trinar and Eurinar. In addition to these several English and American optical manufacturers also provided lenses for the camera.

The Exakta Juniors were often supplied to distributors without lenses. This was to enable them to reduce the retail price by fitting the cameras with more ordinary lenses which were available within their own countries.

Maker	Type	Focal length	Aperture	Number of elements
Zeiss	Tessar Wide Angle	55mm	f/8	4
Meyer	Wide-Angle Anastigmat	56mm	f/6.8	
Berthiot	Olor	59mm	f/5.7	
Dallmeyer	Wide Angle	60mm	f/11	
Zeiss	Tessar	70mm	f/3.5	4
Ihagee	Exaktar Anastigmat	70mm	f/3.5	3
Ihagee	Exaktar Anastigmat	75mm	f/4.5	3
Ihagee	Exaktar Anastigmat	75mm	f/3.5	3
Boyer	Topaz	75mm	f/3.5	3
Zeiss	Tessar	75mm	f/3.5	4
Meyer	Primotar	75mm	f/3.5	4
Schneider	Xenar	75mm	f/3.5	4
Schneider	Xenar	75mm	f/2.9	5
Steinheil	Cassar	75mm	f/2.9	
Zeiss	Tessar	75mm	f/2.8	4
Berthiot	Flor	75mm	f/2.8	
Meyer	Makro Plasmat	75mm	f/2.7	6
Meyer	Primoplan	80mm	f/1.9	
Dallmeyer	Super Six	80mm	f/1.9	6
Schneider	Xenon	80mm	f/2 6	
Zeiss	Biotar	80mm	f/2 6	
Ihagee	Exaktar	105mm	f/4.5	
Meyer	Primotar	105mm	f/3.8	4
Berthiot	Flor	105mm	f/2.8	

Maker	Type	Focal length	Aperture	Number of elements
Ihagee	Exaktar	110mm	f/4.5	
Zeiss	Tele-Tessar	120mm	f/6.3	4
Meyer	Tele-Megor	150mm	f/5.5	
Schneider	Tele-Xenar	150mm	f/5.5	
Berthiot	Tele-Objectif	150mm	f/5.5	
Dallmeyer	Tele-Dallon	6in(152mm)	f/5.6	
Dallmeyer	Tele-Dallon	7in(177mm)	f/6.3	
Zeiss	Tele-Tessar*	180mm	f/6.3	4
Meyer	Tele-Megor*	180mm	f/5.5	
Schneider	Tele-Xenar	240mm	f/5.5	
Schneider	Tele-Xenar	240mm	f/4.5	
Zeiss	Tele-Tessar*	250mm	f/6.3	4
Meyer	Tele-Megor*	250mm	f/5.5	
Schneider	Tele-Xenar	300mm	f/5.5	
Schneider	Tele-Xenar	360mm	f/5.5	

* Useable format: 4x4cm

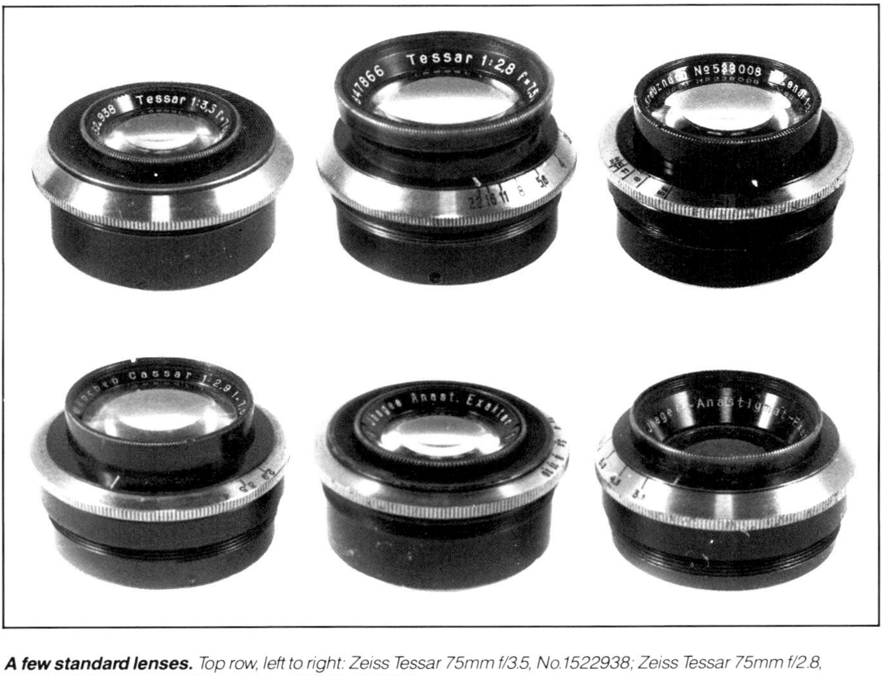

A few standard lenses. *Top row, left to right: Zeiss Tessar 75mm f/3.5, No.1522938; Zeiss Tessar 75mm f/2.8, No.1847866; Schneider Xenar 75mm f/2.9, No.588008.*
Bottom row, left to right: Steinheil Cassar 75mm f/2.9, No.256242; Ihagee Anastigmat 70mm f/3.5, small diameter, No.590709; Ihagee Anastigmat 70mm f/3.5, large diameter, No.692006. These last two are different versions of the same lens.

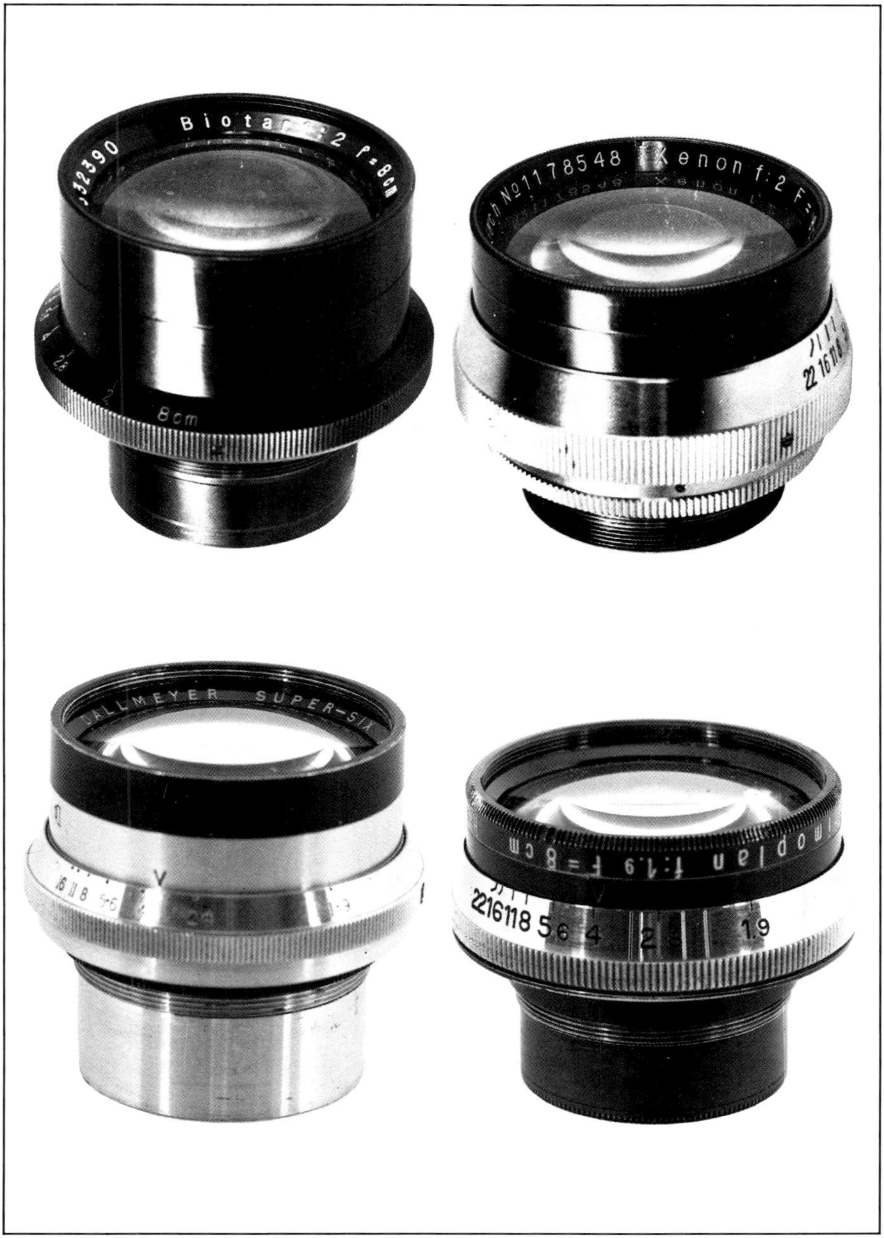

The "Night" lenses. *Top left: Zeiss Biotar 80mm f/2/, No.1632390. Top right: Schneider Xenon 80mm f/2, No.1178548. Bottom left: Dallmeyer Super Six 3in (76mm) f/1.9, No.451464. Bottom right: Meyer Primoplan 80mm f/1.9, No.672032*

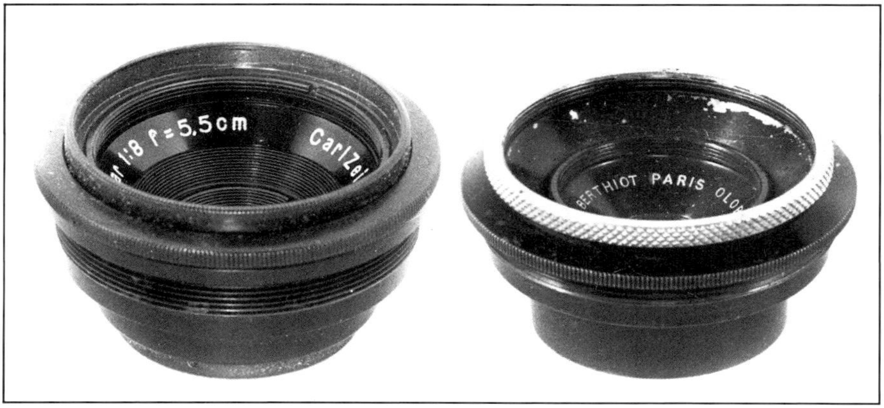

Wide-angle lenses. *Left: Zeiss Tessar Wide-Angle 55mm f/8, No.1508258. Right: Berthiot Olor 59mm f/5.7, No.272154.*

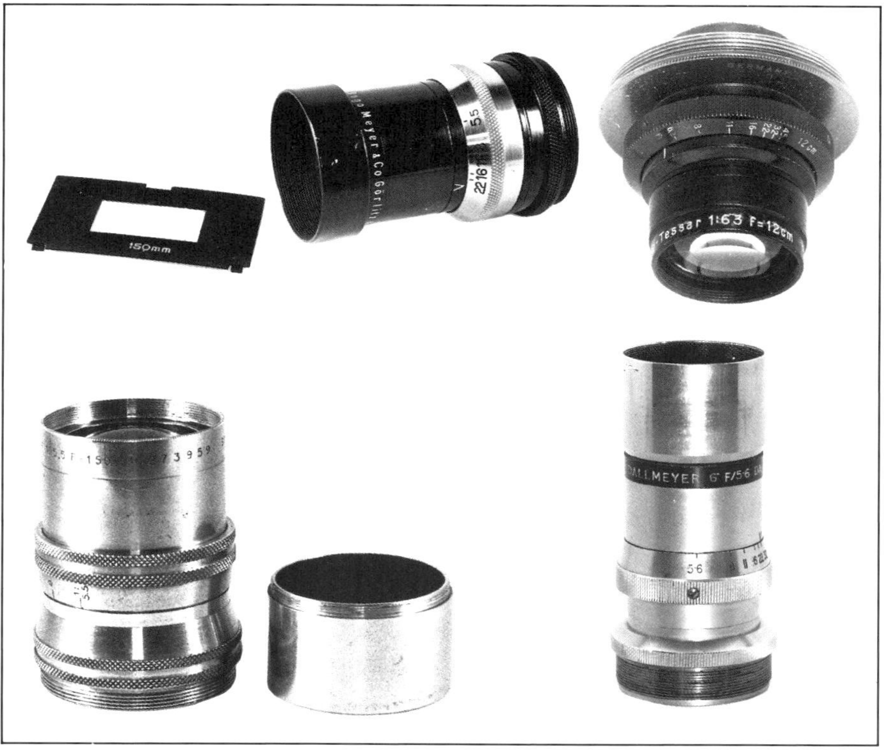

Tele lenses. *Top left: Meyer Tele-Megor 150mm f/5.5, No.662659, with mask for sports viewfinder. Top right: Zeiss Tele-Tessar 120mm f/6.3, No.870172. Bottom left: Berthiot Tele 150mm f/5.5, No.273959. Bottom right: Dallmeyer Tele-Dallon 6in (153mm) f/5.5, No.203383.*

ACCESSORIES FOR THE VP EXAKTA

Hood Extension

This 12cm high leather extension hood was for use with the VP Exakta hood. It made viewfinding and focusing easier in very bright conditions as it prevented incident light from reaching the focusing screen. It had its own retractable focussing magnifier. Another model without magnifier and not so high also existed.

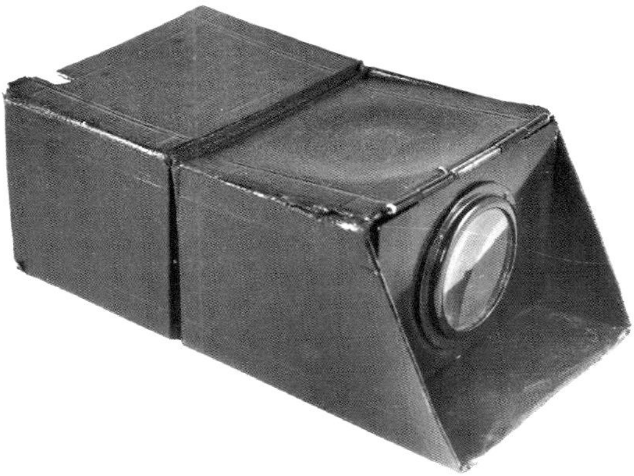

The model with magnifier

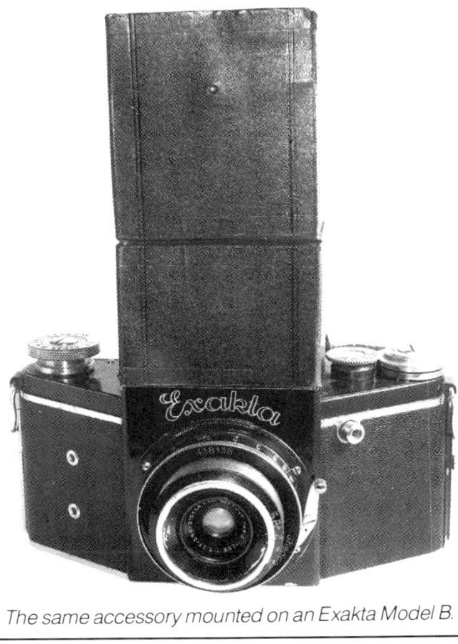

The same accessory mounted on an Exakta Model B.

Extension Tubes

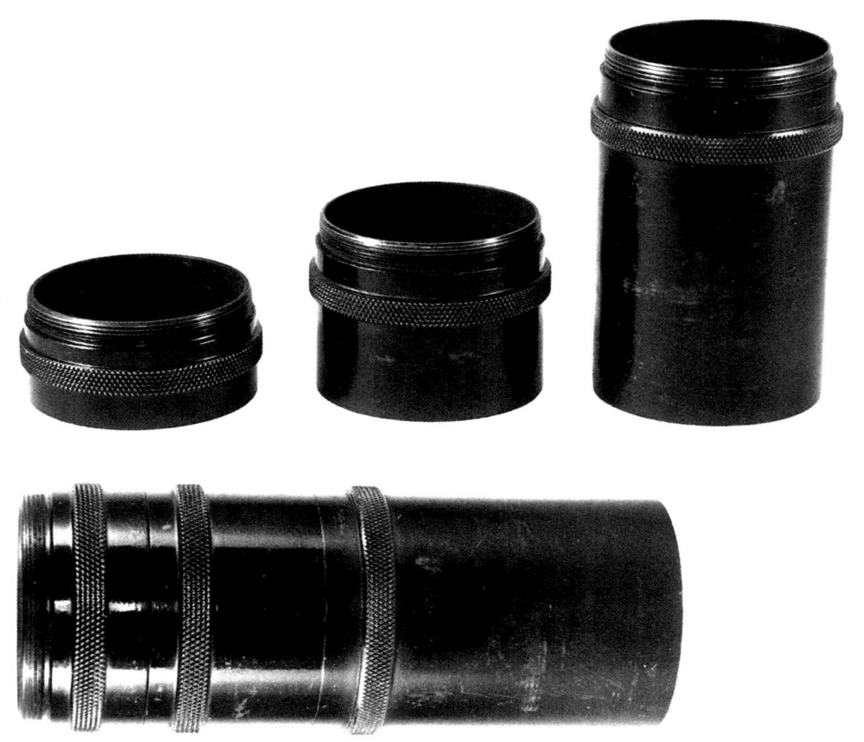

A set of three tubes; separate and joined together
A = 15mm, B = 30mm, C = 60mm

These were intended for close-up photography. Up to three tubes could be inserted between the lens and the focussing mount.

Reproduction ratios with 75mm lens.

Tube combination	*Lens focused at:* Infinity	*1 metre*
A	4.5:1	3:1
B	1.2:1	1.7:1
A+B	1.5:1	1.25:1
C	1.1:1	1:1
B+C	1:1.3	1:1.5
2xC	1:1.7	1:2

The first number in each column refers to the size of the object; the second one to that of the reproduction

Microscope Attachment

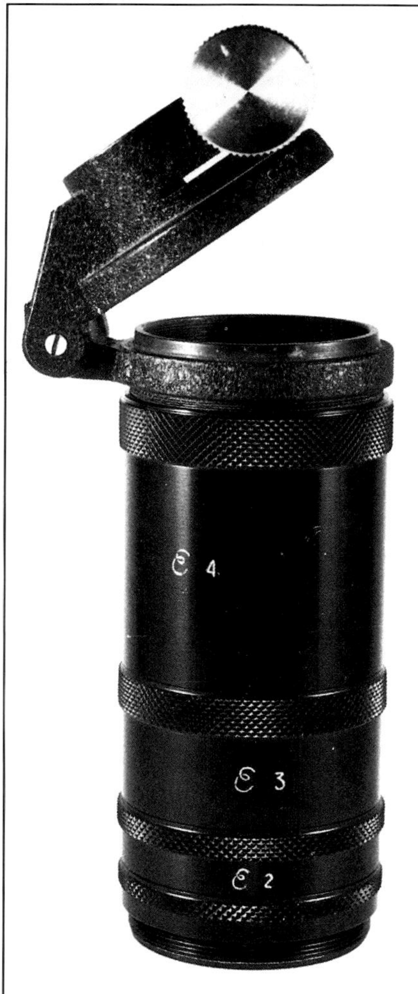

Microscope Attachment, hinge open

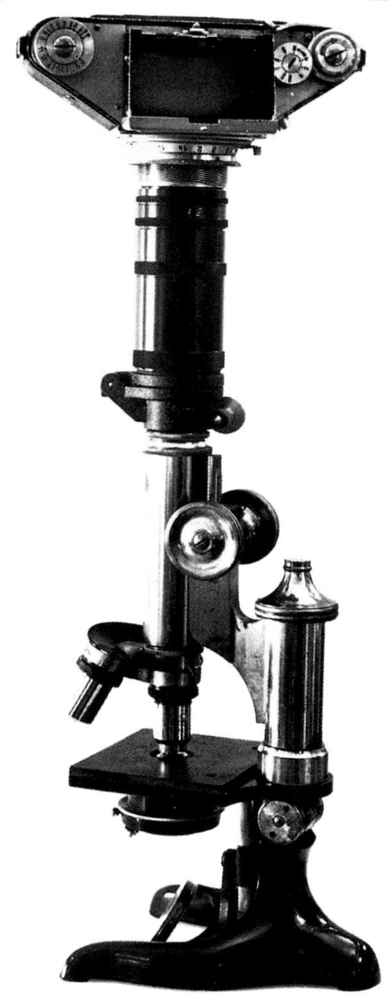

Exakta Model B mounted on a microscope using the Microscope Attachment.

This attachment consisted of four tubes and a hinged connecting eyepiece. In the 1936 catalogue the connecting eyepiece was nickel plated. The black version in the illustration is probably more recent.

After removing the lens, these tubes would be inserted between the body of the camera and the eyepiece of the microscope. The hinge enabled the eyepiece to be changed without removing the camera.

The "Vacublitz" Flash

It was in 1927 that the first flashbulbs appeared in which the filament consisted of a thin sheet of aluminium. In 1929 such bulbs were marketed under the name "Vacublitz". Until that time there existed no, or very few, synchronisation systems between the flashlight and the shutter. This became possible with the new bulbs and

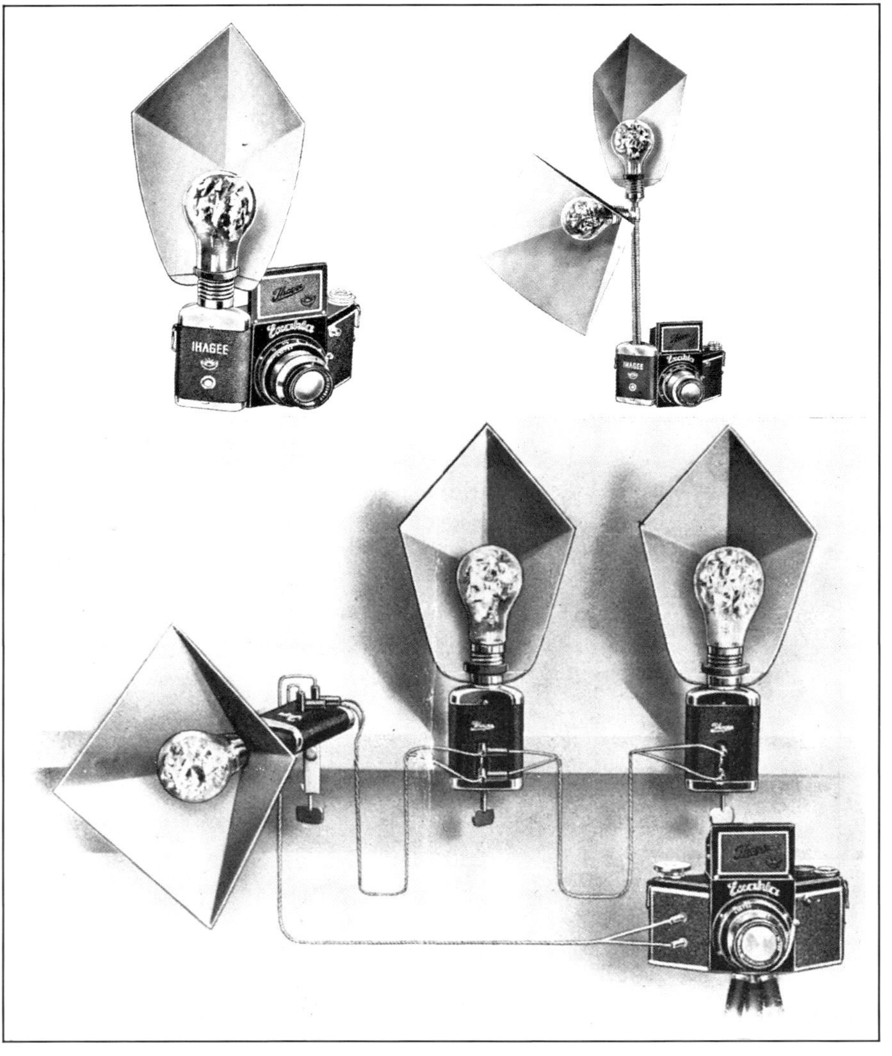

Illustrations from Ihagee catalogue showing the flashgun mounted on the camera, the versatility of the Vacublitz system with the flexible extension and the T piece, and the use of 3 flashguns all fired simultaneously – the clamps were supplied with the equipment.

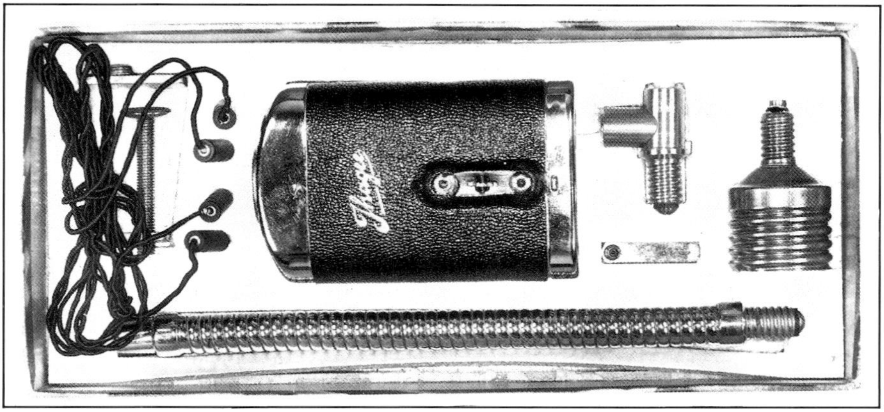

A complete Vacublitz set in its original box (except for the reflector). It comprises, from left to right:- extension lead enabling remote use of the Vacublitz, adjustable clamp for fixing the Vacublitz on any support (visible underneath the extension lead), battery case with fixing screws, T attachment for using two Vacublitz units simultaneously, adaptor pin for the camera, adaptor for large-base bulbs, 16cm long flexible extension. A simplified version of this kit was also offered which comprised:- battery case with bulb, adaptor pin for camera, adaptor for large base bulb, reflector.

Other Accessories

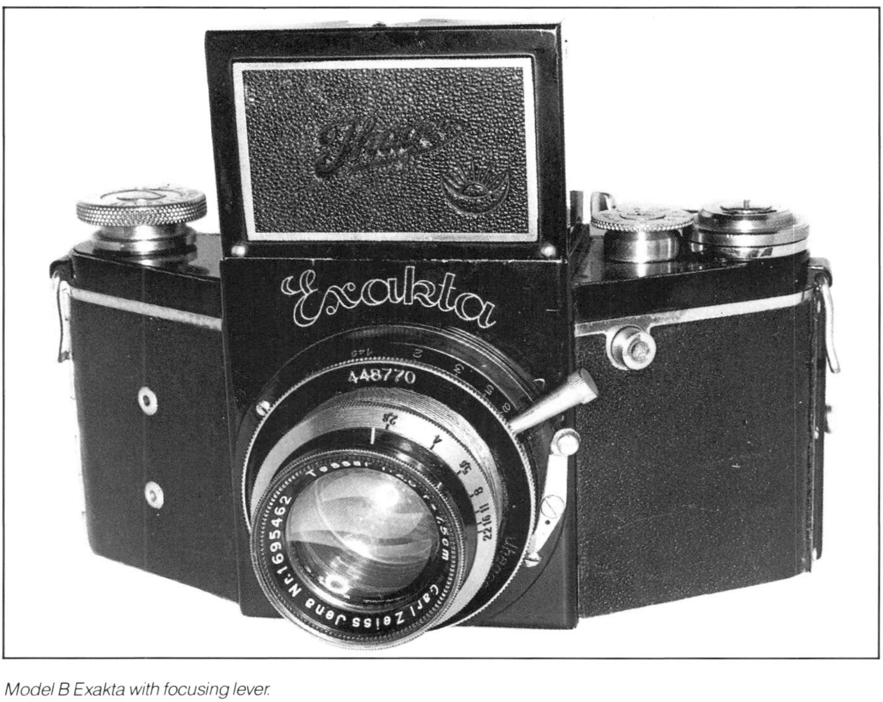

Model B Exakta with focusing lever.

from 1930 numerous external synchronisers and synchronised shutters were patented.

The 1935 Model B Exakta was the first photographic camera to have a built-in socket allowing the flash to be synchronised with the shutter. This two pin socket was directly connected to the flash casing. This was changed to a three pin socket of which the third pin was to give a more secure fixing for the flashgun. Later a coaxial socket was installed in the Kine Exakta. The bulbs were of the slow combustion type and shutter synchronisation was for speeds from 1/25 to 1/1000 second.

Besides the focusing lever, there were seven patterns of lens hood for the different standard lenses, a large diameter shutter release knob, to facilitate release when wearing gloves and a double jointed tilt head for use on a tripod of which both nickel and chrome plated versions exist.

Auxiliary lenses

There were four models, each in four different mountings which could be attached to the following lenses:-

Tessar f/3.5	Diameter 28.6mm
Tessar f/2.8	Diameter 37mm
Exaktar and Makro-Plasmat	Diameter 32mm
Biotar f/2	Diameter 51mm

The four models were:-

Ihagee auxiliary lens enabling close-ups to 30cm

Zeiss Proxar (x2) enabling close-ups to 50cm.

Zeiss Proxar (x1) enabling close-ups to 1 metre.

Ihagee auxiliary tele-lens with x 1.3 magnification. Supplied with special extension tube.

Filters

The filters were available in the four fixtures previously described. Six colours were offered, green, light green, yellow, light yellow, red and blue, as well as ultra-violet and grey sky filters. As with the auxiliary lenses, these were supplied separately or in a pouch containing an assortment.

Enlargers

There were two enlarger models, which actually covered the 6x6 format. The Luminax-Projection was sold with a 75mm f/3.5 Meyer Primotar lens, but could also accomodate the VP Exakta standard lens. There was also the Exakta-Luminax which was cheaper.

Chapter 4
The 35mm EXAKTA: the Early Models

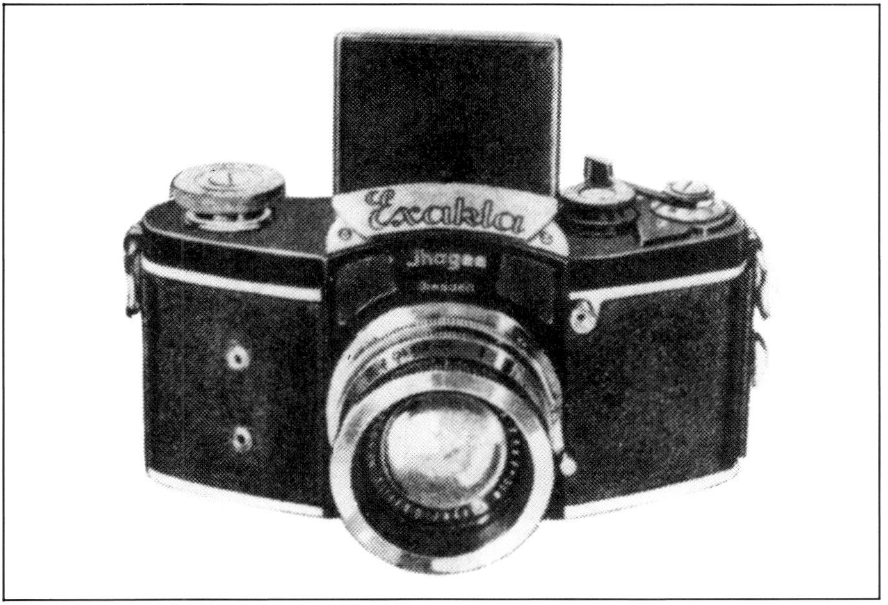

Prototype of the Kine Exakta. Introduced in the catalogue in 1935 and 1936 in black finish like the VP Exakta. It was also called the Kino Exakta. It was not distributed commercially in this form.

Introduced at the annual New Year's Fair in Leipzig in 1936, this was the first single-lens reflex camera on 35mm perforated film. It aroused an enormous amount of interest, but it also had many detractors, especially among the unconvinced users of the Leica and Contax.

The Kine Exakta incorporated the principal technical characteristics of the VP Exakta, Model B. The sceptics at the time believed that it was impossible to reduce a single-lens reflex to the 24x36mm format, that it would be difficult to operate correctly and rapidly with such a camera, and that the idea would fail. The rest is history, and Ihagee themselves earned their place in the history of photography.

The Kine Exakta was very quickly adopted by many amateurs, as well as by technicians and research workers. The sales in the following years rose continuously, whereas those of the 4x6.5 models began to level out and then fall.

The innovation in the Kine Exakta lay in its very precise viewing system. In place of the flat, ground glass, a powerful plano-convex magnifier was substituted, the ground lower face of which gave an excellent view of the image which appeared enlarged. A round, ocular focusing magnifier, hinged to the base of the viewfinder, allowed even more precise focusing. When the magnifier was folded down, the frame of the viewfinder acted as a sports-type viewfinder.

Another innovation was the film cutter. By unscrewing a milled knob, a knife was freed which sliced through the film transversally when the knob was pulled downwards so that the exposed part of the film could be developed after opening the camera in the darkroom. An empty cassette could also be mounted in place of the take-up spool. This avoided rewinding.

Thus the first 35mm reflex camera in the world already possessed all the characteristics of a modern camera and, except for the penta-prism, fifty years on it can still stand comparaison with numerous cameras.

From the first, an entire photographic system was foreseen for the Kine Exakta: special 40 to 500mm lenses, already some as fast as f/1.9 and f/1.5, rings and extension tubes for macrophotography, adaptors for microscopes and astronomical telescopes, a multiflash, a reproduction stand, a swivel tripod, a duplicator for negatives or transparencies, projectors, an enlarger-projector, filters, lens hoods, a magnifier viewing extender, etc...

Kine EXAKTA Version 1, Round Magnifier 1936 ★★★★★

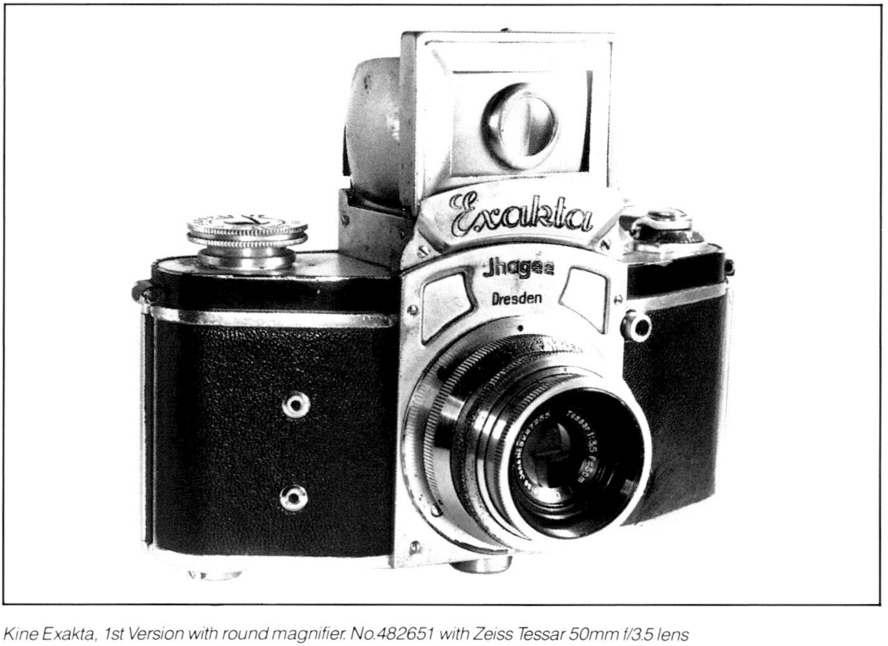

Kine Exakta, 1st Version with round magnifier. No.482651 with Zeiss Tessar 50mm f/3.5 lens

Known range of serial numbers: 455600 - 486000. However, there is an overlap of numbers with the rectangular mangifier Kine Exakta (see below), beginnning from 484000. One also comes across cameras with earlier numbers and a rectangular magnifier, where the owners have had the round magnifier changed. In effect, the latter only enlarged the central area of the screen whereas the rectangular magnifier covered nearly the whole area. The serial number was engraved on the back of the body, on the inside.

The main features of the design of the Kine Exakta were:-

- Metal cast body of trapezoid shape.
- Focal plane roller-blind shutter, running horizontally.
- Shutter speeds B, Z (time), 1/25, 1/50, 1/100, 1/150, 1/500, 1/1000 second
- Slow speeds 1/10, 1/2, 1, 2, 3, 4, 5, 6, 7, 8, 9, 11, 12 seconds.
- Delayed slow speeds 1/10, 1/2, 1, 2, 3, 4, 5, 6 seconds.
- A delay of around 12 seconds could be applied to all speeds from 1/25 to 1/1000 by proceeding in the following mannner: set the mechanism using the lever, choose the shutter speed, then set the slow speed mechanism and place the fixed mark opposite one of the marks engraved in red on this knob (between 1/10 and 6 seconds).
- The fast speeds knob also set the shutter without advancing the film.
- Slow speeds knob above on the right. Slow speeds etched in black, delayed slow speeds etched in red. It should only be set when the shutter itself has already been set.
- Near to the frame counter, at the rear, a lever allows the winding mechanism to be disengaged. Marked V for forward and R for return.
- On the front, at the right, a bipolar plug for flash bulbs, synchronisation at all speeds.

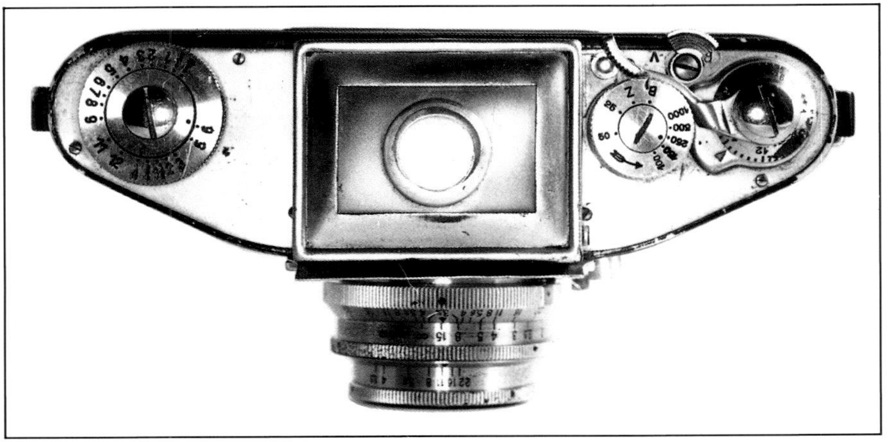

Kine Exakta 1936. In this photograph one can distinguish from left to right: the mechanism cocking lever (The left-hand position wind-on lever is exclusive to Exakta) and the frame counter, the lever for unlocking the rewind mechanism, the fast speeds dial, the folded viewfinder with its round magnifier, the slow speeds dial and its delayed-action release. The lens is a Zeiss Zeiss 50mm f/3.5 and to its left may be seen the shutter release knob.

- Push button release on the left of the front plate.
- Front plate in two parts, the top part engraved "Exakta".
- The folding viewfinder (with round magnifier) had a safety catch on the left which blocked the shutter when the cover was closed.
- On the base there was on the right a rewinding knob with a folding key, next to this the small milled knob of the film cutter, in the centre the tripod socket, on the left a knob with folding key for engaging the film.
- The back was removable. It had the nickel-plated film pressure plate on the inside.
- In the centre of the black leather back was the logo "Ihagee".

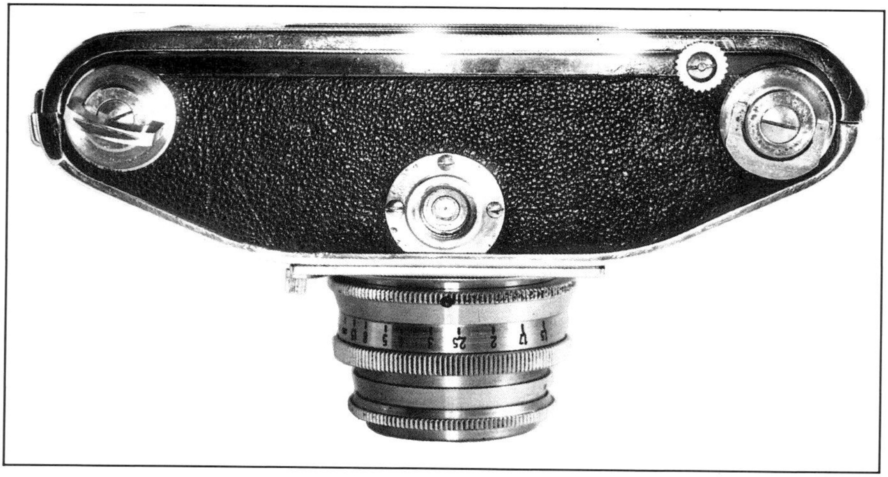

Kine Exakta 1936, seen from below. From left to right: the rewinding knob, the film cutter knob, the threaded tripod socket, the take-up spool axis. In the centre, the lens and its unlocking lever.

Kine Exakta, first version. Right-hand end of the body with the slow speed dial and attachment for shoulder strap.

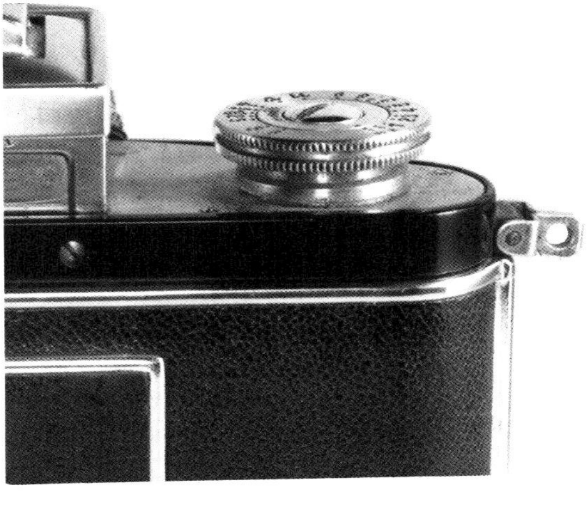

Kine EXAKTA Version 2, Rectangular Magnifier 1937 ★★★

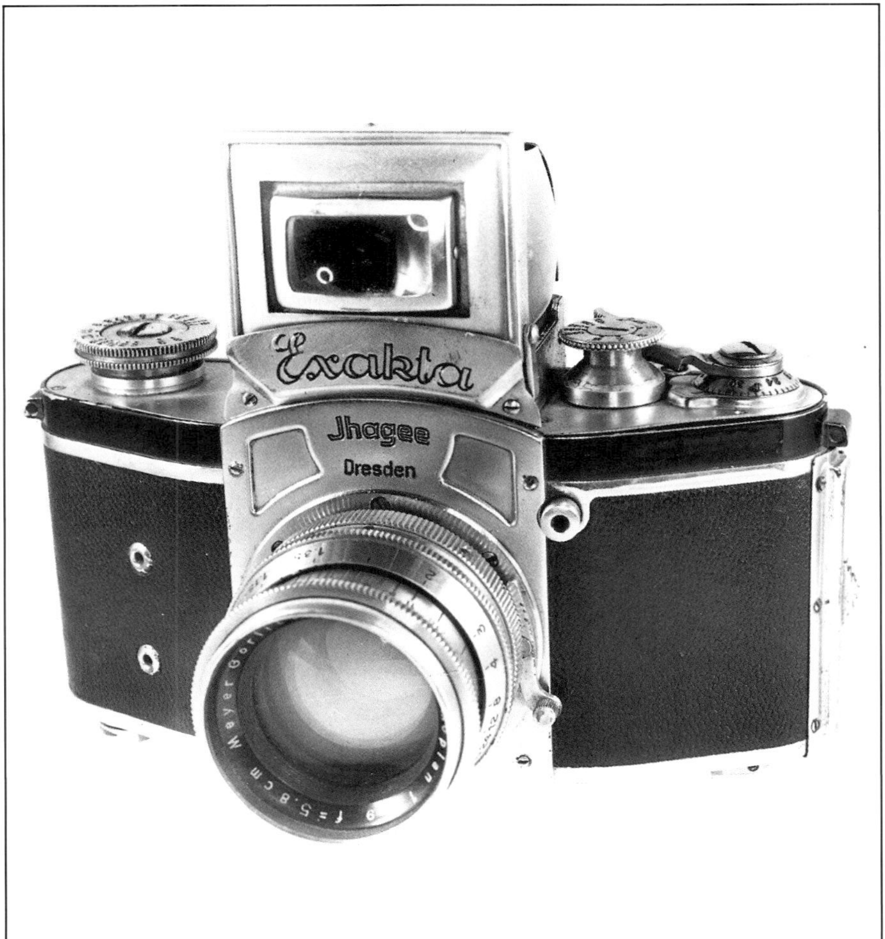

Kine Exakta, 2nd version with rectangular magnifier. Body No.485562, here with a very fine Meyer Primoplan 58mm f/1.9 lens. The front plate was in two parts. The small plate carrying the name "Exakta" was the same as that on the round magnifier version.

Known range of serial numbers: 484000 - 530000.

All the characteristics of this model were identical to those of the first version except for the shape of the magnifier. Its magnifying-power was 4x, the same as that of the round magnifier, but the field covered was greater (18x24mm approx.).

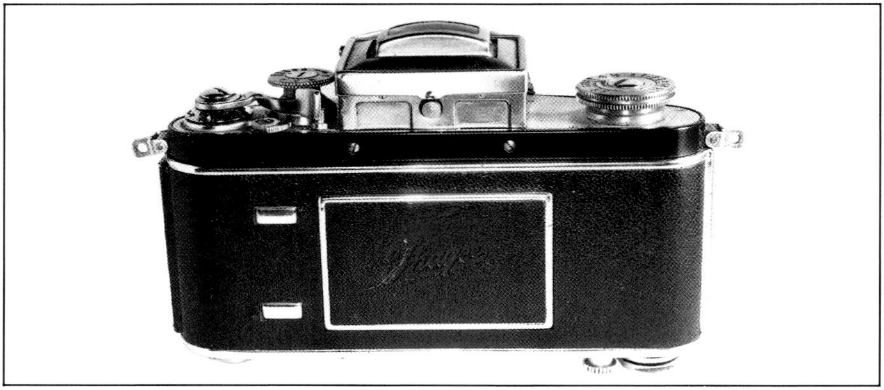

Back of the Kine Exakta, 2nd version. In the central part of the back one can see the logo "Ihagee" embossed in the leather. Only the first four versions carried this detail, it had disappeared from the post-war models.

Kine EXAKTA Version 3, with "C" spelling 1937 ★★★★

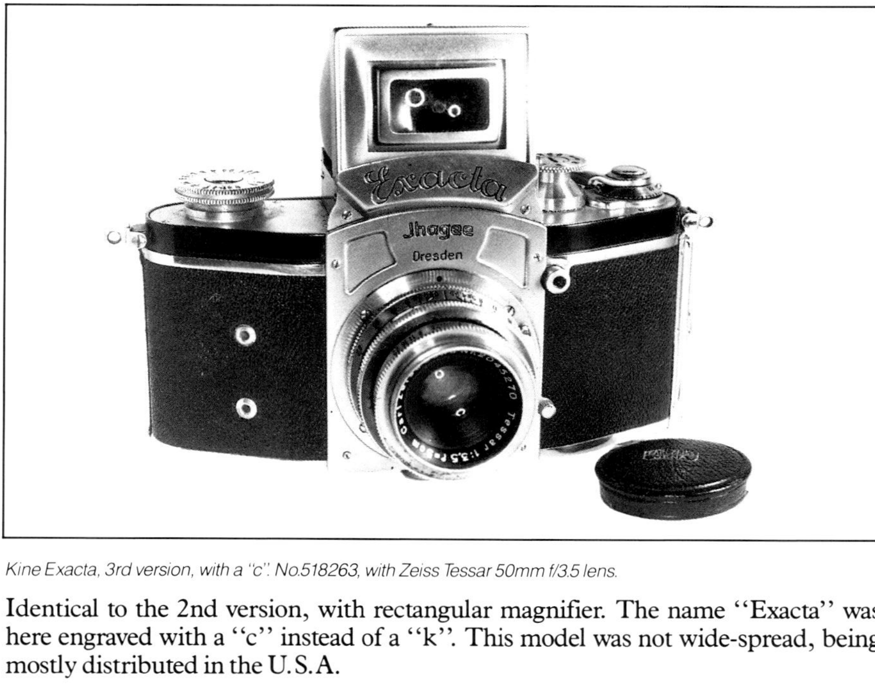

Kine Exacta, 3rd version, with a "c". No.518263, with Zeiss Tessar 50mm f/3.5 lens.

Identical to the 2nd version, with rectangular magnifier. The name "Exacta" was here engraved with a "c" instead of a "k". This model was not wide-spread, being mostly distributed in the U.S.A.

Kine EXAKTA Version 4 1938 ★★★

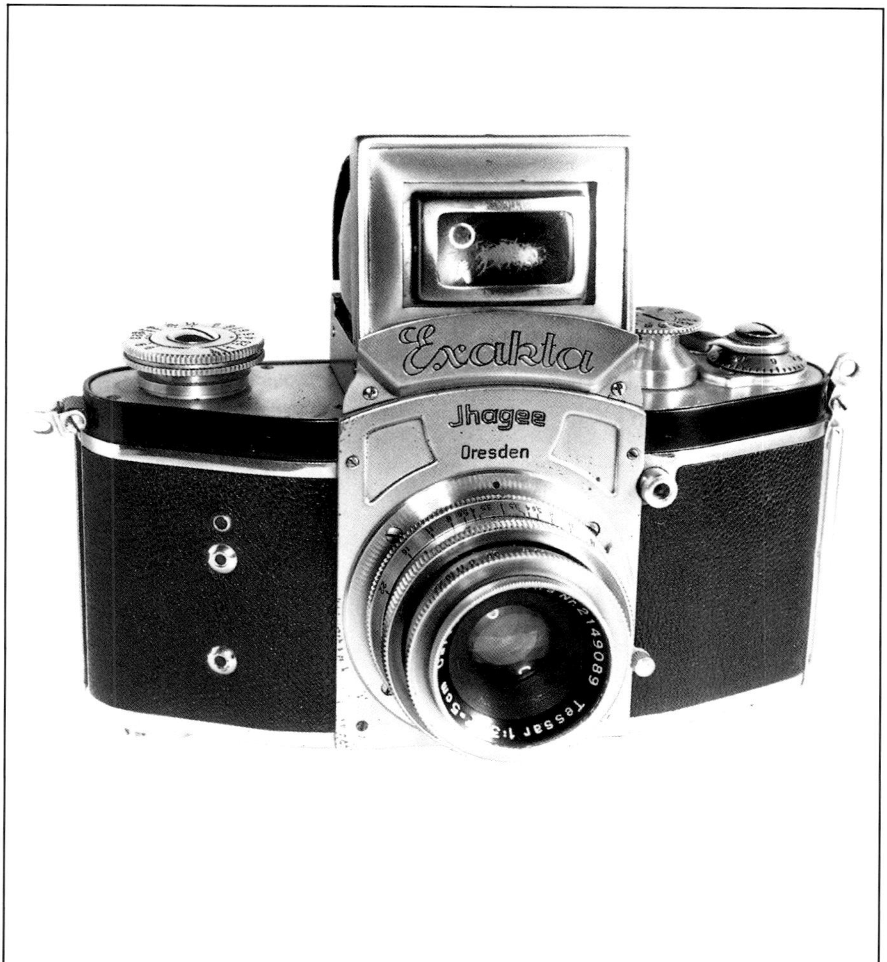

Kine Exakta, 4th version of 1938. No 546875 with Zeiss Tessar lens 50mm f/3.5 lens.

Known range of serial numbers: 530000 - 613000.

Same characteristics as the preceding models; only the bipolar Vacublitz plug was modified. A third hole is visible above the traditional sockets. It was threaded and ensured improved fixing of the Vacublitz flash gun, which was modified accordingly. This threaded hole also appeared on the VP Exakta of the time.

Kine EXAKTA Version 5, with "C" spelling 1948 ★★★

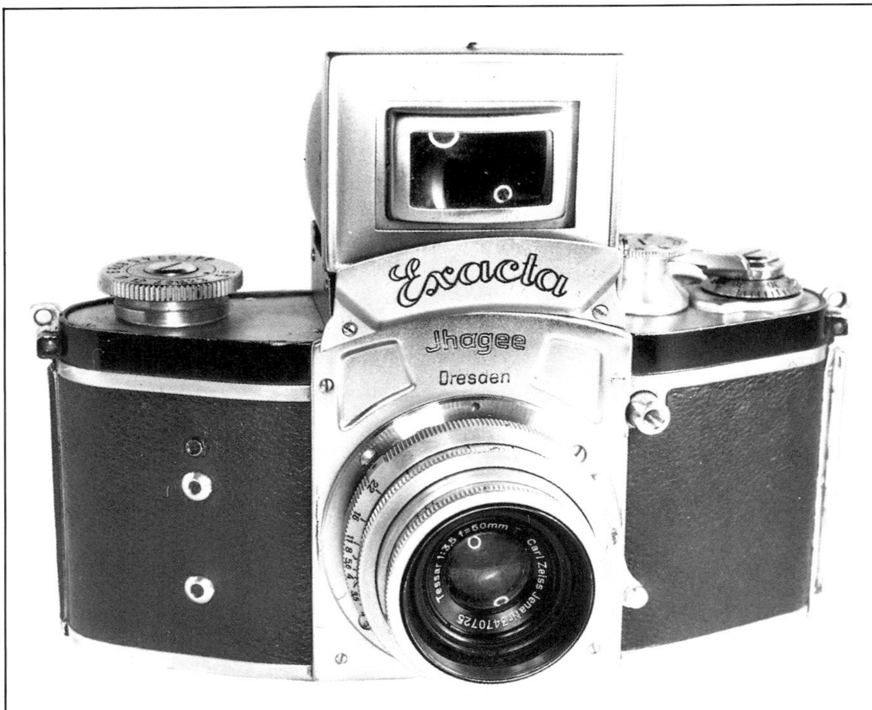

Kine Exacta, 5th version. No.622411, with Zeiss Tessar 5mm f/3.5 lens. Note the nameplate engraved with a "c" instead of of "k".

Known range of serial numbers: 613000 - 650000.

This was the first Exakta model manufactured by Ihagee after the war, despite what seemed to be insurmountable difficulties. It differed from pre-war models in the following respects:-

- The strap attachments were riveted and fixed, whereas they had been hinged.
- The slow speed dial lost its groove round its circumference. The speed 1/5 replaced the 1/10 on the slow and delayed speeds.
- The logo "Ihagee" no longer appeared on the leather at the back of the camera.
- The mirror chamber was slightly modified. The interior, which had been flocked, was now corrugated to cut out stray light more efficiently.
- The tripod bush was more solid and protruded by a half-millimetre, whereas it had been level with the leather on preceding models
- On certain bodies "Made in Germany" was stamped on the leather.

The model was mainly sold in the U.S.A. Very few entered Britain or France because of the import restrictions at the time.

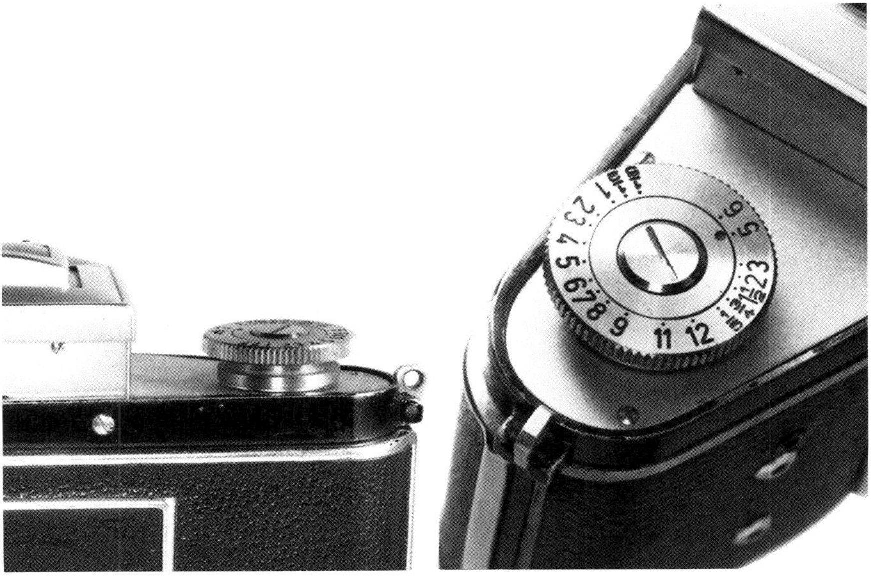

Left: Detail of the slow speed knob, without groove, and of the fixed strap attachment. Right: The slow speeds dial: 1/5, 1/2, 1, 2, 3, 4, 5, 6, 7, 8, 9, 11, 12 seconds. Delayed slow speeds: 1/5, 1/4, 1/2, 2, 3, 5, 6 seconds. The central part of the knob can be flat, as in this photograph (body No. 644146) or convex as on the pre-war models (body No. 618 426).

EXAKTA II Version 1 1948 ★★★★

According to an American specialist, some of the first models were still marked ''Exacta'' with a ''c. The approximate range of serial numbers of this model was from 647000 to 655000. Çertain examples of pre-production runs have a number below 647000. In an Exakta Camera Company prospectus we have found the number 641932.

On this model the name plate was made of a single piece of pressed metal. The upper part had slightly profiled angles. The curved part of the upper edge was thin and did not protrude.

The differences in comparison with the Kine Exakta were as follows:-

- The viewfinder included a hinged cover for protection of the magnifier. However, it remained fixed and retained the shutter release security knob
- The frame counter was built-in, with an indicator window on the top
- There was a small hinged lever for disengaging the mechanism

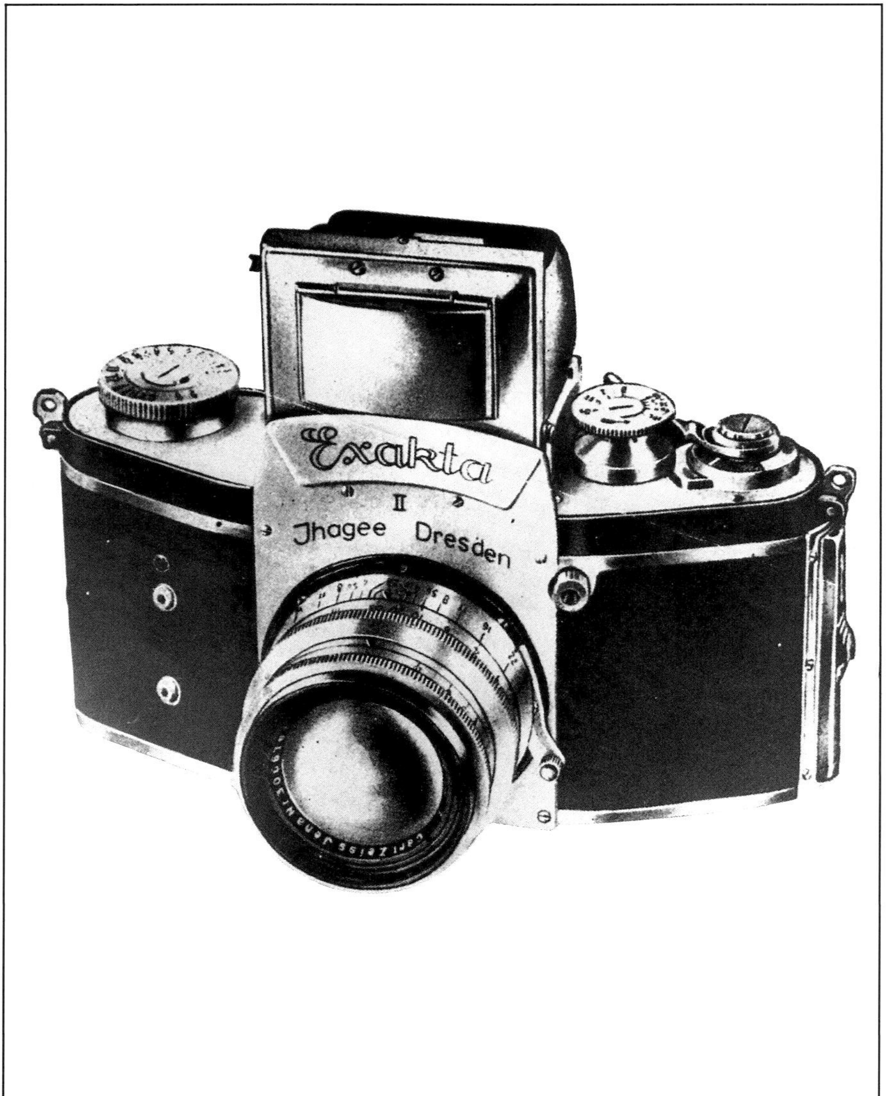

Exakta II, 1st version, No.641932.

- Rewinding was by a knob with key in place of the milled knob
- The ribbed film pressure plate was black, the back still removable
- The flash plug remained unchanged with its third fixing hole.

The speed ranges were the same as those of the Kine Exakta.

EXAKTA II Version 2 1949 ★★★

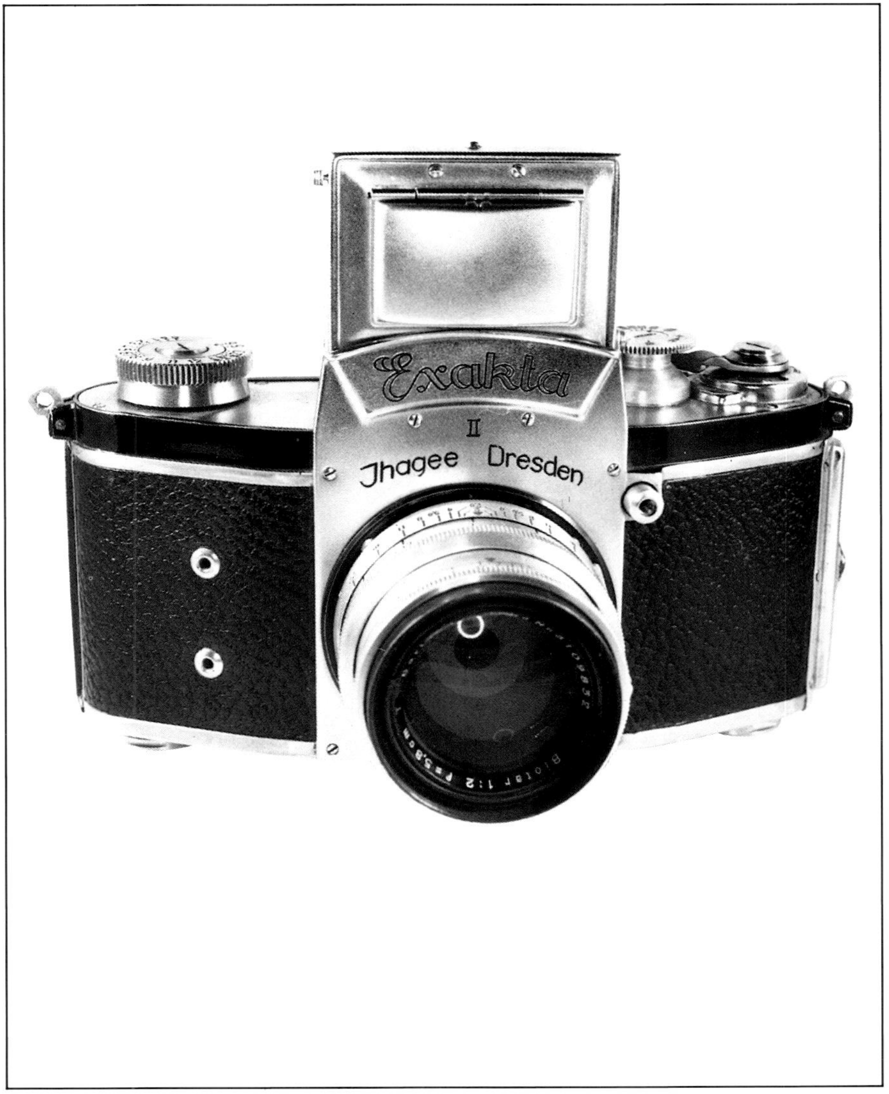

Exakta II, Version 2. No.657377, with Zeiss Biotar 58mm f/2 lens.

Approximate range of serial numbers: 655000 - 672000.

The only major difference between this and the first version was in the front plate, the upper part of which was pressed and shaped to ensure greater rigidity. Another point of detail, a return to the bipolar flash plug without the third fixing hole.

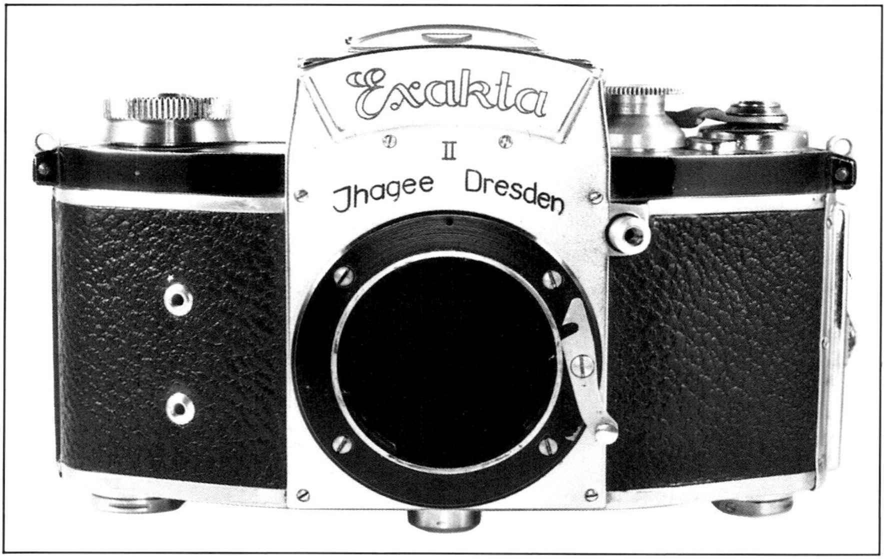

On these cameras, both first and second versions, the lens bayonet was finished in black. However, there are some models with a chromium-plated brass bayonet. Perhaps this was a later modification.

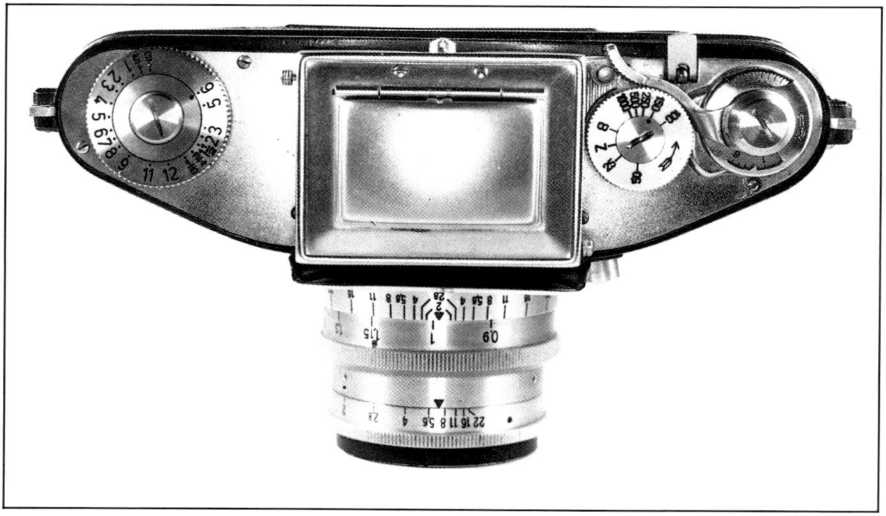

On this photograph of the camera seen from above, one can observe the frame counter, the hinged lever for disengaging the mechanism, the magnifier protection cover and the slow speeds dial.

Chapter 5

The 35mm EXAKTA; the Mature System

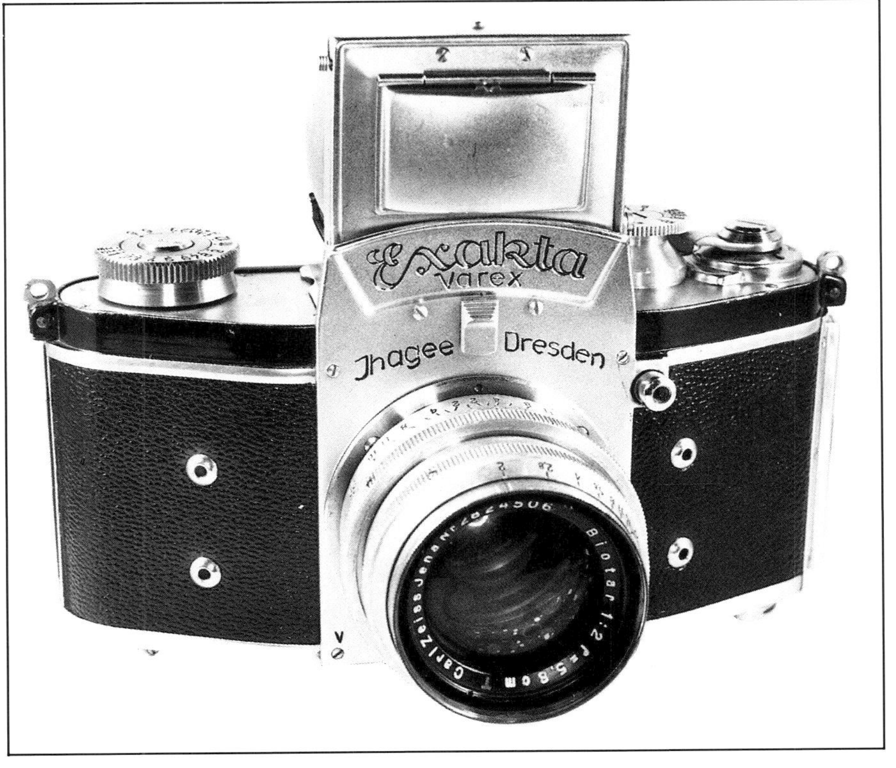

Exakta Varex, 1950. No.674810 with Zeiss Biotar 58mm f/2 lens.

In 1950 Ihagee introduced a new Exakta with a sensational innovation. This was the interchangeable viewfinder so that the photographer had the choice between the waist-level screen or eye-level pentaprism.

EXAKTA Varex 1950 ★★★

Approximate range of serial numbers: 667000 - 692000.

This new Exakta was destined for the European market. The removable viewing hood still retained the lever that prevented release when it was collapsed. It was marked "Varex" on the back and had the same plain ground glass screen, thick and non-removable, as the old viewfinders. The viewing hood, together with the screen, could be replaced by an inverting prism mounted over an interchangeable focusing screen. The prism, called a pentaprism, was the first manufactured by Ihagee. It gave a right-way-round image. When the prism was in place, the release lock was no longer used.

The first cameras to be fitted with a pentaprism were the Pentacon and the Rectaflex. For their part, Zeiss manufactured for the Exakta an early prism which fixed in the viewing hood of the Kine Exakta and the Exakta II.

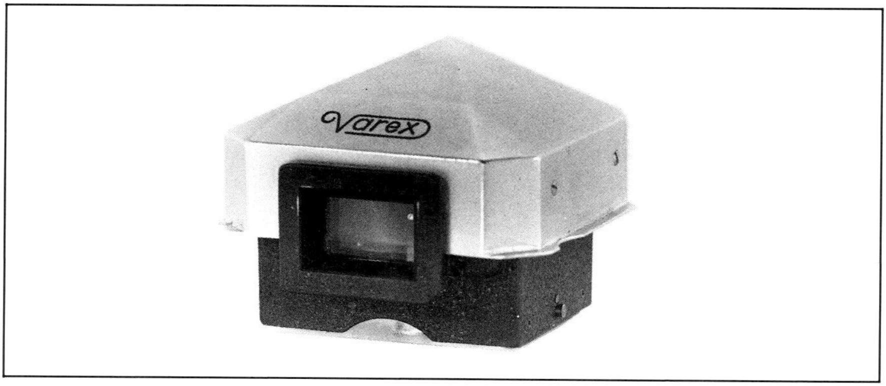

The first Varex prism viewfinder. The casing was matt chrome.

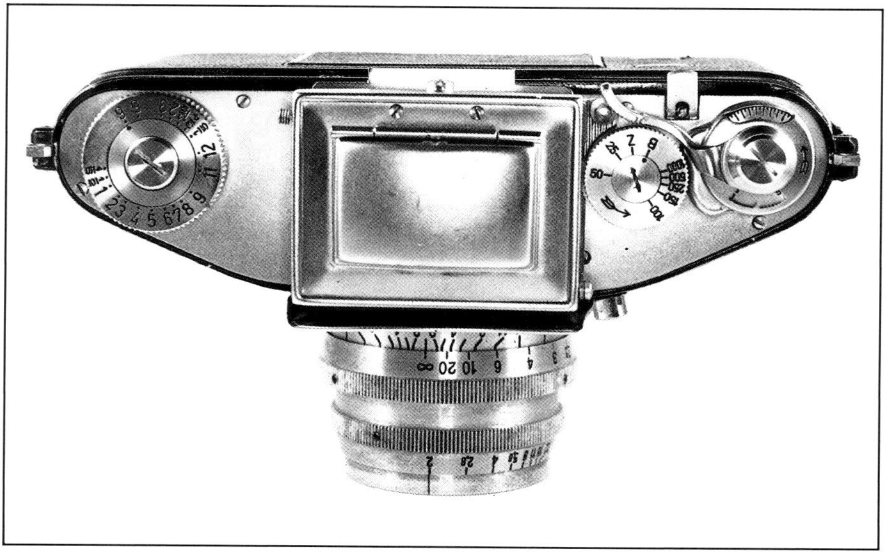

Exakta Varex, No.674810, seen from above.

A safety locking device situated on the front plate held the two viewing systems firmly in place and prevented the play which would undoubtedly have arisen from extensive use. Engraved on this front plate, from top to bottom, was "Exakta", followed by "Varex", then, on both sides of the viewfinder locking button, "Ihagee Dresden".

There were two sets of bipolar sockets for flash synchronisation. There was a "V" pair for bulbs, which allowed for the inertia of flash bulbs by establishing contact 15 milliseconds before the shutter opened. These were used mainly with slow-burning bulbs (FP type) and could be used at all speeds up to 1/1000 second. The "E" pair was for electronic flash, giving synchronisation at 1/50 second.

The lens bayonet was of chromium-plated brass. The shutter-tensioning/wind-on lever was curved. The removable back of the body was identical to that of the Exakta II and the speed ranges were unchanged.

To sum up, apart from the viewing system and the synchronisation plug for the electronic flash, the rest of the camera was the same as the Exakta II.

EXAKTA V 1950 ★★★

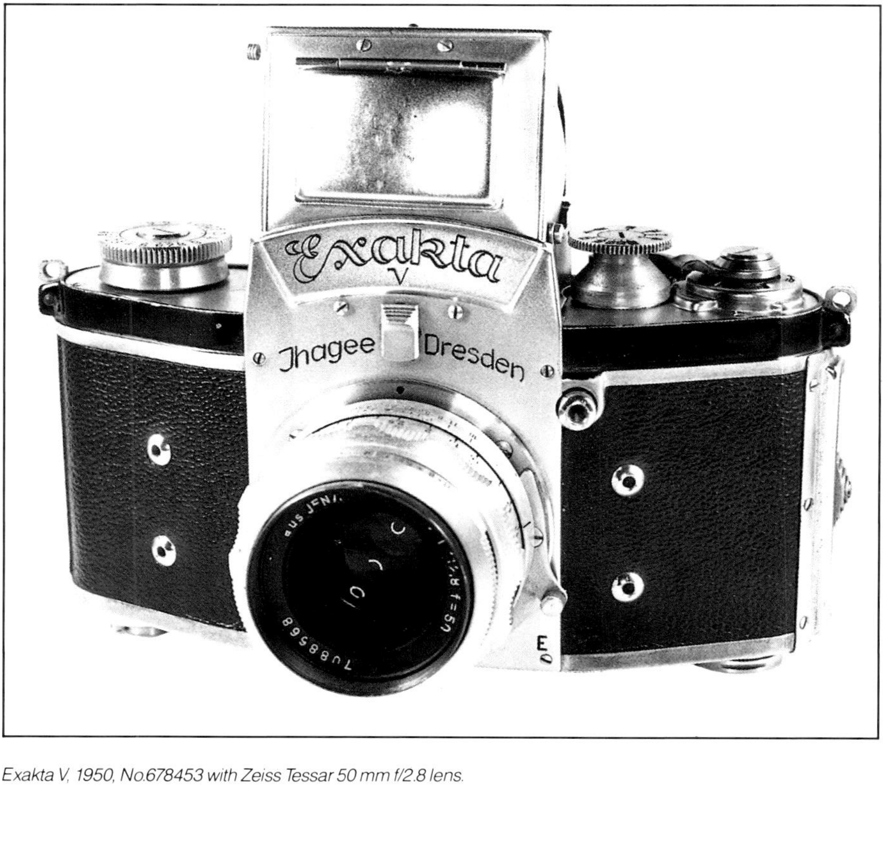

Exakta V, 1950, No.678453 with Zeiss Tessar 50 mm f/2.8 lens.

Approximate range of serial numbers: 667000 - 692000.

These models named "Exakta V" were destined for the American market; the name "Varex" was a trade mark already registered in the USA and hence unavailable to Ihagee. The removable viewing hood had a release blocking lever and was marked "Ihagee" at the back. It had a plain ground glass screen, thick and non-interchangeable. The alternative viewfinder was the inverting prism with interchangeable ground glass screen. It was marked "Ihagee". Other features were:-

- Safety lock for the viewing systems, on the front plate
- Removable back
- Curved wind-on lever
- Two bipolar flash plugs marked "V" and "M"
- Lens bayonet in chromium-plated brass
- The body of the camera was cast from a single piece, but the back part which kept the film flat was separately fitted
- The range of speeds was identical to those of the Varex.

Exakta V. Detail of the left top-plate: the curved wind-on lever with the frame counter, the fast speeds dial, and the lever for unlocking the rewinding mechanism between them.

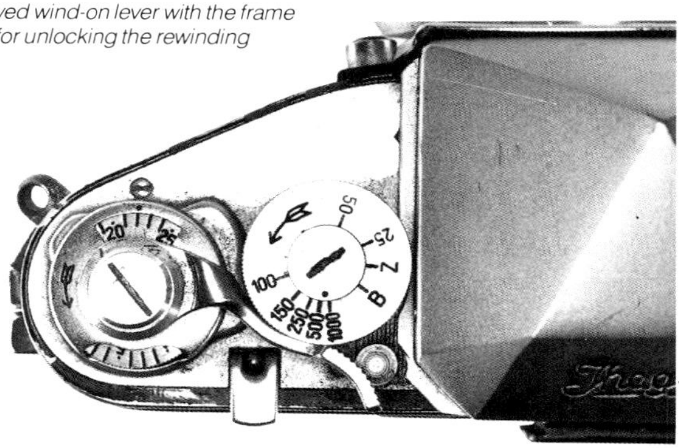

EXAKTA VX Version 1 1951 ★★

Appromimate range of serial numbers: 692000 - 730000.

These cameras were marked "VX" on the front plate and were destined for the American market. The fast, slow and delayed speeds were identical to those of the preceding model. The bipolar flash plugs were marked "M" for bulbs and "X" for electronic flash. For the first time the back was hinged, but it could be removed by lifting its spindle. The closing system of the back was modified. The rewinding key was replaced by a milled knob. On the opposite side there was an identical knob which served to lock the closing system; it was a part of the back of the camera. The strap attachments were changed in appearance and moved forward.

A film transport indicator, seen through a small round window on the top right of the body, enabled the advance of the film to the controlled during loading. The frame counter henceforth indicated the number of exposures made and not the number of exposures available. Intentional double or multiple exposures were numbered twice

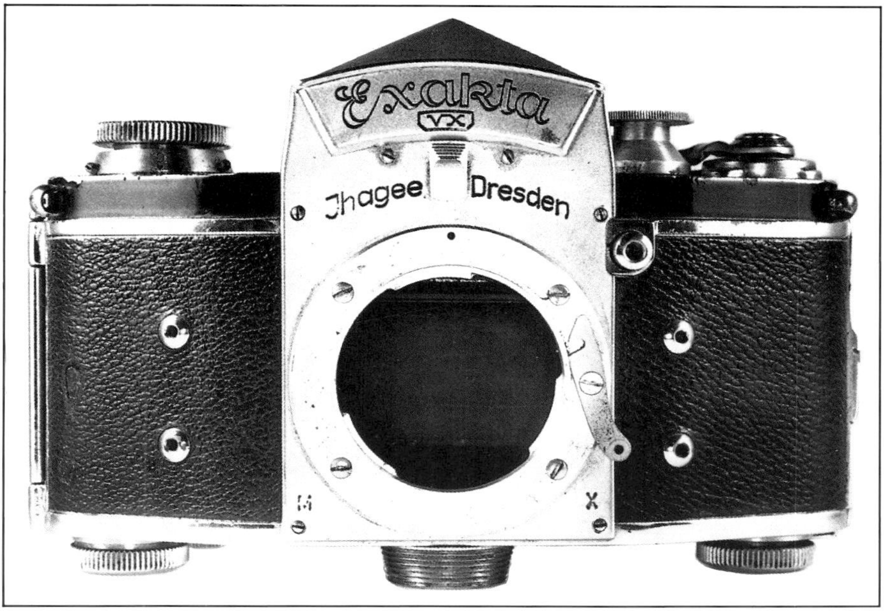

Exakta VX, 1951, No.693766 without lens.

or more. The film speed reminder was on the ring under the slow speed knob and was calibrated in Weston and ASA.

The appearance of the tripod fixing socket was modified and was now corrugated. The film-guide on the inside of the back was omitted. The exposure time marked "Z" on the first VX's became "T" on the later ones, around No.695000. Starting with the VX model, the body of the camera was cast in a single piece, front plate and film gate, which gave the whole thing greater rigidity and fool-proof parallelism. The base-plate was now in two parts so that the take-up spool would now slide in, the section of the base-plate was part of the back instead of the body as previously.

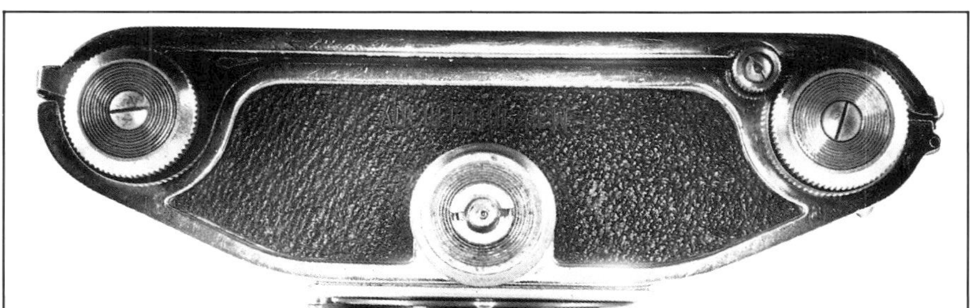

Exakta VX, 1951, seen from below. From left to right: the rewind knob, the film-cutter knob, the threaded tripod socket, the milled knob for opening the back. Note the division in the base in comparison with the Kine Exakta.

EXAKTA
Varex VX Version 1 1951 ★★

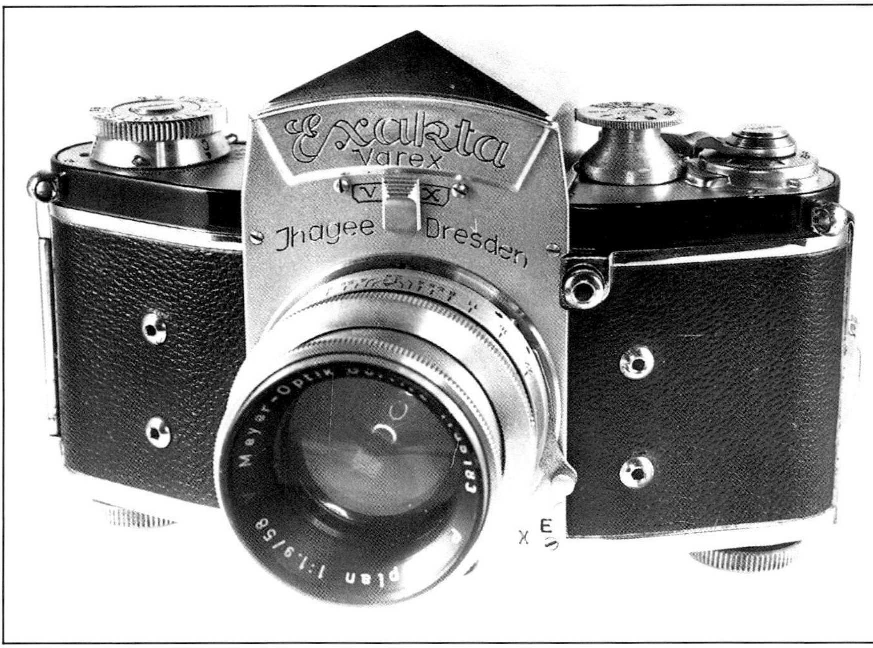

Exakta Varex VX, 1st Version, No.695480 with Meyer Primoplan 58mm f/1.9 lens.

Approximate range of serial numbers: 692000 - 730000.

These cameras were destined for the European market. Their characteristics were identical to the preceding VX model. The two bipolar flash plugs were marked "VM" for bulbs and "XE" for electronic (from approx. No.720000, marked "M" and "X"). The film speed reminder under the slow speed knob was calibrated in DIN.

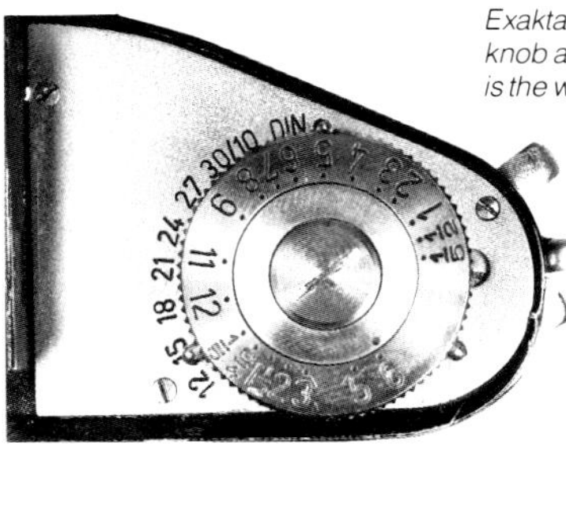

Exakta Varex VX. Detail of the right-hand section of the body. Slow speeds knob and film speed reminder in DIN. On the right of the slow speeds knob is the window of the film transport indicator.

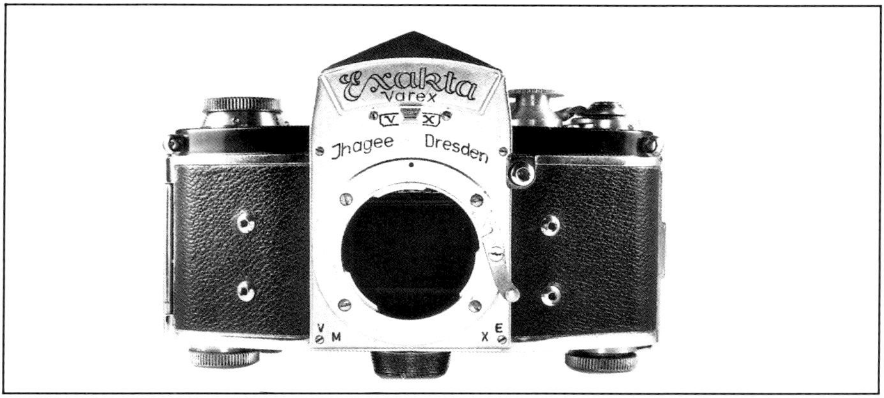

The body without lens. Left, the flash bulb plugs engraved "VM", on the right, the electronic flash plugs, engraved "XE".

EXAKTA Varex VX Version 2 1954 ★★

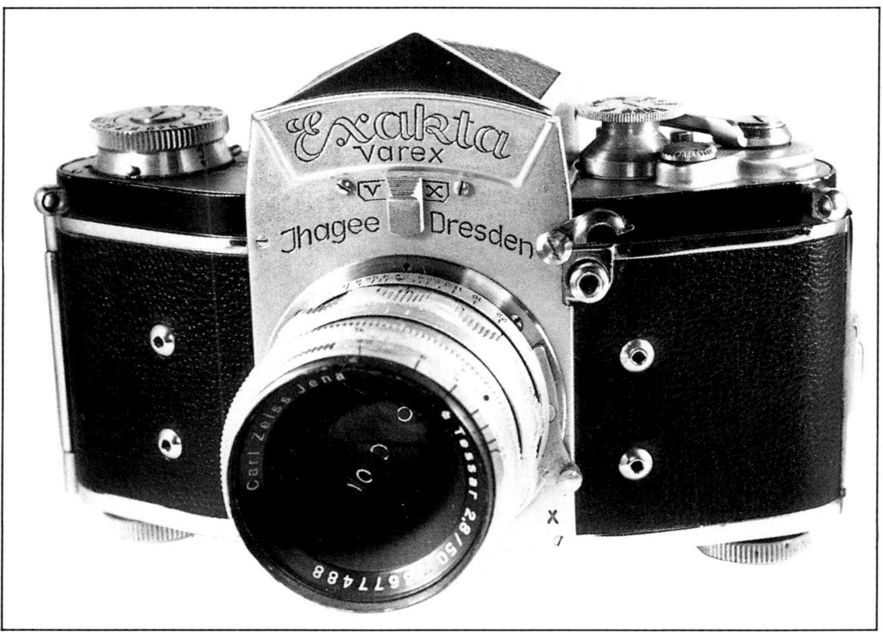

Exakta Varex VX, 2nd version, No.733843 with Zeiss Tessar 50mm f/2.8 lens.

Approximate range of serial numbers: 730000 - 770000.

These cameras were destined for the European market. The film speed reminder was marked in DIN. There was also a version for the USA, marked "Exakta VX", but otherwise identical. The film speed reminder was marked in Weston and ASA and it was known as the Exakta Automatic VX.

In 1953 the introduction of the split-image focusing aid on the screen, which hitherto had been plain ground glass, had given a convincing argument to rebut critics of the reflex who complained of the slowness in focusing compared with rangefinder cameras.

Exakta Varex VX, 2nd version. Detail of the left-hand side of the body with the new frame counter and the straight lever.

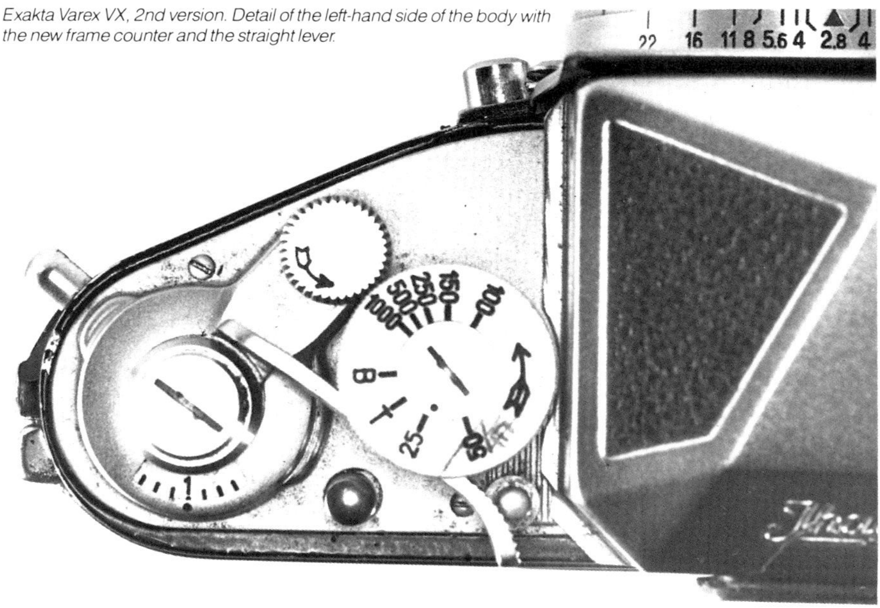

The camera had the following modifications in comparison with the first version:
- Integral exposure counter with indicator window at the back.
- Zero adjustment of counter by milled knob.
- Introduction of a push-button for disengaging the mechanism, in the place of the lever.
- Straight tensioning lever replacing the curved shape used since the beginning.
- The film pressure plate flat and smooth once more.
- The two flash synchronisation plugs marked "M" and "X".
- A second bayonet outside the first appeared on the casing. This allowed better connection of long-focus lenses.
- The security lever for the shutter release had been removed from the viewing hood. From this model onwards, a hinged cover appeared on the release button. This was a safety measure; this cover was cleverly hinged to allow the use of a cable release. All other characteristics were similar to those of the preceding model.

One of the drawbacks of the single-lens reflex cameras had been the black-out of the image when the aperture was closed before the shot. At this time a system of external preselection appeared. A lever on the lower half of the lens allowed a mechanism to be set which held the diaphragm open at its greatest aperture. A plunger, external to the lens, when pressed, closed the aperture to the chosen setting just before its rear end impinged on the release button on the camera body and released the shutter. After release it was necessary to reset the mechanism in order the re-open the aperture.

The external preselection lenses offered were the 50mm f/2 Schneider Xenon, the 58mm f/2 Zeiss Biotar and the 50mm f/2.8 Zeiss Tessar. They were called "automatic" lenses. The mechanism was further developed so that resetting was done automatically.

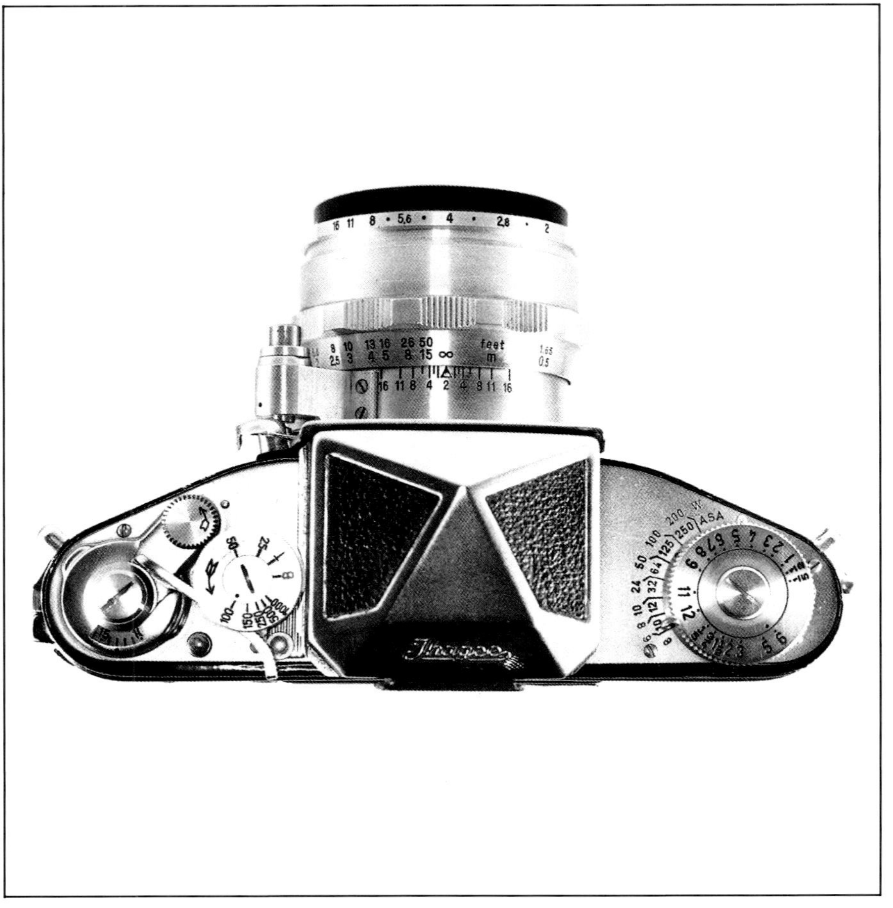

Exakta VX, 2nd version, for the American market, equipped with a Zeiss Biotar automatic lens. The plunger for operating the aperture-closing mechanism can be seen.

EXAKTA
Varex VX Version 3 1954 ★★★

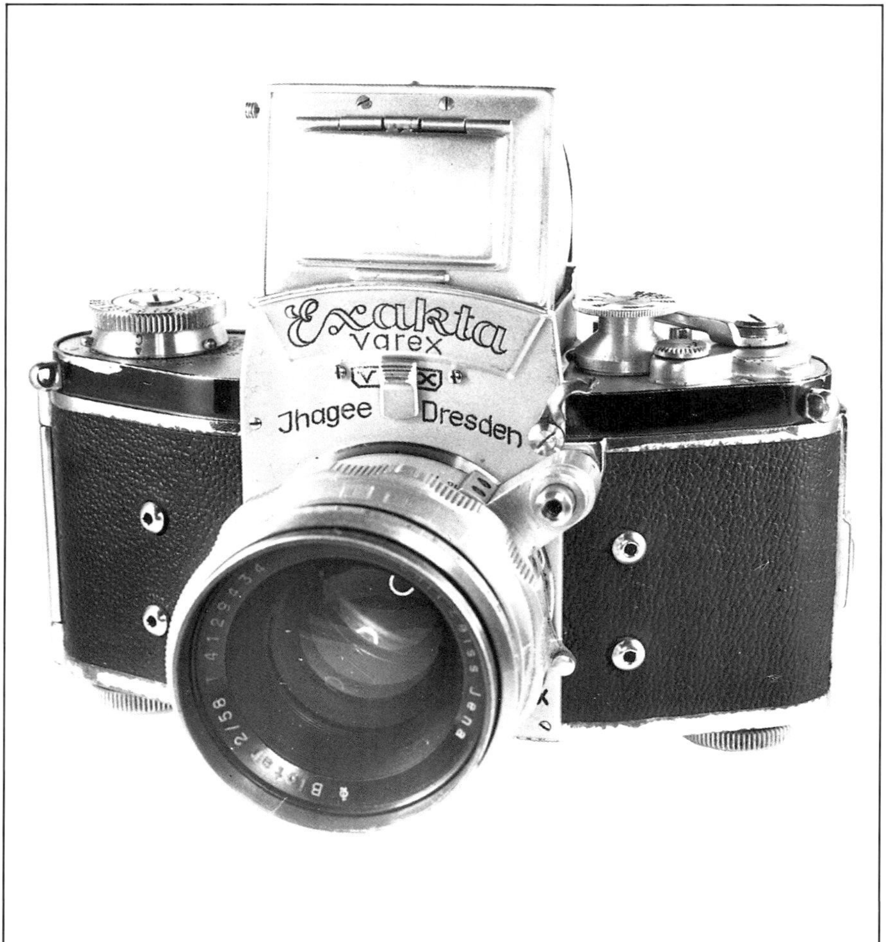

Exakta Varex VX, 3rd version, No.765394 with 58mm f/2 Zeiss Biotar lens.

Approximate range of serial numbers: 765000 - 774000.

This model was identical to the second version, except that the film speed reminder under the slow speeds knob was graduated in Weston and ASA.

The same model was sold in the USA, engraved "Exakta VX". It was also called the Exakta Automatic VX.

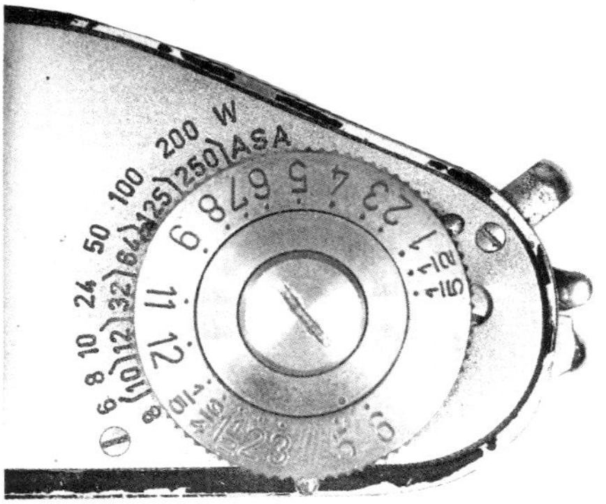

The engraving in Weston and ASA of the film-speed reminder.

Numerous automatic external preselection lenses were manufactured from 1954 onwards.

EXAKTA Varex VX Version 4 1956 ★★

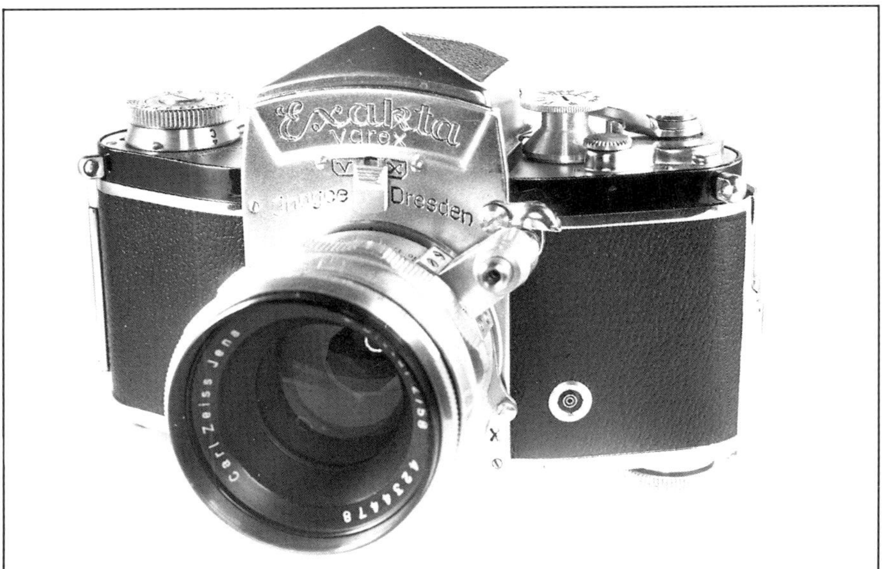

Exakta Varex VX, No.780296, with Zeiss Biotar 58mm f/2 lens.

Approximate range of serial numbers: 775000 - 817000.

The bipolar flash plugs were replaced by two standardised 'synchro' plugs on Version 4. On the right of the body, engraved in black, was "M" for bulbs, and on the left in red "X" for electronic. The small protecting cover of the release button, which hitherto had had a cut-out on previous models, was now half-moon shaped so that it was now necessary to raise it in order to use a cable release. The film speed reminder was graduated in Weston and ASA.

An identical model was sold in the USA, marked "Exakta VX".

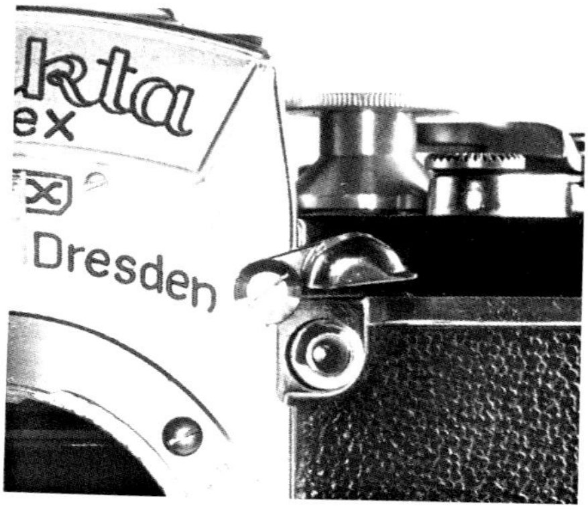

Detail of release button and its protective cover

EXAKTA Varex VX Version 5 1956 ★★

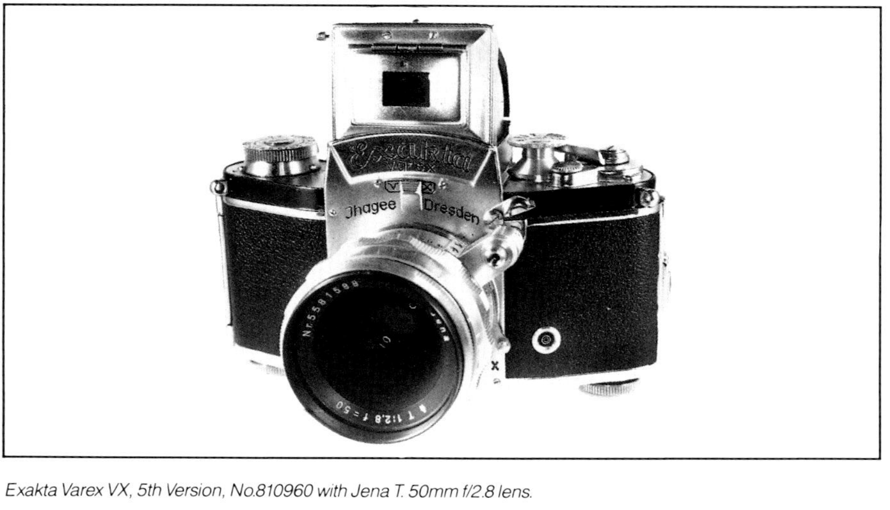

Exakta Varex VX, 5th Version, No.810960 with Jena T. 50mm f/2.8 lens.

Approximate range of serial numbers: 775000 - 817000.

This camera was identical to the preceding version, except for the film speed indicator which was graduated in DIN.

From this time onwards the Exakta Varex became the universal camera. An extraordinary number of accessories appeared on the market: lenses, focusing screens, viewfinders, rings, bellows, reproduction benches. It was adapable to all the problems presented by medical, scientific, industrial and astronomical photography. It became the most highly developed camera system of the 50's.We will study these lenses and accessories in detail in Chapters 7 and 8.

EXAKTA Varex IIa Version 1 1957 ★★

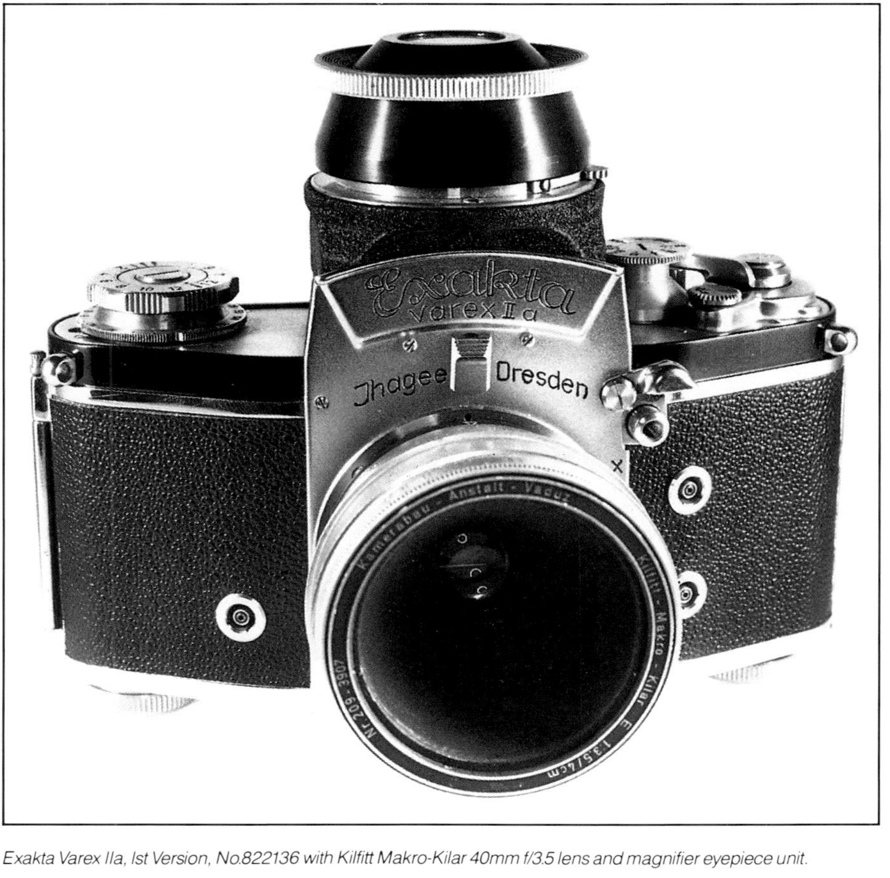

Exakta Varex IIa, Ist Version, No.822136 with Kilfitt Makro-Kilar 40mm f/3.5 lens and magnifier eyepiece unit.

Approximate range of serial numbers: 818000 - 850000.

On this model "Exakta Varex IIa" was engraved on the front plate. A change immediately noticeable is the addition of a third flash plug marked "F". This permitted the use of instantaneous flash bulbs, with synchronisation of the shutter at 1/25 second. It is very important to note that on this first model the setting 1/150 second still existed. The film pressure plate, which was smooth and not removeable on previous models, was replaced by a removeable type with stippled embossing.

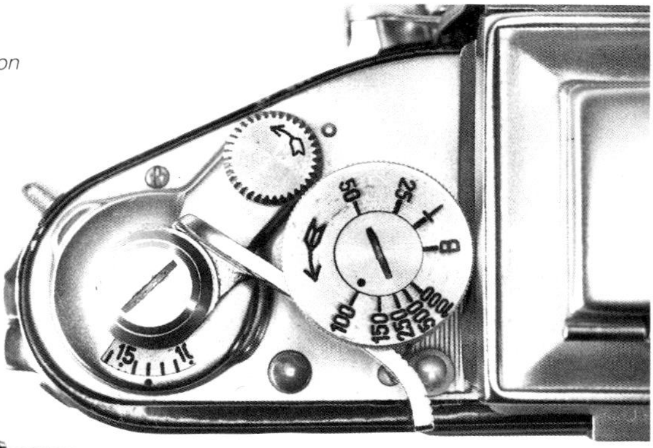

The left-hand top plate with the tensioning lever and the shutter-speed dial for 1/25 to 1/1000 second. Note the intermediate position of 1/150.

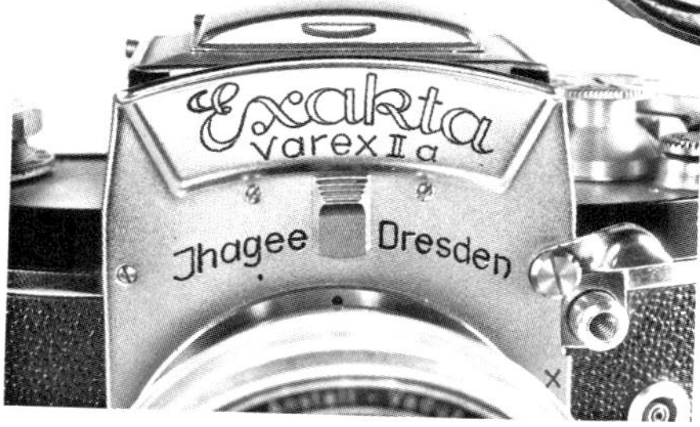

The front plate of the Varex IIa.

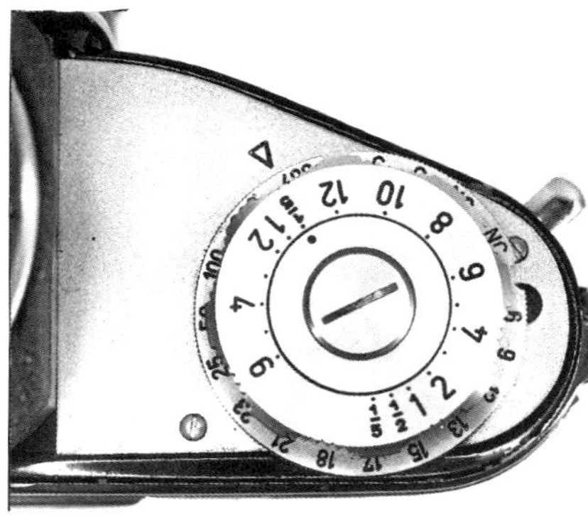

The slow speeds dial with the film speed reminder ring underneath. On the right, the control window for unwinding the film.

The mechanism for the slow speeds was modified on the Varex IIa. An especially silent centrifugal governor replaced the escapement of the preceding models. The range of the slow speeds was: 1/5, 1/2, 1, 2, 3, 4, 5, 6, 8, 10 and 12 seconds. The 7, 9 and 11 seconds had been dispensed with and the 10 seconds added. The range of delayed slow speeds was: 1/5, 1/2, 1, 2, 3, 4, 5 and 6 seconds, with the 3 and 5 represented by a full stop. The 1/2 second replaced the 3/4 and the 1 1/2 disappeared.

The shape of the slow speeds dial was modified: it became octagonal and was easier to grip. The film speed reminder was no longer engraved on the top part of the casing, but on a flat ring under the slow speeds dial. The remainder of the camera is unchanged.

An identical model was sold in the USA marked "Exakta VX IIa".

Sychronisation options with the three flash plugs

Plug "M"	*Plug "F"*	*Plug 'X'*
1/50 to 1/1000	to 1/25	1/50 or slower
Slow-burning bulbs	Instantaneous bulbs	Electronic flash
Osram Vacublitz-SO	Osram Vacublitz XM-1, XM-5	
Philips Photoflux PF-24, PF-45	Philips Eclair PF-1, PF-5	
RFT Eclair DF-20	RFT Eclair F-19	

It was possible to use an electronic flash and flash bulbs simultaneously.

EXAKTA
Varex IIa Version 2 1957 ★★★

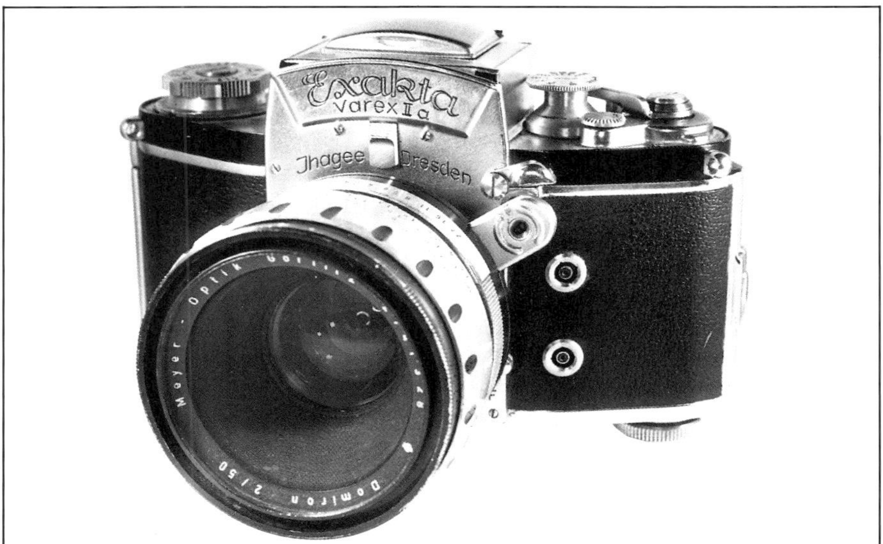

Exakta Varex IIa, 2nd Version. No.857102 with 50m f/2 Meyer Domiron lens.

Approximate range of serial numbers: 850000 - 860000.

This version was identical to the preceding model except that the shutter was slightly modified. The 1/150 was discarded.

An identical model was sold in the USA marked "Exakta VX IIa".

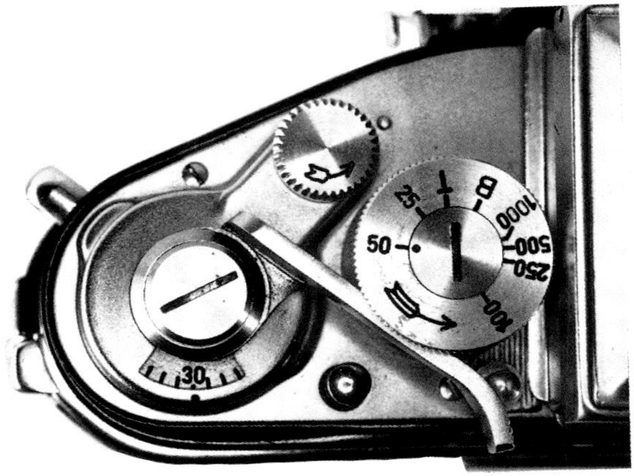

Note the disappearance of the 1/150 from the speed dial.

EXAKTA Varex IIa Version 3 1958 ★

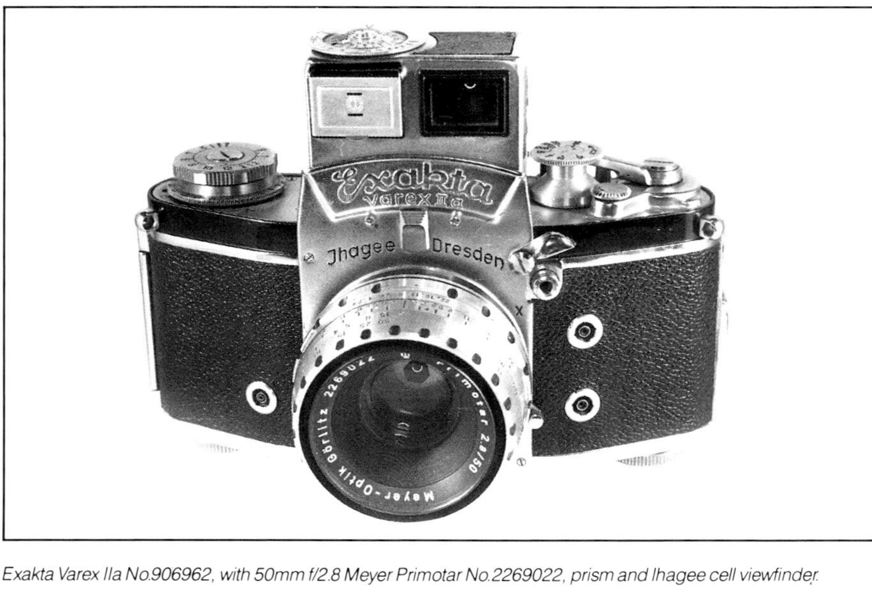

Exakta Varex IIa No.906962, with 50mm f/2.8 Meyer Primotar No.2269022, prism and Ihagee cell viewfinder.

Approximate range of serial numbers: 860000 - 935000.

Only the front plate differentiated this version from the other Varex IIa models. The name "Exakta Varex IIa" appeared embossed rather than engraved. All the characteristics remained identical to those of the preceding (2nd version) models.

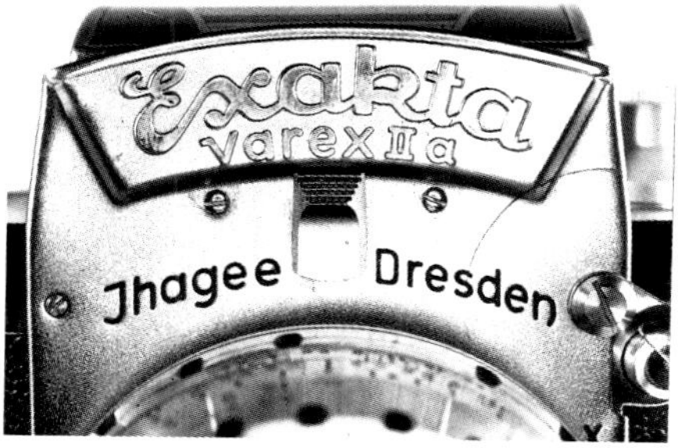

Detail of the front plate of the Varex IIa, 3rd Version.

The various versions with the rounded plate and the name in relief were made until 1961. All collectors agree in considering this camera the most attractive of all the Exakta 24x36 models. It seems that Ihagee anticipated it, because from 1961 they issued a viewing hood and prism which were even more attractive. These viewfinders, black and metal striped, were called Jubilee hoods and prisms. They marked the twenty-fifth anniversary of the Kine Exakta. We should point out that the first cell pentaprism manufactured by Ihagee was also put on sale that year under the name of "Light Meter IIa"

EXAKTA VX IIa Version 3 1958 ★

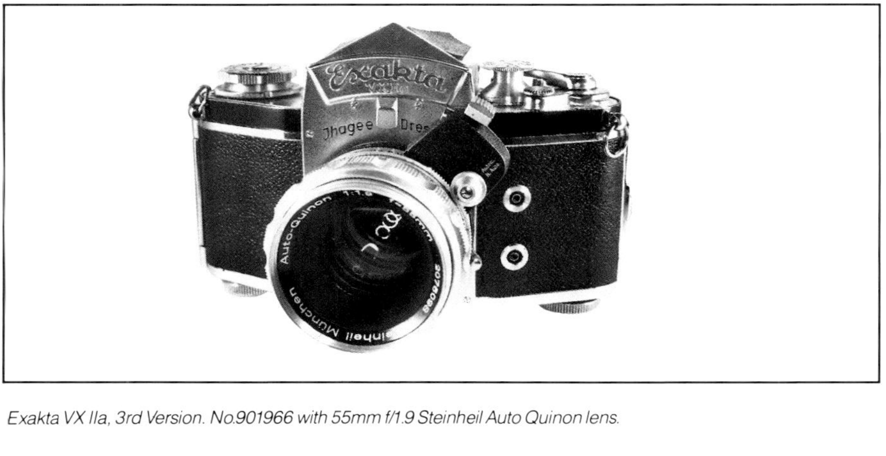

Exakta VX IIa, 3rd Version. No.901966 with 55mm f/1.9 Steinheil Auto Quinon lens.

Approximate range of serial numbers: 860000 - 935000.

Destined for the American market, this model did not differ in any way from the preceding model, only the name plate was in relief and carried the inscription "Exakta VX IIa".

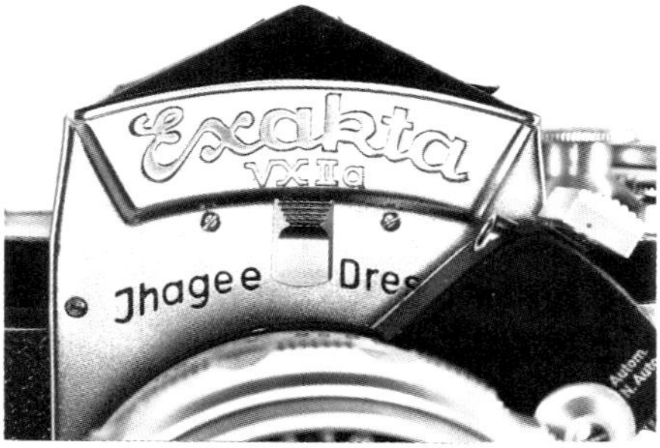

Detail of the front plate, marked "VX IIa".

EXAKTA IIa Version 4 1958 ★★★★

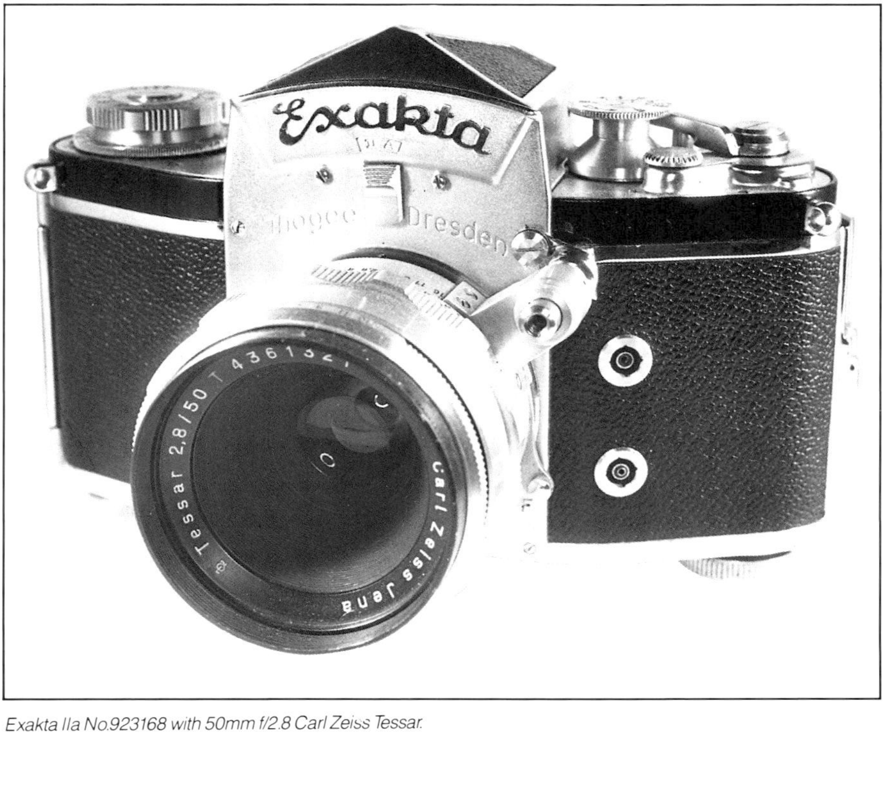

Exakta IIa No.923168 with 50mm f/2.8 Carl Zeiss Tessar.

This version, on which the name "Exakta" was in relief and "IIa" was engraved on the front plate, was mechanically identical to the other versions but was not very numerous. The inscription "VX II" was also engraved on the inside of the body.

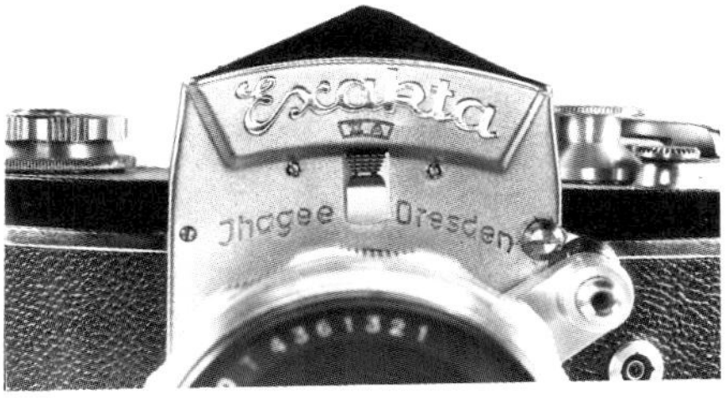

Detail of the front plate.

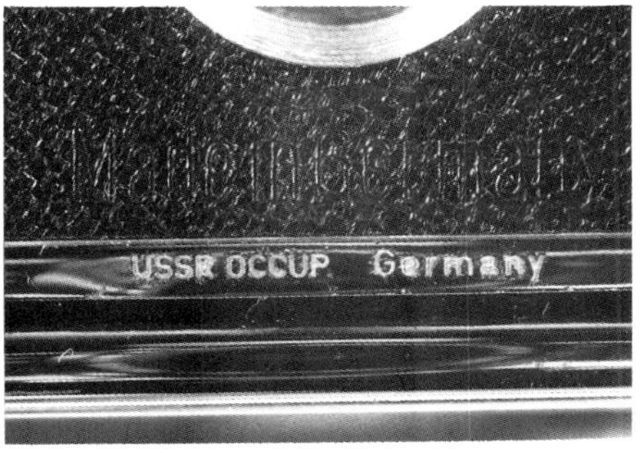

The model shown here has "USSR OCCUP Germany" engraved on the chrome-plated part of the lower housing.

EXAKTA Varex IIa Version 5 1961 ★

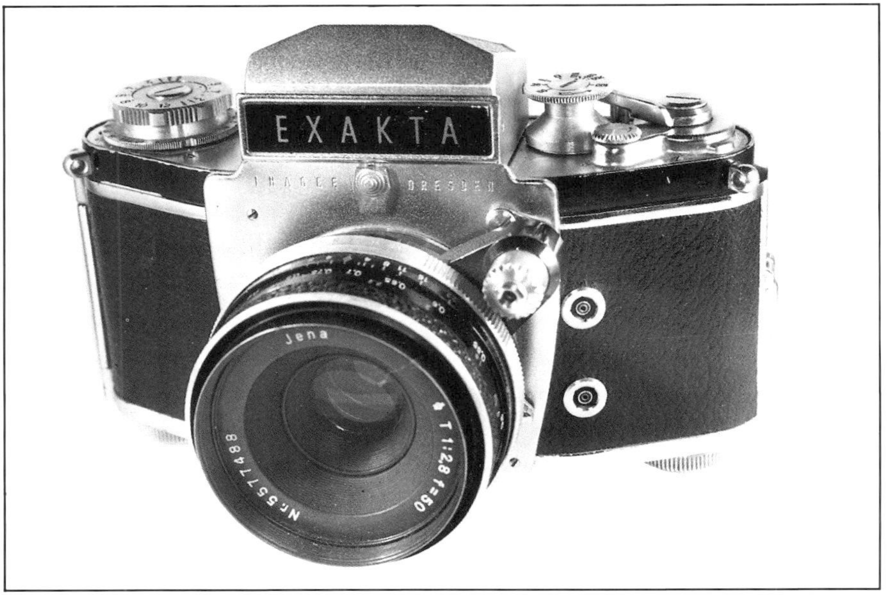

Exakta VX IIa, 5th Version. No.938895 with 50mm f/2.8 Jena T lens. This lens was a Zeiss Tessar without the name.

Approximate range of serial numbers for versions 5 to 8: 935000-1005000.

This new version of the Exakta camera was to see no further modifications to its general aspect until the 1967 "VX 1000". "VX IIa" was engraved on the inside of the body. There had been a complete modification of the front panel which was now wider and extended as far as the shutter release knob. Above it the name "Exakta" appeared in upper case letters, in a new modern typeface, in white on a black background. On the front plate "Ihagee Dresden" was engraved in smaller upper case characters on either side of the locking control for the viewfinding system. However, all the mechanical characteristics remained identical to those of the Varex II which was already on the market. New lenses, in black mountings and leather trimmed, were planned. The viewfinders, which were also leather trimmed, and collapsible at the touch of just one finger, replaced the chrome ones. The pyramid-shaped prism was replaced by a model which was higher and of trapezoid shape. In the USA, with a 50mm f/1.9 Schneider Xenon lens, the price was 375 dollars.

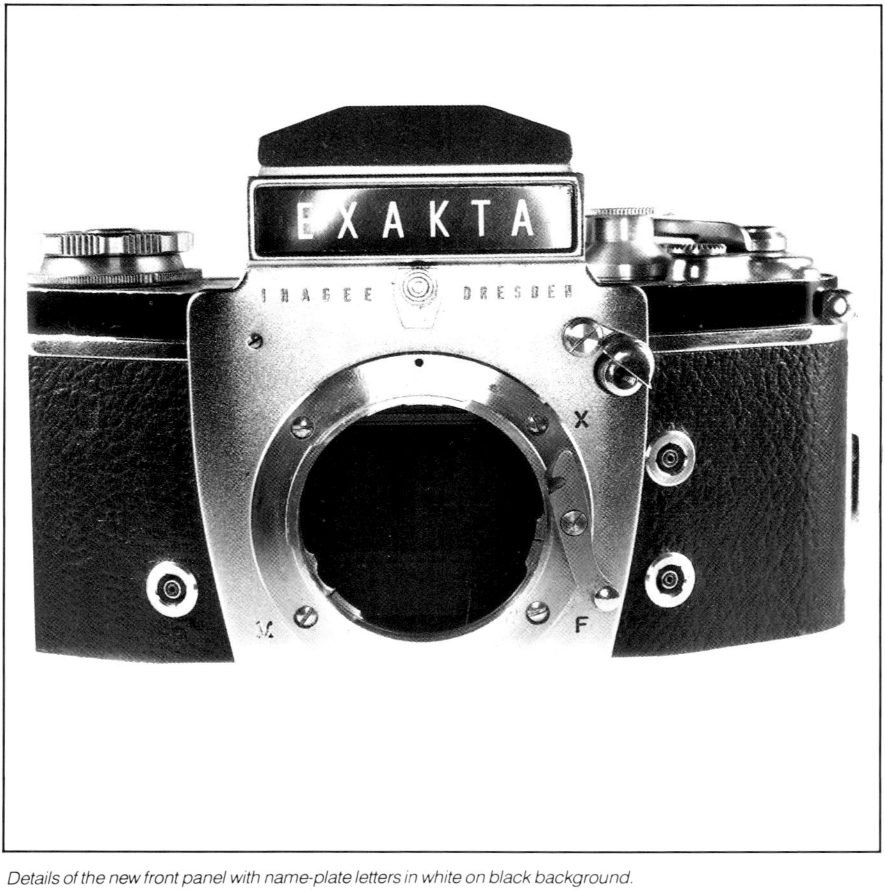

Details of the new front panel with name-plate letters in white on black background.

EXAKTA
Varex IIa Version 6 1961 ★

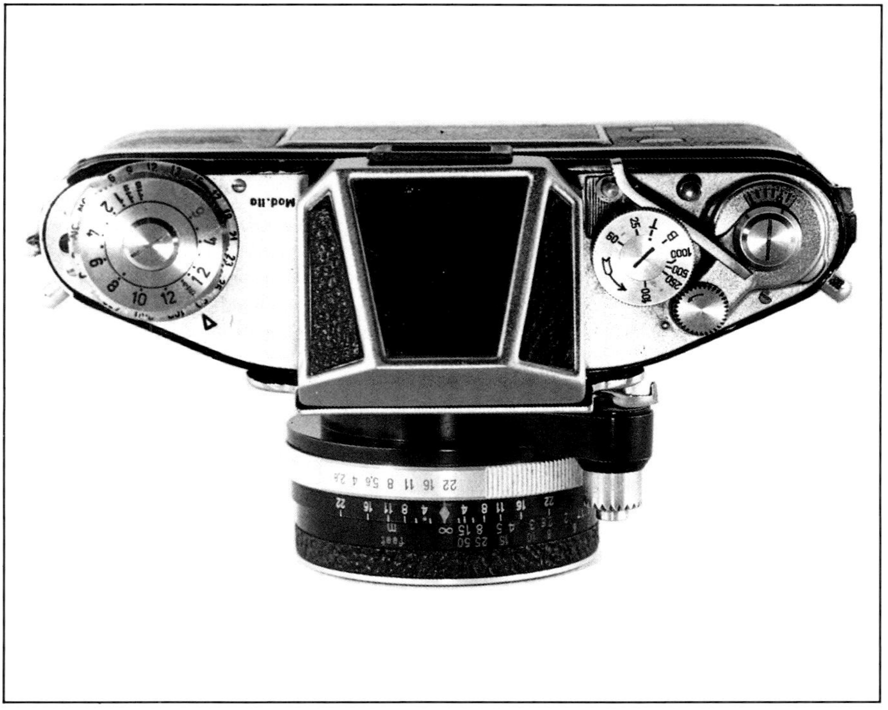

Exakta Varex IIa (Mod. IIa) No.943720.

A model identical to the previous one exists, with the only difference being that it had "Mod IIa" engraved on the rear of the top plate, between the viewfinder housing and the slow speeds knob. This version appears in all the catalogues and advertisements of that period.

EXAKTA
VX IIa Version 7 1961 ★

This version, intended for the American market, was identical to the previous models, but fitted with the new front plate. Under the name "Ihagee Dresden", we also find "VX IIa" engraved in small characters. The trade name "Varex" was never used in the US market.

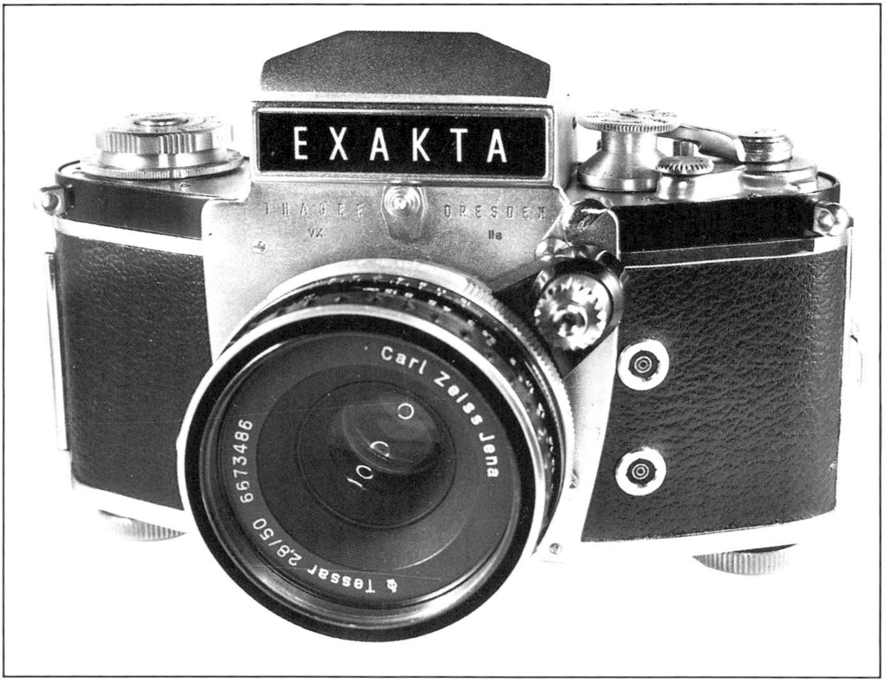

Exakta VX IIa, No.947476 with 50mm f/2.8 Carl Zeiss Tessar.

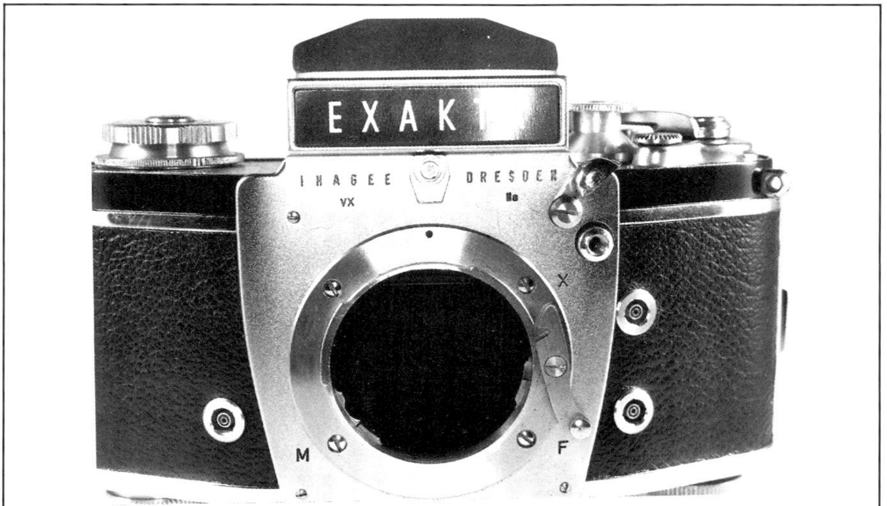

Detail of the front plate with "VX IIa" engraved.

EXAKTA
Varex IIa Version 8 1962 ★

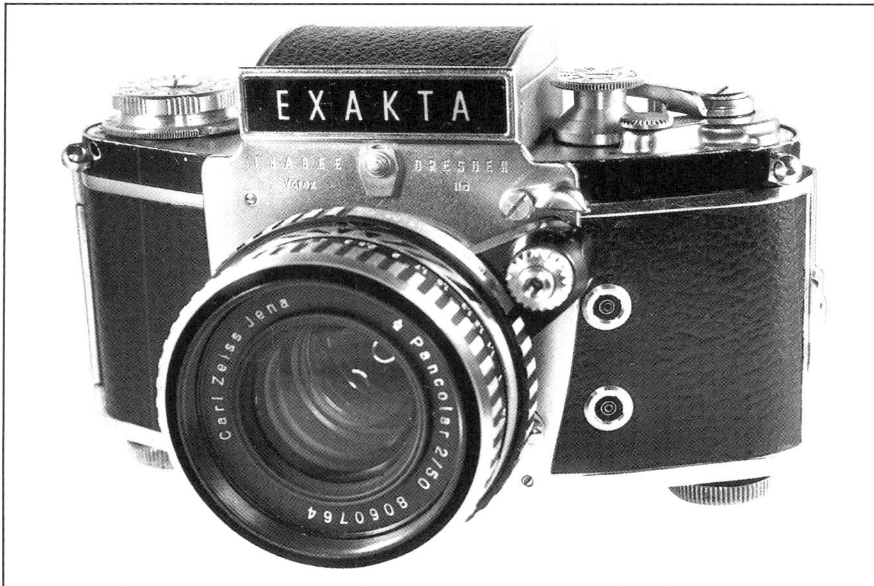

Exakta Varex IIa, No976705 with 50mm f/2 Carl Zeiss Pancolar.

This model was identical to the previous models fitted with the new front plate. Below the name "Ihagee Dresden", we also find "Varex IIa" engraved in small characters.

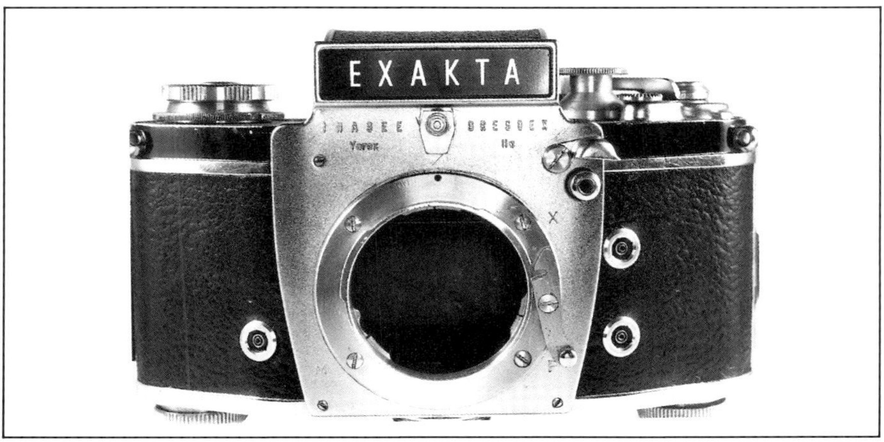

Detail of the front plate bearing the name "Varex".

To summarise, four variants of this IIa model exist with the new style. From serial No.978000 (approx), the knob for locking the mirror in the viewfinding position was replaced by a hook-shaped lever.

EXAKTA Varex IIa Marked "USSR OCCUP. Germany" ★★★

We have noted three different types of lettering over four different models. It is very likely that others exist.

1. On an Exakta IIa, 4th version, "USSR OCCUP. Germany" is engraved on the chrome edge of the base. (See Exakta Varex IIa above.)
2. On an Exakta Varex IIa, 3rd version (serial number not recorded), "GERMANY U.S.S.R. OCCUPIED" was engraved on the top plate. The engraving was very neat and clean. It was identical to that on the following model, but very light.
3. On a VX IIa, 5th version, with the new front plate, the engraving was bolder. This version was originally intended for the American market.
4. On a VX IIa, 7th version, with the new front plate, the non-engraved legend "GERMANY U.S.S.R. OCCUPIED", presumably etched, can be found on the right hand side of the top plate. This inscription is much less tidy than the engraved one. Top right hand picture.

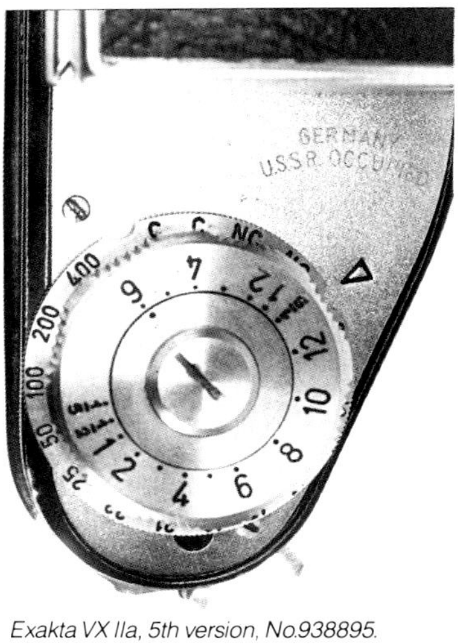

Exakta VX IIa, 5th version, No.938895.

Editor's note: It appears that these markings were put on cameras to be sold on US territory because at that time the US Government did not recognise the GDR. The markings are assumed to have been applied by the US Customs. (Private communication)

EXAKTA Varex IIb 1963 ★

Approximate serial number range: 1005000 to 1125000.

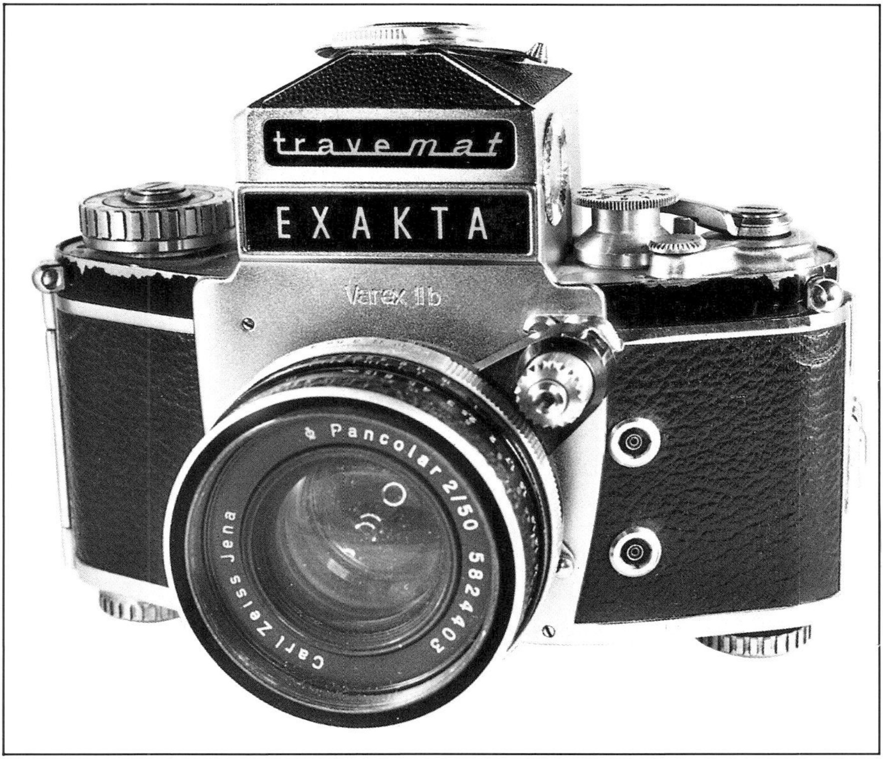

Exakta Varex IIb. No. 1112866 with 50mm f/2 Zeiss Pancolor, No.5824403, and prism "Travemat"

Presented at the 1963 Leipzig fair, this model went on sale at the end of the same year. The general aspect remained the same as the previous model Varex IIa.

Here are the points of detail which differentiated the Varex IIb from its predecessors:

- On the top plate, right hand side, there was no film speed reminder ring; the plate was now engraved with "Ihagee Dresden".
- The aspect of the slow speed knob changed. It became round with a milled circumference and the film speed reminder appeared on a central black disk.
- A centrifugal governor improved the slow speed mechanism, giving it a higher precision. The speed range was changed and becomes: $1/8$, $1/4$, $1/2$, 1, 2, 4, 6, 8, 10 & 12 seconds. The delayed speeds were $1/4$, $1/2$, 1, 2, 4 & 6 seconds.
- Complete rearrangement of the fast speeds which for which the standard range: $1/30$, $1/60$, $1/125$, $1/250$, $1/500$, $1/1000$, plus B & T, was adopted. - The flash

synchronisation sockets have became: "FP" for slow combustion bulbs (synchronisation to 1/30 second) and "X" for electronic flash (synchronised to 1/60 second).

- On the base of the camera, the rear cover opening knob was different. It was also milled, same as the film rewind knob which also incorporated a little collapsible crank handle. The tripod fixture knob was also modified.
- On this model, Ihagee did away with the front viewfinder release knob. The removal of the viewfinder was simpler, but its locking was no longer quite so efficient. Consequently, this system was abandoned for the following model, the VX 1000, for which Ihagee returned to the original system.

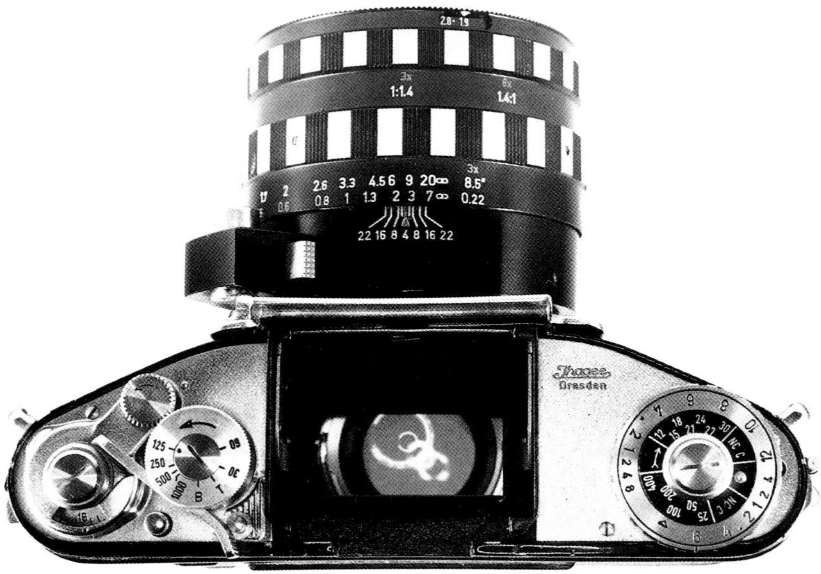

Exakta Varex IIb, without viewfinder, with 55mm f/1.9 Steinheil Macro Quinon.

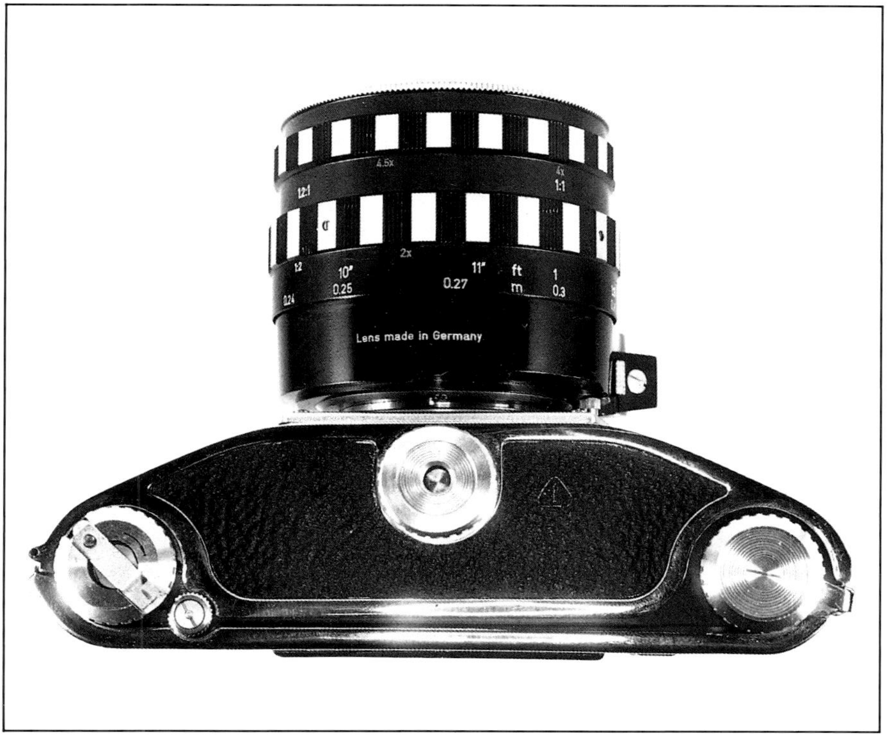

Exakta Varex IIb with Steinheil Macro-Quinon lens. Seen from underneath.

EXAKTA VX IIb 1963 ★

For serial number range see the Varex IIb

This model, which was intended for the American market, was identical in all respects to the Exakta Varex IIb described previously except for the chrome front plate, which was engraved "VX IIb". The name Varex was never used on the American market.

EXAKTA VX 1000 1967 ★

Approximate range of serial numbers: from 1125000 to 1185000.

This camera was introduced at Photokina in October 1966. The specifications were more or less similar to those of the Exakta Varex IIb.

The camera body was a different casting and the back cover was modified. The

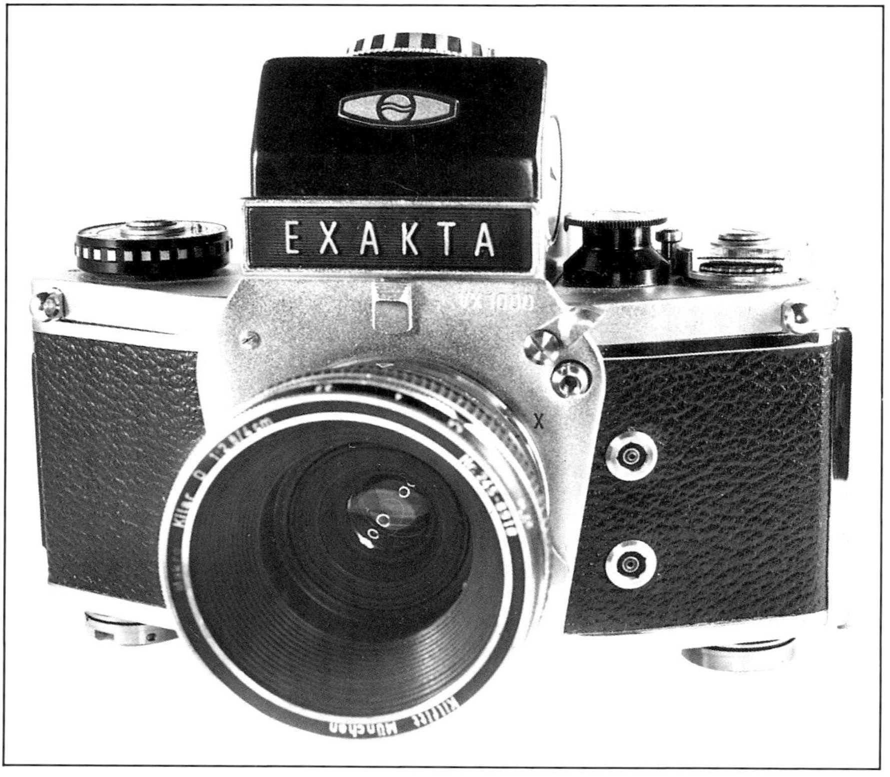

Exakta VX 1000 No.1126404, with 40mm f/2.8 Kilfitt Makro Kilar lens No.2458910 and Examat penta-prism.

general shape had become more angular. In addition, the following details gave a new external appearance:-

- The Exakta logo was shown in relief on a scored black background.
- The front plate receiving the bayonet was modified and the viewfinder was given a new appearance.
- The top plates, which had been inset on the previous models, were matt chrome and returned over the top part of the camera body. On the early models "Ihagee Dresden" was engraved on the right-hand plate whereas "Aus Dresden" appeared on the following models.
- A new design of slow-speeds knob was introduced. The fast-speeds dial was black with white-painted figures, which had been engraved on the early models and photoengraved on the following ones.
- The same applied to the counter (black background with white-painted figures) which showed the number of exposures left in the camera.
- A new cast metal winding lever with reduced stroke (235° instead of 300°) was introduced.

- The knobs located on the base of the camera were changed to show the film-type on one side and to lock the rewind crank on the other.
- The film-cutter knob, which previously was screwed out, was now equipped with a catch.
- A lateral rod allowed automatic locking of the camera back. The hinge spindle was no longer removeable.
- Finally, Ihagee introduced the mirror with automatic return after release. However, we must point out that all the reflex cameras at the time had this facility. When the shutter was not cocked, a red warning signal appeared on the right-hand side of the viewfinder.

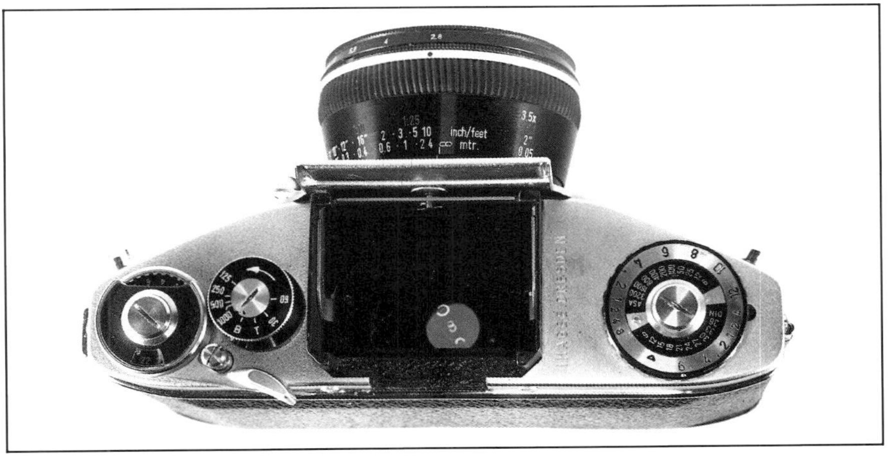

Exakta VX 1000 with Kilfitt Makro-Kilar. The viewfinder has been demounted.

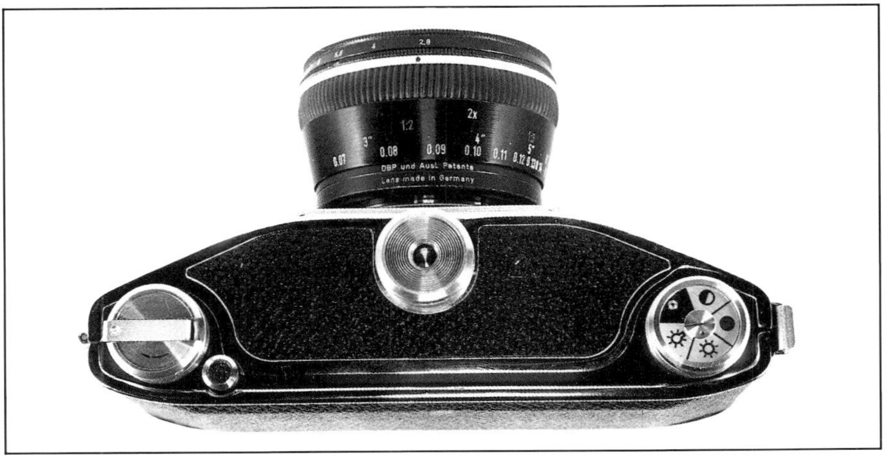

Exakta VX 1000, bottom view. Note the film-type reminder on the right, shown by symbols.

Although the Exakta VX 1000 brought some improvements in the world of photography, the design was ageing and held no scope for progress. The main specifications were all based on the same model and therefore new designs and techniques were needed. It was is on the VX 1000 that the first penta-prisms with through-lens (TTL) metering was seen. These were specially manufactured for Ihagee by Schacht for the Travemat and by Harwix for the Examat.

In the USA, as from 1969, the importer, the "Exakta Camera Company", added the letters "TL" on the front plate.

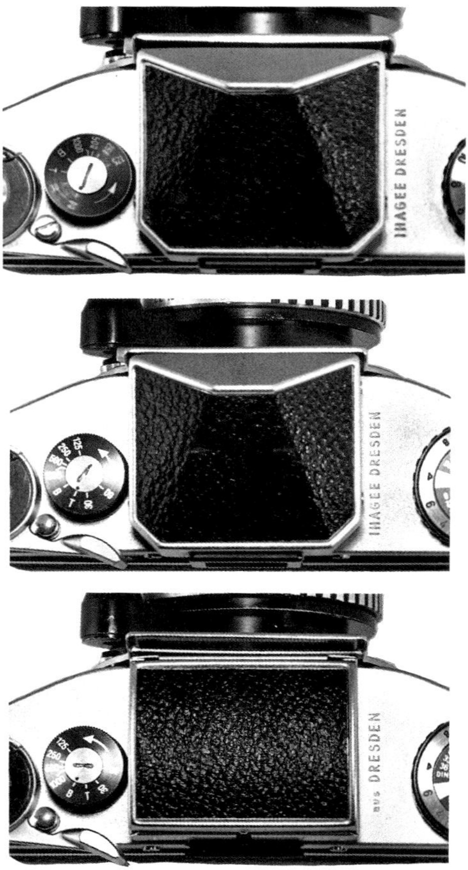

Development of the VX 1000 (3 versions)
Top: VX 1000 No.1132280: speeds-knob engraved with white letters on black; release button with slot; "Ihagee Dresden" engraving.
Middle: VX 1000 No.1179465: photo-engraved and all-black speed knob; smooth release button; "Ihagee Dresden" engraving.
Lower: VX 1000 No.1183065: photoengraved and fully black speeds-knob; smooth release button; "Aus Dresden" engraving.

ELBAFLEX VX 1000 1967 ★★

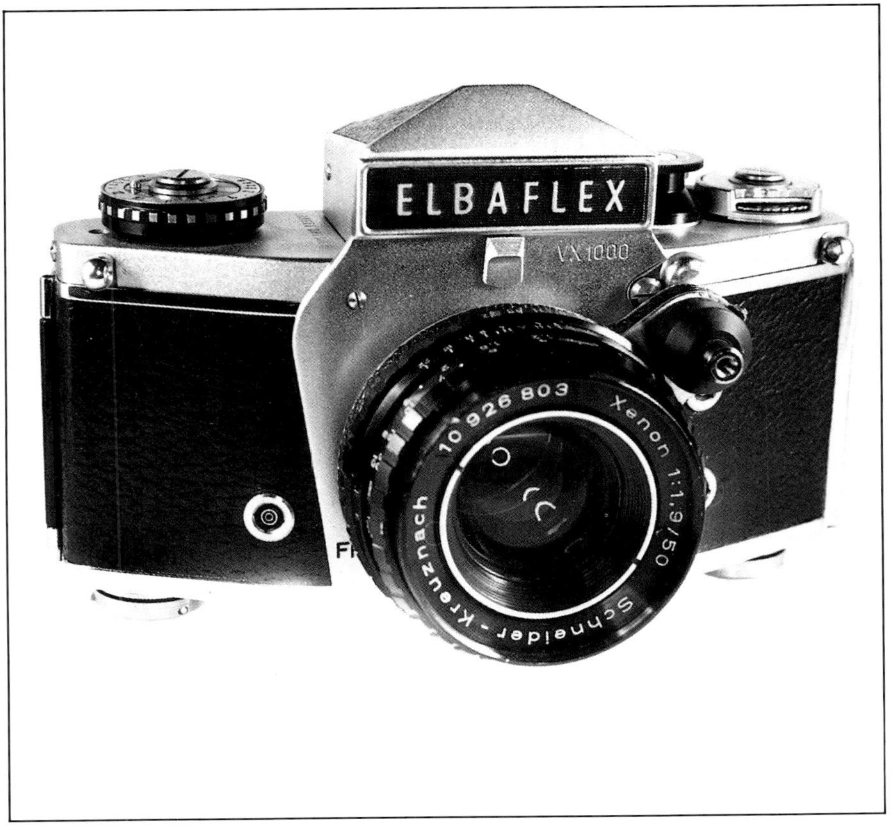

Elbaflex No.1157075 with 50mm f/1.9 Schneider Xenon lens No.10926803.

Approximate range of serial numbers: 1150000 to 1230000.

The Elbaflex was really the Exakta VX 1000 under a different name. The characteristics were identical, except for the name-plate which appeared on a scored metallic black background with white-painted letters. This plate was to be made of plastic at the later stages of production.

We must point out that the Exakta VX 1000, the VX 1000 and the Elbaflex were included in this range of serial numbers. For reasons of control and commercial considerations, the name-plates were affixed at the final stage of assembly. The Elbaflex was marketed in European countries only.

"Ihagee Dresden" was engraved on the early models and "Aus Dresden" on the later ones.

EXAKTA VX 500 1969 ★

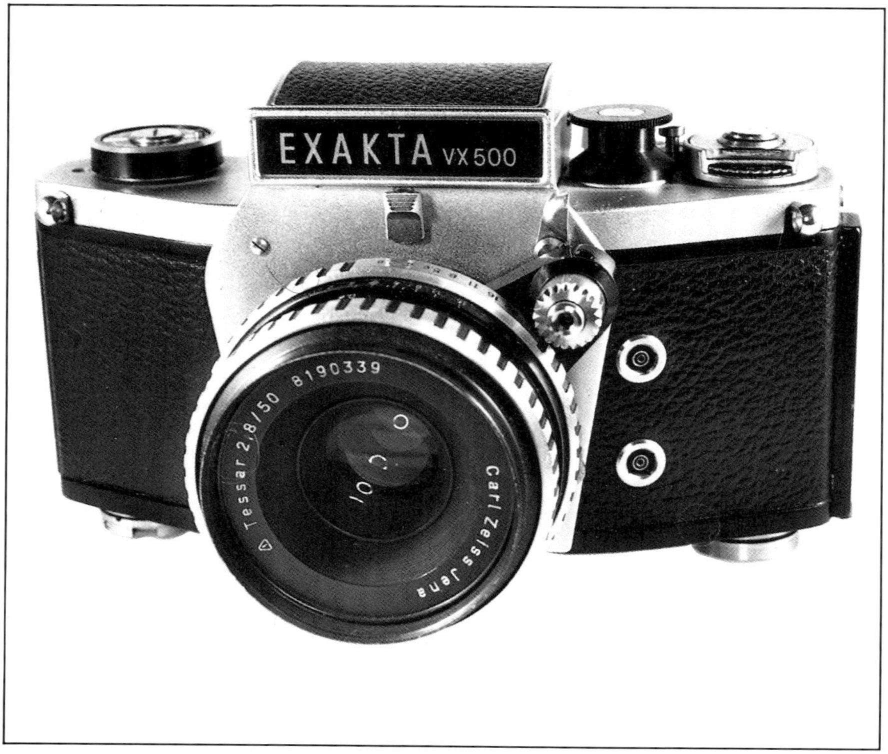

Exakta VX 500 No.1504085 with 50mm f/2.8 Zeiss Tessar No.8190339.

Approximate range of serial numbers: 1500000 to 1590000.

This model was to be the last Ihagee to appear in the VX range. The manufacturer wanted this model to be cheap and popular. The Exakta VX 500 was a simplified version of the Exakta VX 1000. In the USA there was some confusion when the importer advertised the 1966 Exa 500 as "Exakta 500".

Compared to the Exakta VX 1000, the camera body and the back cover were the same. On the body the chrome strips were omitted and replaced by gloss black paint. The film-cutter was also omitted. The shutter speed range was limited to: B, 1/30, 1/60, 1/125, 1/250 and 1/500 second. The slow-speeds and delayed speed functions and the FP flash socket disappeared altogether. The speed-dial was modified later on and an intermediate speed of 1/40 second was added for electronic flash, and marked by a flash symbol.

After 35 years of existence, with limited changes in specification, the era of the famous trapezoid reflex camera with left-hand operated release came to an end with this model.

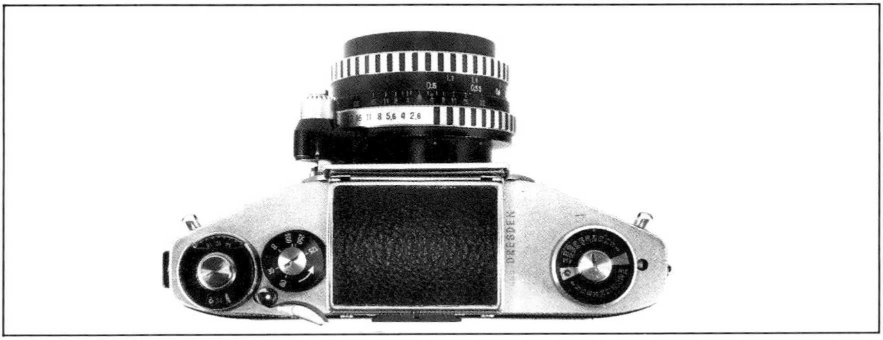

Exakta VX 500, top view. The right-hand end knob shows the film speed only.

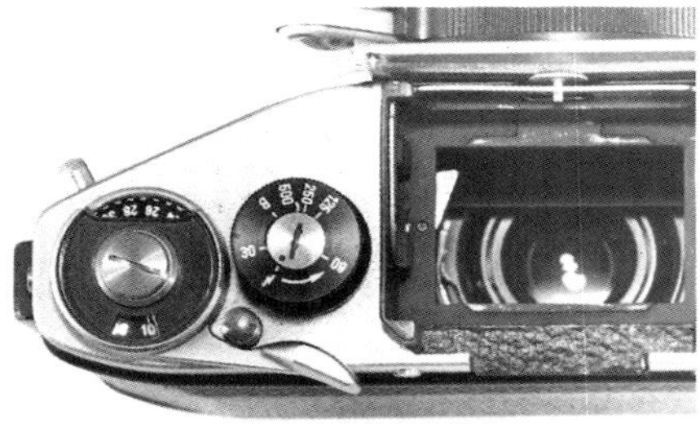

Exakta VX 500, Later model. The shutter speed-dial features an intermediate position between 1/30 and 1/60 indicated by a flash symbol.

VX 500 1970 ★★

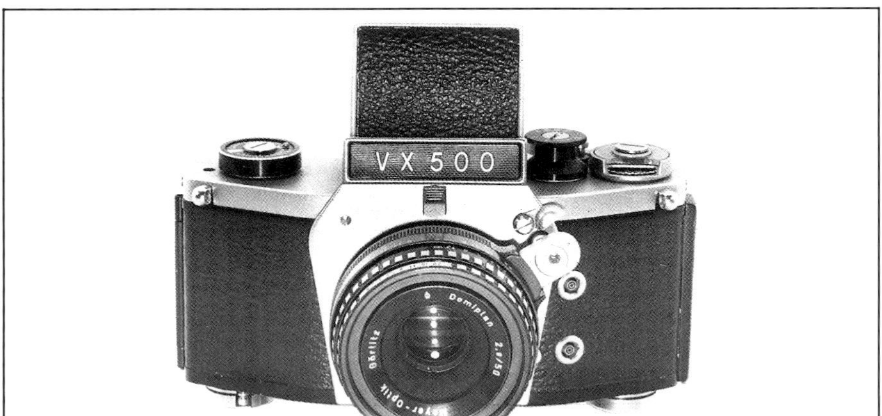

VX 500 No.1520466 with 50mm f/2.8 Meyer Domiplan No.4370433.

The serial numbers are in the same series as the Exakta VX 500.

This model was identical to the previous model except for the Exakta trade mark which did not appear on the front of the camera. It had a name-plate marked "VX 500" with letters shown in relief on a scored background. On the shutter speed-dial, the intermediate position between $^1/_{30}$ and $^1/_{60}$ was represented by a flash symbol.

EXAKTA RTL 1000 1970 ★

Approximate range of serial numbers: 200000 to 290000.

This model was a slightly modified version of the Praktika VLC and was manufactured by VEB Pentacon. When Ihagee was absorbed by Pentacon the Exakta name brought them a considerable asset for a while.

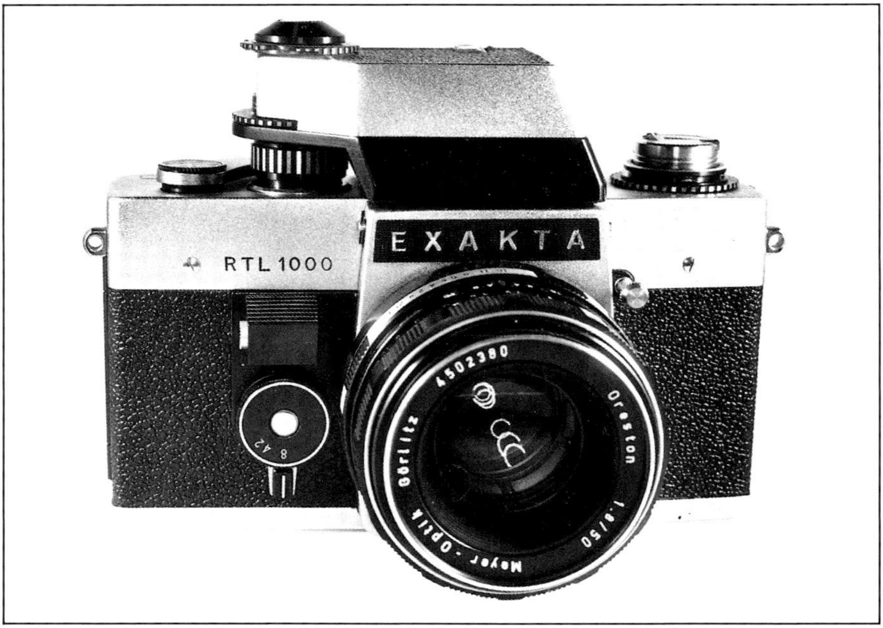

Exakta RTL 1000 No.201460 with 50mm f/1.8 Meyer Oreston lens No.4502380.

In order to be named Exakta RTL 1000, the Practica VLC was equipped with slow-speeds at 2, 4 and 8 seconds., and a left-hand operated release so that it could receive Varex optics.

The Exakta RTL 1000 had a body with instant-return mirror, focal-plane shutter with metal blinds and vertical movement, speeds ranging from 8 to $^1/_{1000}$ seconds and a single flash socket with $^1/_{125}$ synchronised for electronic flash and $^1/_{30}$ for bulbs.

The lens bayonet was similar to that of the Exakta, with internal preselection for the new range of lenses. Release was by pressing a large knob, placed on the right for this type of lens and on the left for the old Varex lenses with the external preselection system. The camera could be connected to any Exakta Varex accessory, except for the viewfinders and screens. There was a new range of interchangeable viewfinders, one of them equipped with a light-measuring prism for TTL light metering. The focusing screens were also interchangeable. Except for this TTL prism, the other viewfinders were interchangeable with those of the Praktica VLC. A wide range of lenses with internal preselection was available (see Chapter 8).

RTL 1000 1970 ★★

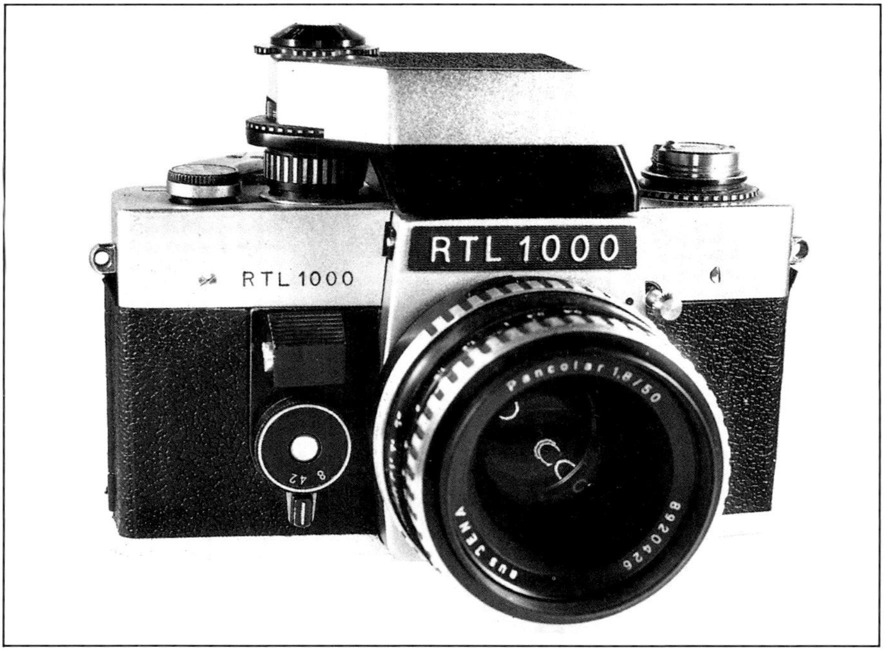

RTL 1000 No.207269 with 50mm f/1.8 "aus Jena" Pancolar lens No.8920426.

Approximate range of serial numbers: 205000 to 290000.

This camera was identical to the Exakta RTL 1000 in all respects, apart from the name-plate.

After several legal actions, Pentacon had finally given up using the Exakta name. This model was intended for marketing mainly in the Eastern Block and in Central Europe.

There was another version of this model with "RTL 1000" appearing in the centre of the camera instead of the right-hand side (see Abring, H.D, Von Daguerre bis Heute, Vol 2, entry no. 1647).

Chapter 6
The "Western" EXAKTA'S

EXAKTA Real 1966 ★★★★★

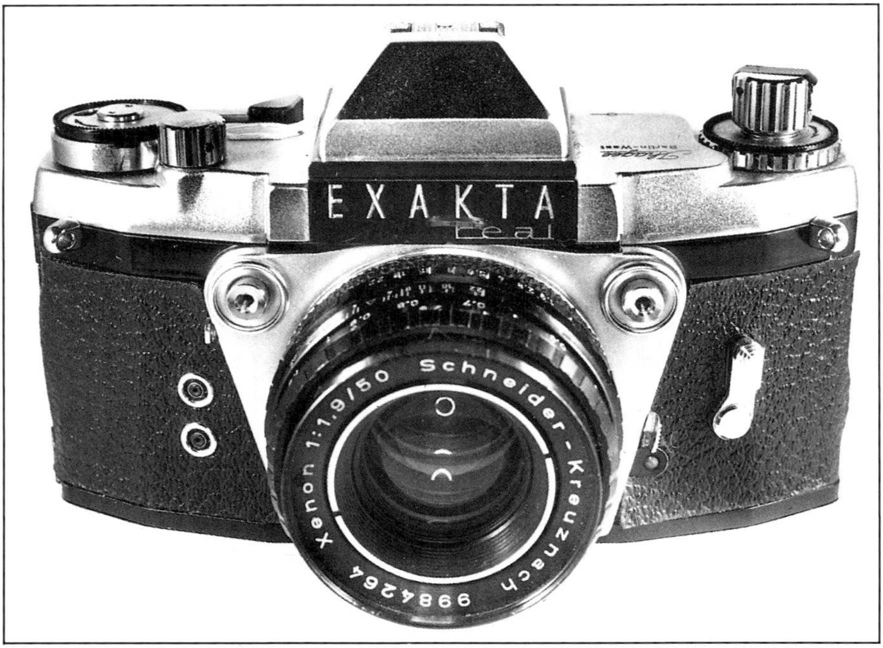

Exakta Real, No.1007, equipped with 50mm f/1.9 Schneider Xenar No.9984264.

Approximate range of serial numbers: 001 to 2500

This model was manufactured by Ihagee Kamerawerk AG, 1 Berlin 65, Koloniestrasse 133-135, and introduced at Photokina, 1963. The company had been formed by a regrouping the Steenbergen heirs and shareholders. The distribution of the camera did not commence until 1966, and then it was only on the market for a year. It was a very modern-looking camera, with a very oval trapezoid shape and interchangeable viewfinders.

The cloth-blind shutter operated horizontally from right to left. The speed range was: B and T, 2, 1, $^1/_2$, $^1/_4$, $^1/_8$, $^1/_{15}$, $^1/_{30}$, $^1/_{60}$, $^1/_{125}$, $^1/_{250}$, $^1/_{500}$, $^1/_{1000}$, with an intermediate position for flash between $^1/_{30}$ and $^1/_{60}$. The speed control knob was milled and did not carry any graduations. A mechanism located under the hood drove a graduated disc which displayed the speed opposite a window. There was a 15 second delay mechanism operated by a lever located in the front of the body. The two flash sockets, "F" and "X", were synchronised at $^1/_{40}$ second.

The lens mount was of bayonet type, but of an entirely new design. It had a diameter of 46mm, instead of the 38mm of the Varex, and a lateral lever-operated internal locking device. Closing of the diaphragm was by an internal linkage. An adapter was available for mounting Exakta Varex lenses on the new camera.

The body carried two shutter releases on the front. The left-hand one was reserved for the external diaphragm control of the Varex lenses. The right-hand one was for the new internally controlled lenses and was fitted with a locking device. The exposure meter could be automatically reset when opening the back of the camera. The camera had a chrome finish, but a black model also became available.

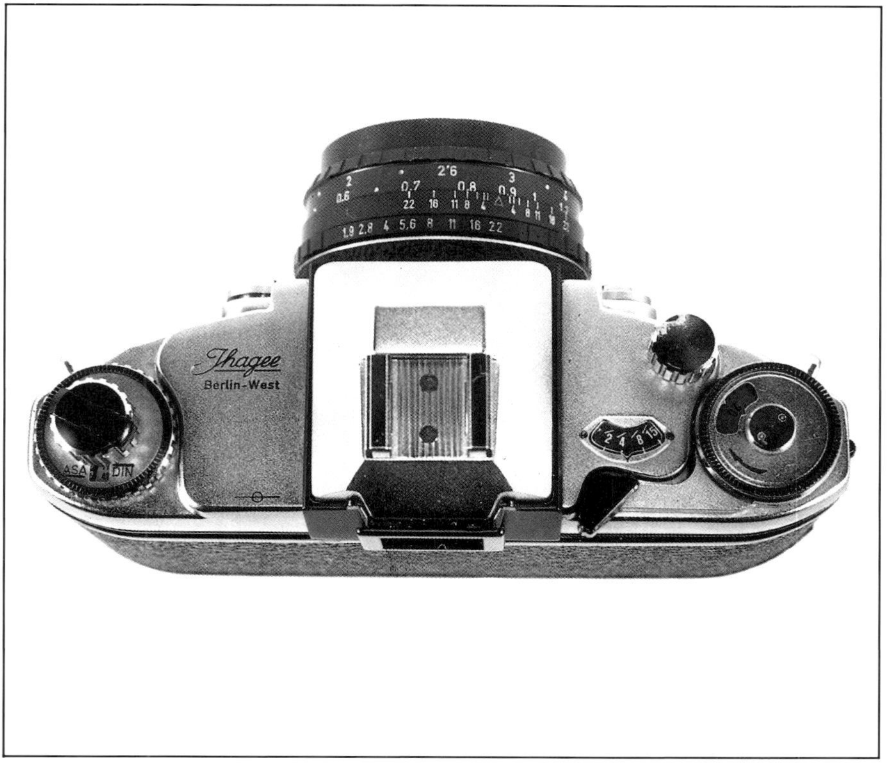

Exakta Real,top view. On the left: film speed reminder located concentrically to the rewind knob. In the centre: prism viewfinder equipped with its accessory shoe On the right: shutter speed knob with display window and wind-o lever with frame counter.

The viewfinders were of a new type, fitted with slides for interchangeability. Three types were available:-

- a hooded viewfinder with magnifier.
- a standard prism viewfinder.
- a prism viewfinder equipped with a TTL meter. To our knowledge, this one was never distributed.

The focusing screens, which werea similar to those of the Varex, were interchangeable and mounted in the body.

For unknown reasons, presumably technical or commercial, the experience of the new Ihagee team was to be short-lived: production ceased in 1967. Needless to say, at the time Japanese models were penetrating European markets and this was probably a factor.

It is interesting to compare some catalogue prices:

- Exakta Real with 50mm f/1.9 Xenon and standard prism: FF 1882
- Asahi Pentax Spotmatic with 55mm f/1.8 lens: FF 1998
- Nikkormat FT with 50mm f/2 lens: FF 1830

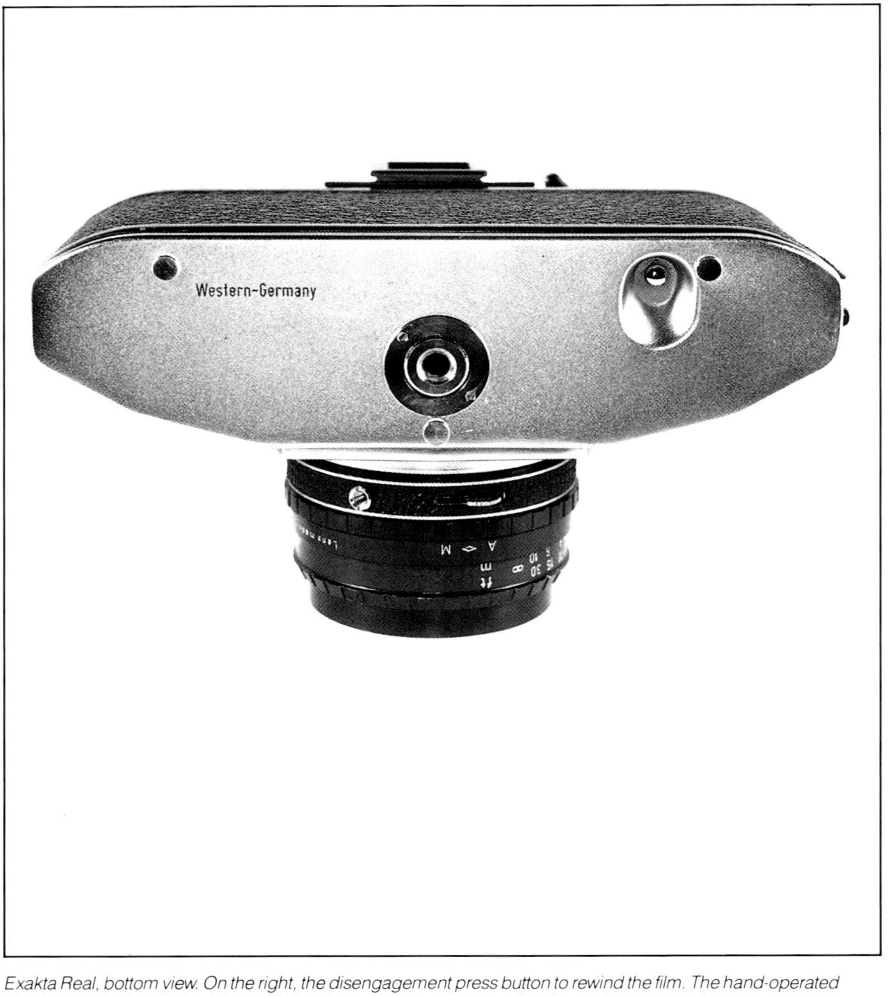

Exakta Real, bottom view. On the right, the disengagement press button to rewind the film. The hand-operated diaphragm closing device is located directly on the lens, together with a flange for a cable-release.

VIEWFINDERS FOR THE EXAKTA REAL

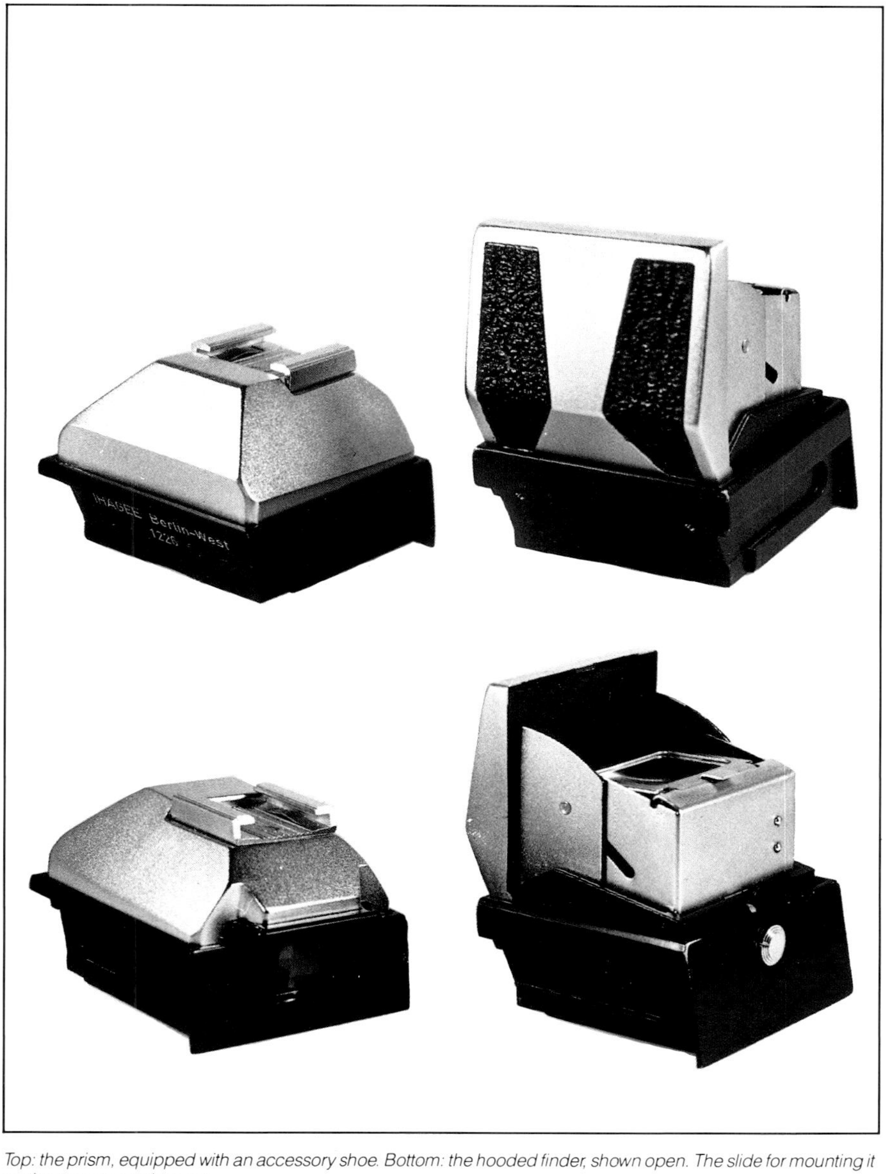

Top: the prism, equipped with an accessory shoe. Bottom: the hooded finder, shown open. The slide for mounting it on the camera can be seen.

LENSES FOR THE EXAKTA REAL

The lenses relating to the Exakta Real ranged in focal length from 28 to 200mm, plus a 80-240mm zoom

Maker	Lens	Focal Length	Aperture
Schneider	Curtagon	28mm	f/4
	Curtagon	35mm	f/2.8
	Xenon	50mm	f/1.9
	Xenar	50mm	f/2.8
	Tele-Xenar	135mm	f/3.5
	Zoom Tele-Variogon	80-240mm	f/4
Schacht	Travegon	35mm	f/2.8
	Travelon	50mm	f/1.8
	Travenar	50mm	f/2.8
	Travenar (Macro)	50mm	f/2.8
	Travenar	90mm	f/2.8
	Travenar	135mm	f/3.5
	Tele-Travelon	200mm	f/4

The following accessories were also available :

Macro bellows bench
Set of extension rings
Adapter for microscope
2x and 3x Schacht focal length extenders

EXAKTA Twin TL 1970 ★★

The West Berlin Exakta company turned to Japan for their next camera. This was the Exakta Twin TL. It was made by Cosina and it was the only Exakta camera to be made in Japan which remained close to Exaktas made in Germany. The bayonet mount was similar to that of the Exakta Real and the camera could be equipped with Varex optics by means of an adapter collar. There was another version with a 42mm screw mount called the Exakta Twin TL 42.

The camera measured 145x65x95mm and weighed 770g (without lens). There was one adapter for Varex optics and another one for 42mm screw-mount lenses. The French importer recommended a 38-80mm f/3.5 zoom as a standard lens. There was auto-preselection of the diaphragm and depth of focus control. The shutter was a horizontally-running Copal with metal blinds. The speeds ranged from 1 second to 1/1000, plus B, and a delay of about 8 seconds. The Twin TL had the special feature of having two shutter releases. The first one was located on the top right corner of the camera body and the second one on the left hand side of the front. This additional shutter release was designed for automatic-diaphragm Varex lenses with external

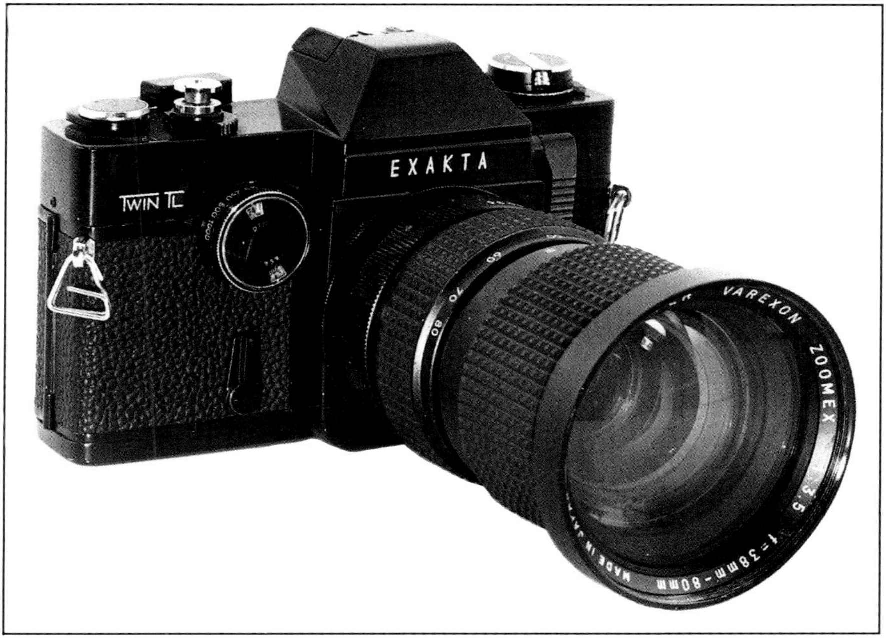

Exakta Twin TL No.25465, with 38-80mm f/3.5 Super Varexon Zoom lens.

diaphragm coupling. There were two flash sockets, "X" and "M", synchronised at 1/125, and a hot-shoe.

The viewfinder was a fixed prism and there was automatic mirror-return. The focusing screen was ground-glass with a microprism disc in the centre. The eyepiece could be fitted with an eye shade. The exposure meter was a CdS cell behind the lens with semi-automatic exposure setting at actual aperture. Its sensitivity range was from 25 to 1600 ASA. The needle and scale were visible through the viewfinder.

The lenses offered for the camera were by Schneider and Schacht and are listed in the table:

Schneider	Curtagon	28mm f/4
Schneider	Curtagon	35mm f/2.8
Schacht	Travegon	35mm f/2.8
	Exaktar	28mm f/2.8
	Exaktar	35mm f/2.8
Schneider	Xenon	50mm f/1.9
Schacht	Travelon	50mm f/1.8
	Exaktar	50mm f/1.8
	Exaktar	55mm f/1.4
	Exaktar	58mm f/1.2

Schacht	Travenar	90mm f/2.8
Schacht	Travenar	135mm f/3.5
Schneider	Tele-Xemar	135mm f/3.5
	Exaktar	135mm f/2.8
	Exaktar	200mm f/3.5
	Exaktar	300mm f/5
	Vario-Exaktar	45-135mm f/3.5
	Vario-Exaktar	78-205mm f/3.5
Schneider	Variogon	45-100mm f/2.8
Schneider	Tele-Variogon	80-240mm f/4

The range of accessories was rather limited, but the adapter for the Varex lenses had the advantage of adapting all the macro accessories of the previous camera bodies to the Twin TL. Accessories with the Twin TL mount included a microscope attachment, a set of extension tubes and a macro bellows with inner diaphragm locking device.

EXAKTA TL 500 1976

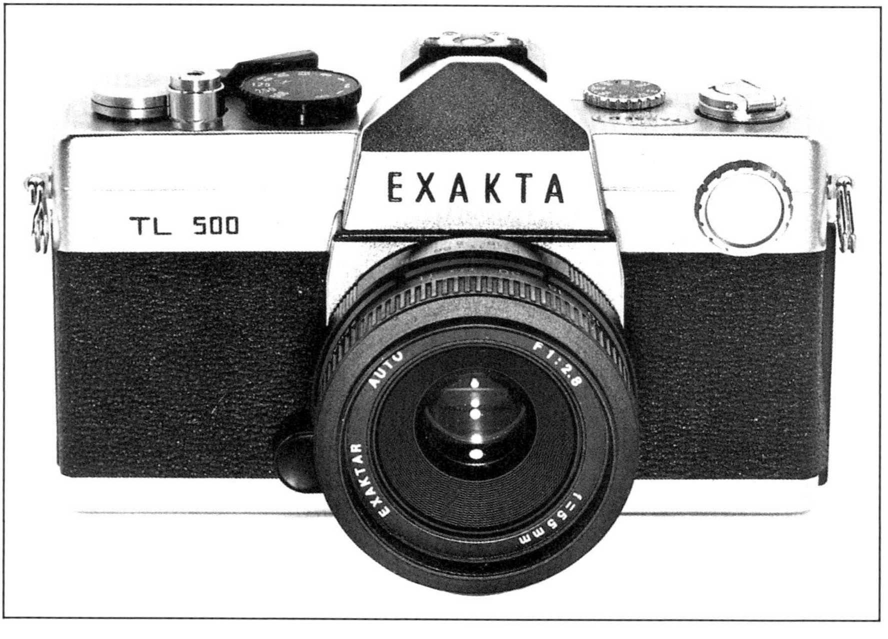

Exakta TL 500 No.829117 with 55mm f/2.8 Exaktar lens No.770324.

This camera was manufactured in Japan for the West German Ihagee company using the same specifications as those of the Petri body. The logo "Ihagee Kamerawerk A.G." appeared in the manual provided with the camera. There was a very similar model called the Exakta TL 1000 with shutter speeds up to 1/1000.

The TL 500 had a CdS TTL light-meter with a sensitivity range from 25 to 1600 ASA. Shutter speeds were from 1 second to 1/500, plus B. FP and F flash synchronisation was provided, together with a hot-shoe. The fixed prism viewfinder had a ground-glass screen with a central microprism disc. The lens mount was a 42mm screw.

EXAKTA FE 2000 1978

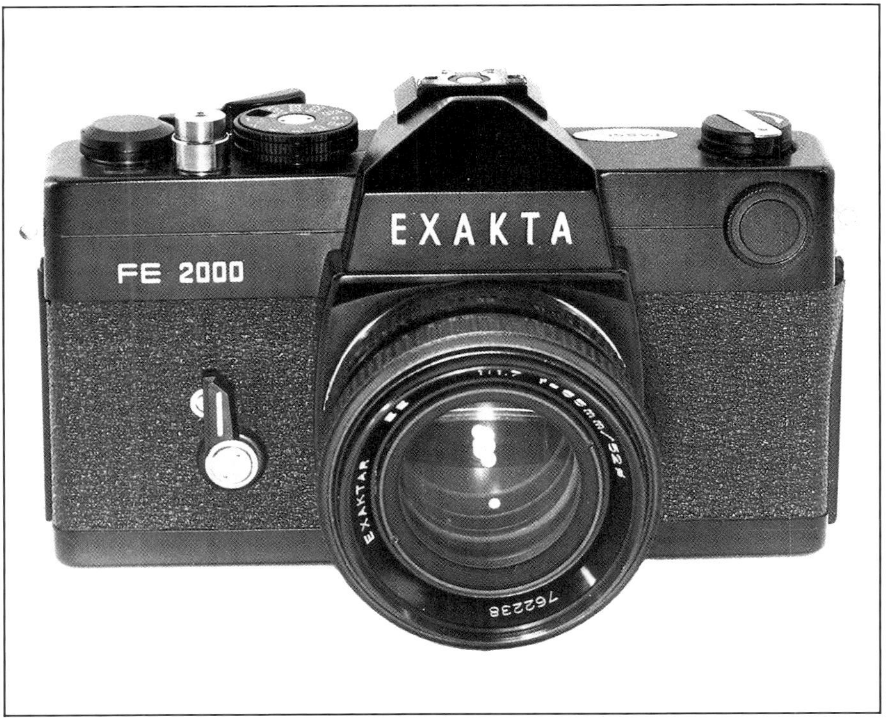

Exakta FE 2000 No.524476, with 55mm f/1.7 Exaktar EE lens No.762232.

This camera was also manufactured in Japan to a Petri specification. On the right-hand side of the eyepiece "Ihagee West" was engraved on the top hood.

It was basicly similar to the TL 500, but the lens diaphragm automatically closed down on pressing the shutter release if the lens was set on the "EE" position. The aperture scale was visible in the viewfinder. The shutter was speeded from 1 second to 1/1000, plus B. Flash synchronisation was by hot-shoe.

Chapter 7
The 35mm EXA

EXA, Version 1   1952   ★★

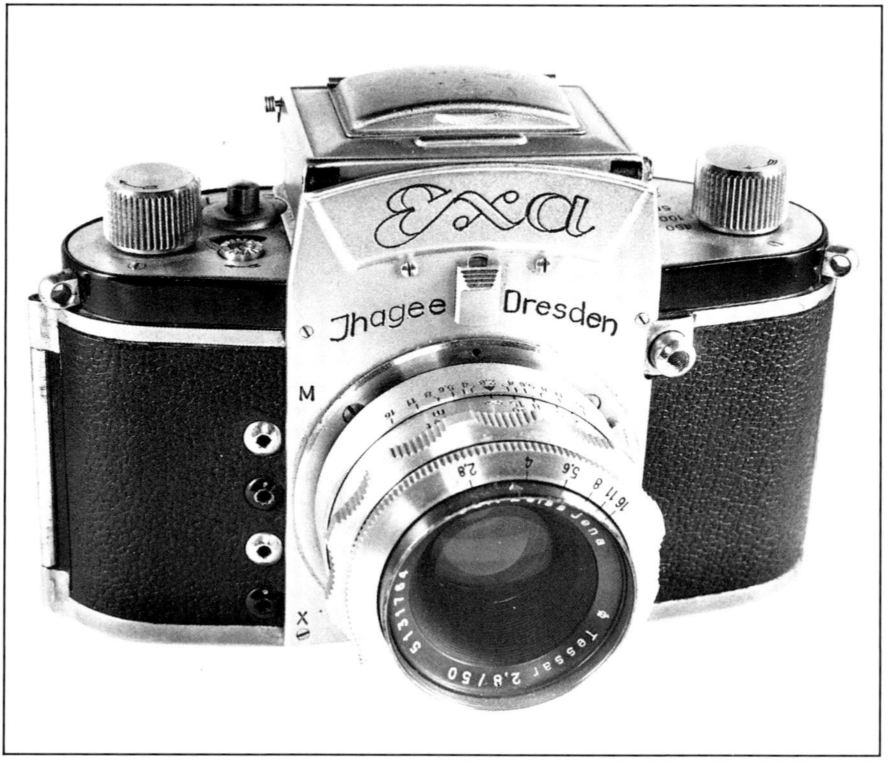

Exa No.227811 with 50mm f/2.8 Zeiss Tessar lens No.5131764.

Approximate range of serial numbers: 200000 to 235000.

In 1951 many amateurs were delighted to see a new reflex camera advertised at a very reasonable price. Up to then the cost of a reflex camera had been the equivalent of several months' pay. Marketed from 1952, the first Exa was a great success. The simplicity, sturdiness and compactness of the Exa turned out to be a technical triumph.

Some people thought of the Exa as a separate instrument entirely from the contemporary Exakta Varex, whereas others considered it as an extra body for their Exakta lenses. In reality, it was an independent reflex camera with a more limited scope, but of unquestionable sturdiness.

The main characteristics of the camera were:-

- Exakta Varex viewfinders and viewing optics could be used on the Exa.
- It had a metal sector shutter.
- Shutter wind and film wind-on were coupled.
- It measured 130x85x48mm and weighed 465g without viewfinder.

One can immediately recognise the early Exa models by the two bipolar flash sockets which were located on the right-hand side of the camera body. One socket was chrome-plated and marked "M" for use with flash bulbs (synchronisation at all speeds with FP bulbs), and the other one was glossy black and marked "X" for electronic flash (synchronisation at 1/50). "Exa" was engraved on the front-plate and "Ihagee Dresden" on each side of the viewfinder locking button. The hood of this early model had the release blocking rod.

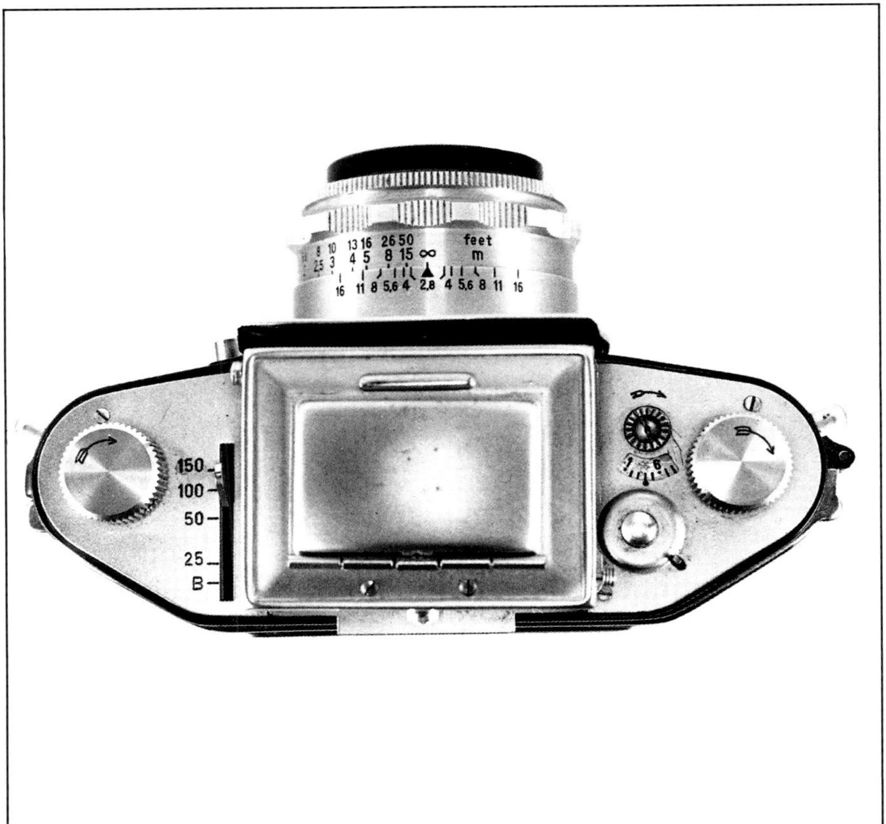

Top view of the Exa. From left to right: rewind button, shutter-speed lever, collapsible hooded viewfinder, (front to back) frame counter zero adjustment button, counter window and rewinding release button, and, far right, wind-on knob.

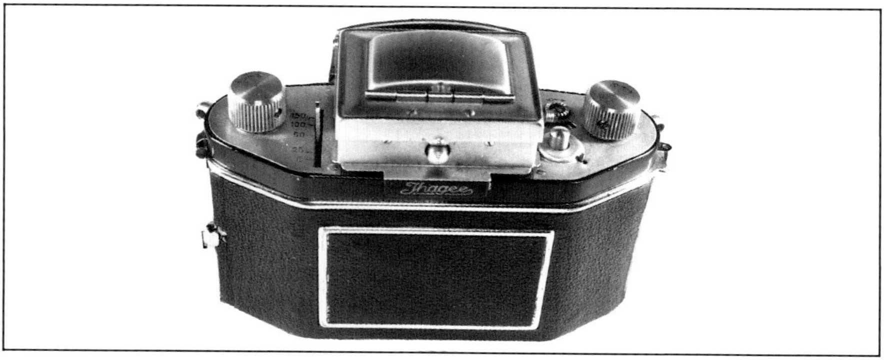

Exa, Version 1, back view.

On the right-hand side of the top plate was a milled knob which advanced the film and cocked the shutter. Contrary to most modern 35mm cameras, the Exa wound the film with the emulsion to the inside. The take-up spool was removable and could be replaced with an empty cassette. This model featured a hinged back and a large size film pressure plate. Like its elder brother, the Exa was of trapezoid shape, but unlike the Exakta the flat part was at the front. The camera body was remarkably rigid.

The Exa shutter was remarkable because of its simplicity. Being of a sector type, it could be mirror and shutter at the same time. Its motion was vertical. The speed range was: B, 1/25, 1/50, 1/100, 1/150 second.

The camera was often supplied with a Meyer Trioplan or Ludwig Meritar lens. The Exa could also accept all the lenses designed for the Exakta, but vignetting occured with focal lengths greater than 100mm, with extension tubes and with macro-bellows.

EXA, Version 2 1955 ★★★

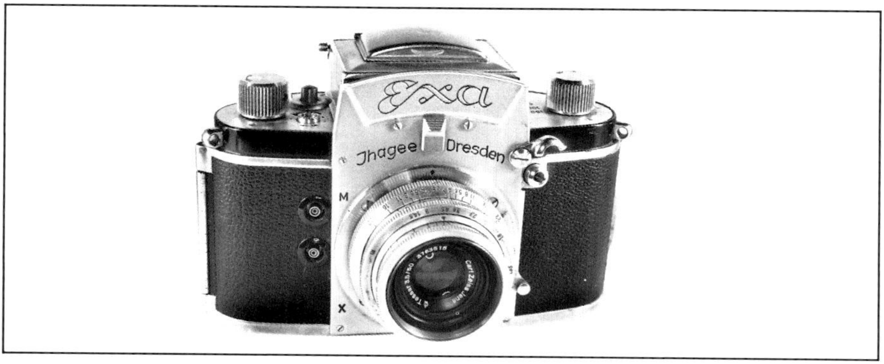

Exa No.235926 with 50mm f/3.5 Zeiss Tessar No.3763513.

Approximate range of serial numbers: 235000 to 245000.

This camera was similar to the first version of the Exa except for the flash sockets. The Exa Version 2 was provided with two glossy black sockets of a standard coaxial type, marked "M" and "X".

The viewing hood lost its release blocking rod, which was replaced by a protective cover which hinged over the shutter release button in the same way as on the Exakta Varex of that time. Like the Varex, the cover had a cut-out to allow the use of a cable release when it was in the safety postion.

EXA, Version 3, Rheinmetall 1956 ★★★

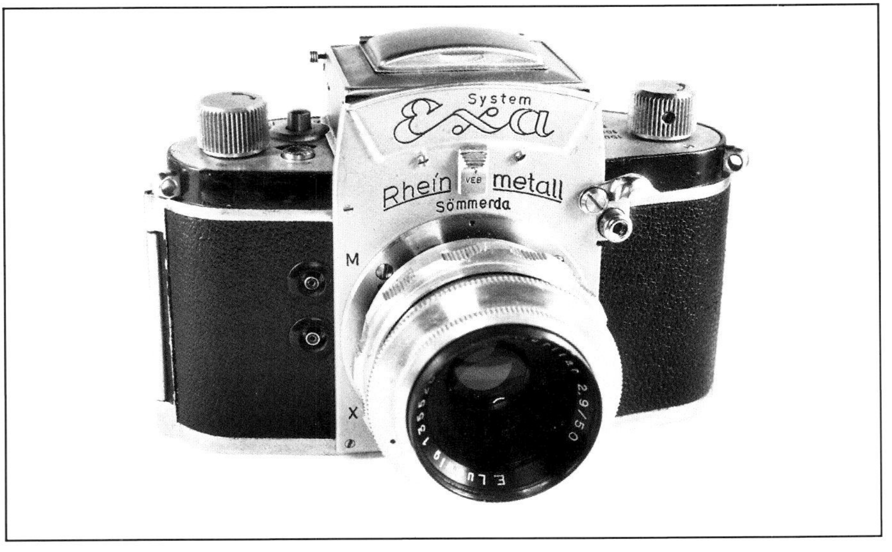

Exa Rheinmetall, No.255874, with 50mm f/2.9 Ludwig Meritar lens No.1355205.

Approximate range of serial numbers: 245000 to 275000.

This camera, named "System Exa Rheinmetall", was identical to the second version of the Exa, except for the name-plate, the viewfinder locking button which was marked "VEB", and the shutter release safety cover which had no cut-out. Also the viewfinder hood was engraved "Rheinmetall" on the rear instead of "Ihagee".

At that time the factory in Dresden was working at full capacity and the ever-increasing production of the Varex and the many accessories was monopolising the whole production. In order to relieve the overloaded factory Ihagee entrusted Sommerda with the production of the Exa.

Contrary to legend, the Rheinmetall is not the rarest of the Exa models.

EXA, Version 4 1957 ★

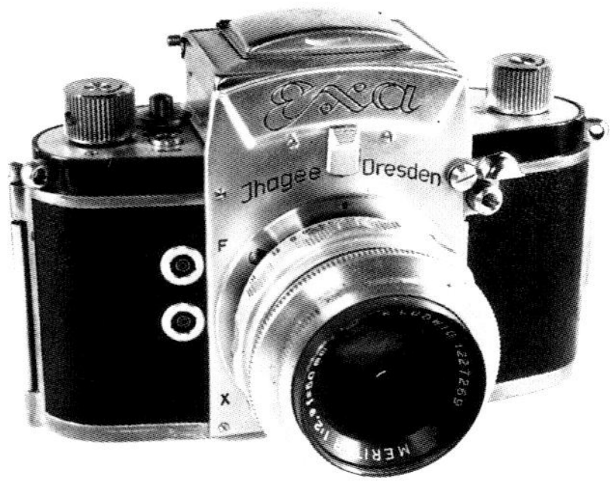

Exa No.514580 with 50mm f/2.9 Ludwig Meritar lens No.1227269.

Approximate range of serial numbers: 400000 to 520000.

Ihagee regained production of the Exa, which had been temporarily entrusted to Sommerda, and curiously reused the serial numbers already given to the Exakta A, B and Kine models.

This 4th version was distributed mainly in the USA. It differed in the following ways from Version 2:-

- The flash sockets were finished in chrome instead of black.
- The spindle of the hinge holding the back could be withdrawn and the back removed.
- The film guides on each side of the film pressure plate were omitted.

EXA, Version 5 1958 ★★

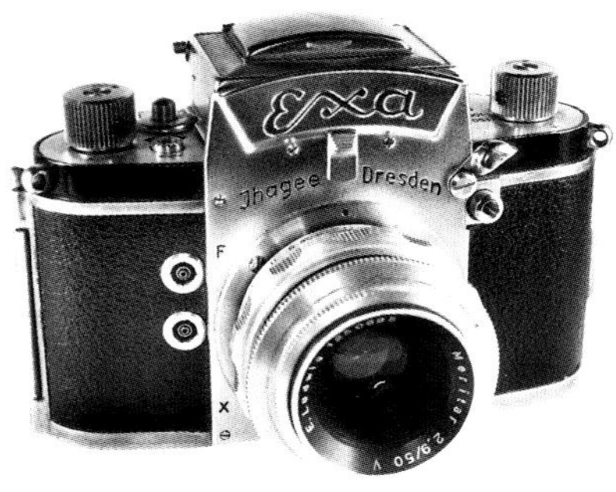

Exa No.534506 with Ludwig Meritar lens No.1250695.

Approximate range of serial numbers: 520000 to 560000.
The Exa, 5th version, employed the same graphics as its "elder brother", the Exakta Varex IIa: the name "Exa" was not engraved but appeared in relief on the front plate. In all the other respects it was identical to the previous model.

EXA, Version 6 1961 ★

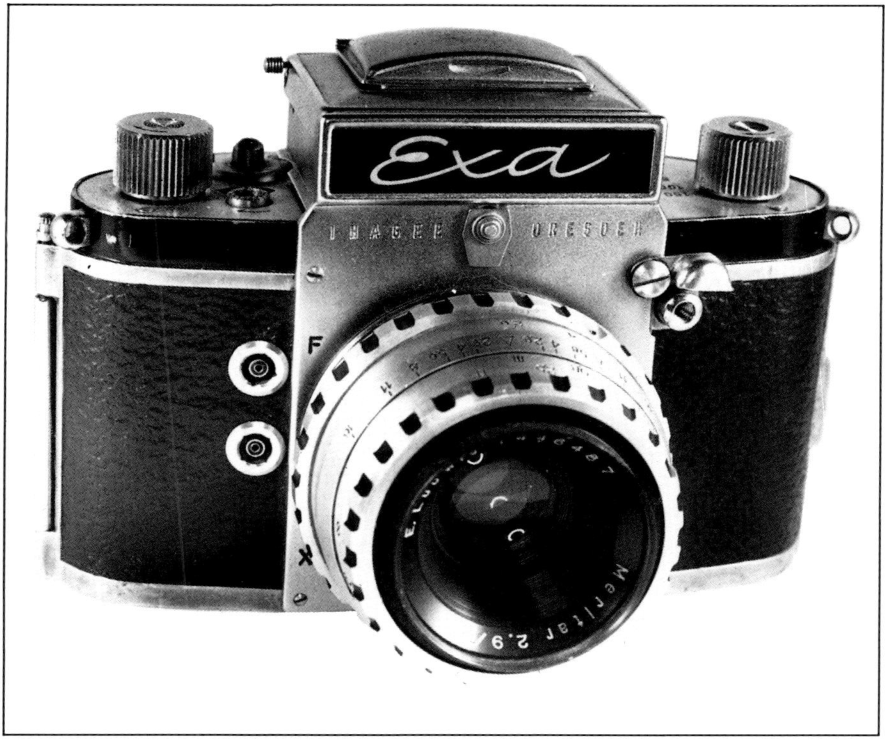

Exa No.613545 with 50mm f/2.9 Ludwig Meritar lens No.1446487.

Approximate range of serial numbers: 560000 to 620000.

Although this 6th version had been updated, it still retained the specification of the previous model. The new name plate had a rectangular shape. The name "Exa" was in white letters on a black background. Below this plate, on each side of the viewfinder locking button, "Ihagee Dresden" was engraved in capital letters. This model featured the new black leathered covered prisms and hoods. On various advertisements of the time the camera was shown with the Jubile prism or hooded viewfinder.

EXA I, Version 1 1963 ★

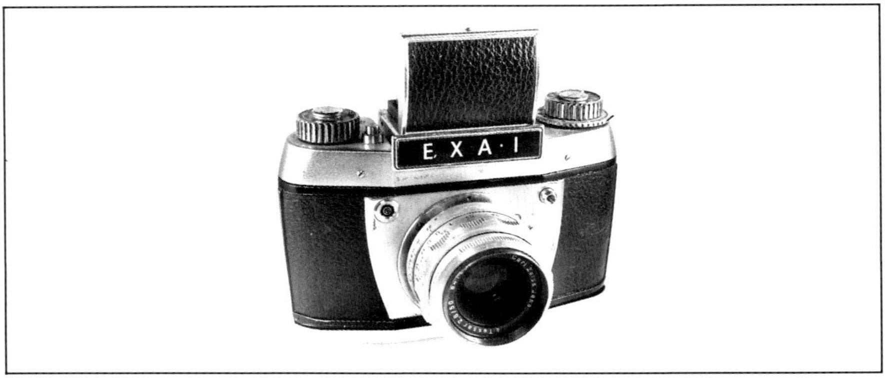

Exa I, No.122160, with 50mm f/2.8 Zeiss Tessar No.6475825.

Approximate range of serial numbers: 100000 to 150000.

The Exa I had a completely new body shape, but it was still basically the same camera as the previous models. It remained a small but sturdy reflex camera. Without viewfinder and lens, it measured 135x90x48mm and weighed 520g. The Exa I still had a trapezoid shape but with a more oval profile. The chrome front plate was in the shape of a shield with a cut off base. The new logo, Exa I, appeared in white capital letters on a black background. The single socket for electronic flash or bulbs was on the right of the front plate. Synchronisation was at 1/60 and 1/30 respectively. The shutter-release was on the right of the front plate. A lever located on the rear of the camera body, left of the viewfinder, acted as a shutter-release safety device.

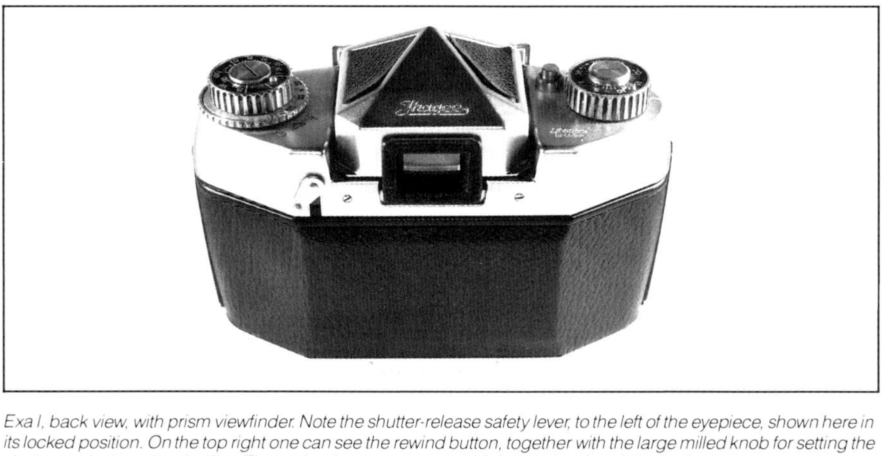

Exa I, back view, with prism viewfinder. Note the shutter-release safety lever, to the left of the eyepiece, shown here in its locked position. On the top right one can see the rewind button, together with the large milled knob for setting the shutter and advancing the film. The set-back exposure counter is located on top of this knob.

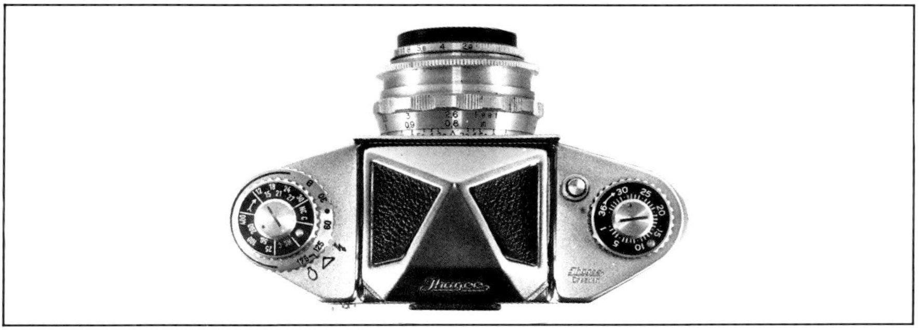

Exa I, top view, with prism viewfinder. On the left of the camera one can see the rewind knob with the film speed reminder on top. The shutter speed dial is concentric with the rewind knob offering the following range: B, 1/30, 1/60, 1/125 and 1/175 second. Time exposures could be set by selecting B and using the shutter-release locking lever. When pushed back, this lever locked the shutter.

The camera back and baseplate could be removed as a unit by giving a half turn to the ring that was concentric with the tripod socket, and then sliding the back downwards. The film pressure plate, which was similar to that in the Exakta was also detachable. One film guide roller was fixed on the camera back and the other on body to the left of the film gate. The shutter was of the same sector type as earlier Exa models. The film wound with emulsion inside and the take-up spool was detachable and could be replaced with an empty cassette. Strangely enough, there were no strap eyelets on the camera.

EXA I, Version 2 1964 ★★

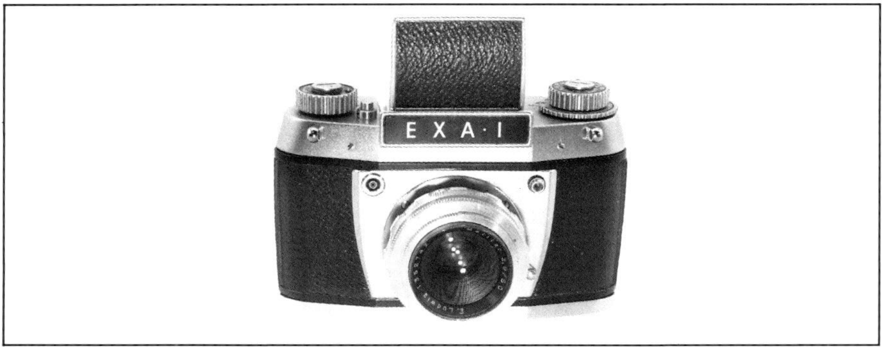

Exa I. No.172275, with 50mm f/2.9 Ludwig Meritar lens No.1352742.

Approximate range of serial numbers: 150000 to 175000.

This model was almost identical to the previous version, except that strap eyelets were provided on the front of the top plate.

EXA Ia 1965 ★

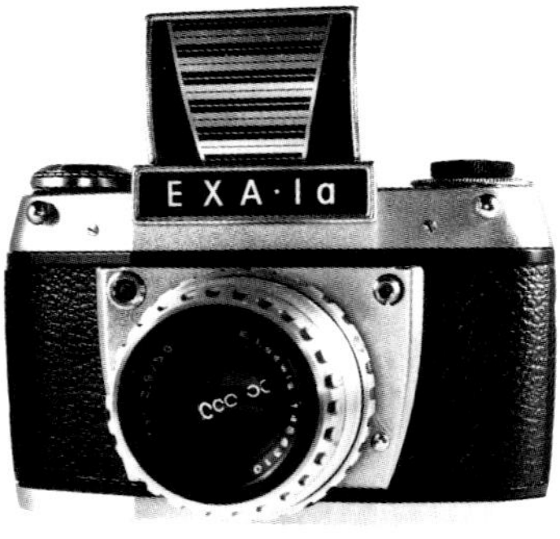

Exa Ia, No.212753, with 50mm f/2.9 Ludwig Meritar lens No.1458310 and equipped with Jubile hooded viewfinder.

Approximate range of serial numbers: 200000 to 440000. Once again, Ihagee had repeated the numbers given to a previous model, the Exa of 1952.

The production run of this model was considerable, and in fact the Exa Ia was manufactured under this name until the end of 1968. Later, when VEB Pentacon stopped making use of the names "Exakta" and "Exa", the same model continued to be manufactured under the new name of VX 100.

The Exa Ia was similar to the Exa I but differed from it in the following respects:-

- the disengagement press button was moved to the rear of the camera.
- the rewind knob was reduced in thickness.
- the shutter and film wind-on knob was replaced by a lever.
- the film speed reminder was moved to the top of the rewind lever.
- the shutter-release locking lever was also modified.

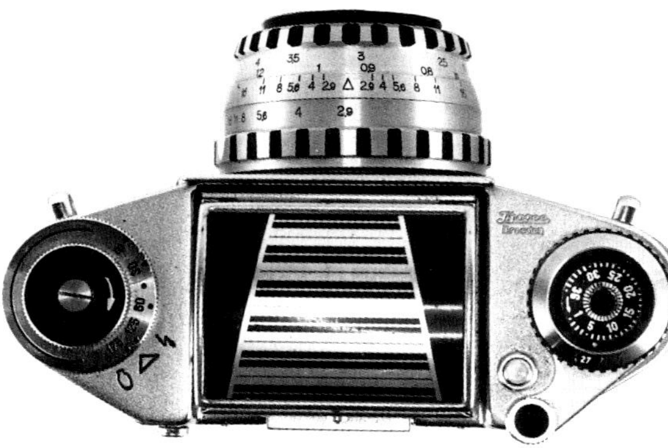

Exa Ia, top view.

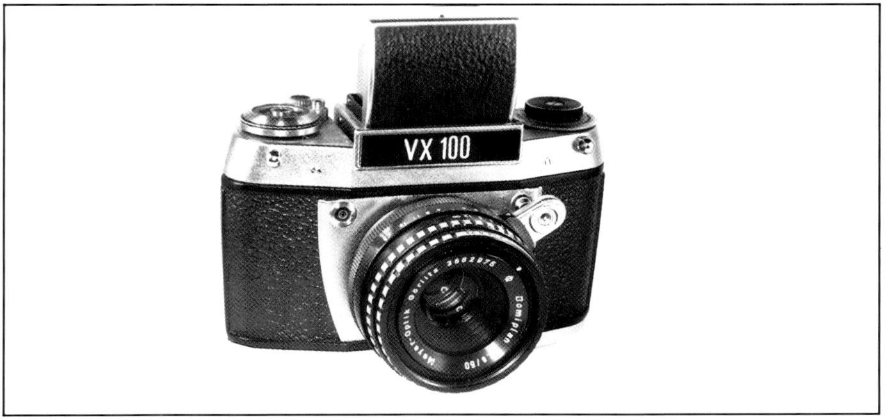

VX 100. Similar to the Exa Ia except for the name. This model was not distributed in France.

EXA Ib 1977 ★

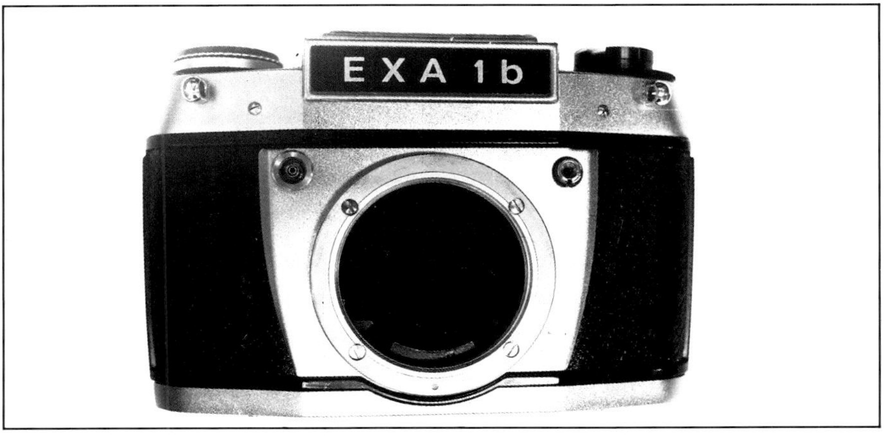

Exa Ib, without lens.

This model was still being distributed at the time of writing.

In 1977 VEB Pentacon either made use of the remaining stock, or re-started production of the Exa Ia, which became known as the Exa Ib. The only modifications were the introduction of the 42mm screw mount of the Praktica and replacement of the rewind knob with a crank. The rest of the specification remained the same. The Exa Ib, which is available with a Domiplan lens, is equipped with the Exakta VX 1000 viewfinder or prism. However, we must point out that in 1973, the Exa I was already distributed with a 42mm screw mount.

EXA II 1959 ★

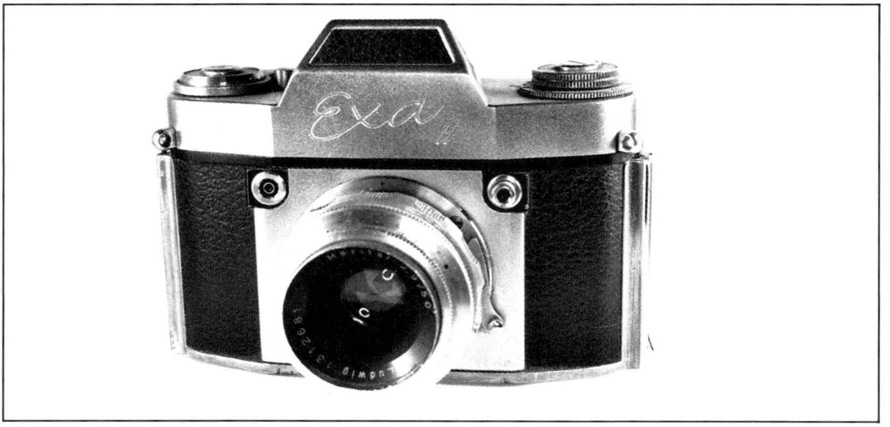

Exa II, No.234239 with 50mm f/2.9 Ludwig Meritar len No.1312681.

Approximate range of serial numbers: 200000 to 290000.

Although it was similar in many respects to the Exa and Exa I, the Exa II differed in its shutter and viewing system.

The sector shutter, which offered limited possibilities, was replaced with a vertical-motion cloth focal-plane shutter. The speed range of the new shutter was: B, 1/2, 1/4, 1/8, 1/15, 1/30, 1/60, 1/125, 1/250 second. The bulb and electronic flash synchronisation speeds were 1/15 and 1/30 respectively. With this new shutter there were no more of the vignetting problems that occured with the Exa and Exa I with certain lenses. All the long focal length lenses designed for the Exakta could be used on the Exa II. However, whereas the viewfinders had been interchangeable on the Exa models, the Exa II was equipped with a fixed, inverting prism.

Previous Exa cameras had had a plain frosted-glass screen, but this model was equipped with a central optical-wedge split-image rangefinder.

The front plate, of a new type, carried the Exakta bayonet mount. The single flash socket was located at the top right and the shutter-release on the top left. The release safety device was placed on the back of the camera, to the left of the eyepiece. This device could be used to lock the shutter when it was open and set on "B". The wind-on lever was under the exposure counter and with the disengagement button was located on the top right of the camera body. On the top left was the rewind knob with the film speed reminder. The shutter speed setting dial was placed concentrically under this knob. The dimensions were 130x95x48mm and the weight 670g.

By removing the spindle from the hinge the back could be removed. It opened when the catch on the left side of the body was pushed upwards. The film guides and pressure plate were similar to those of the Exa Ia. The take-up spool was removable and could be replaced with an empty cassette. Above serial number 250000 the rewind knob was modified by removing the ridge located on the milled part.

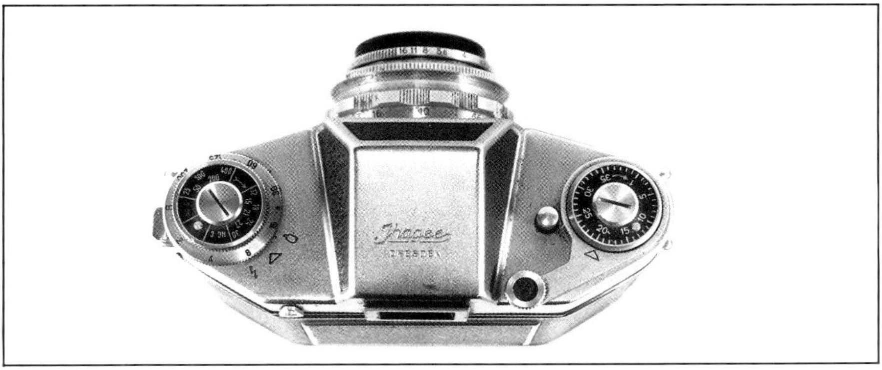

Exa II, top view.

EXA IIa, Version 1 1963 ★★

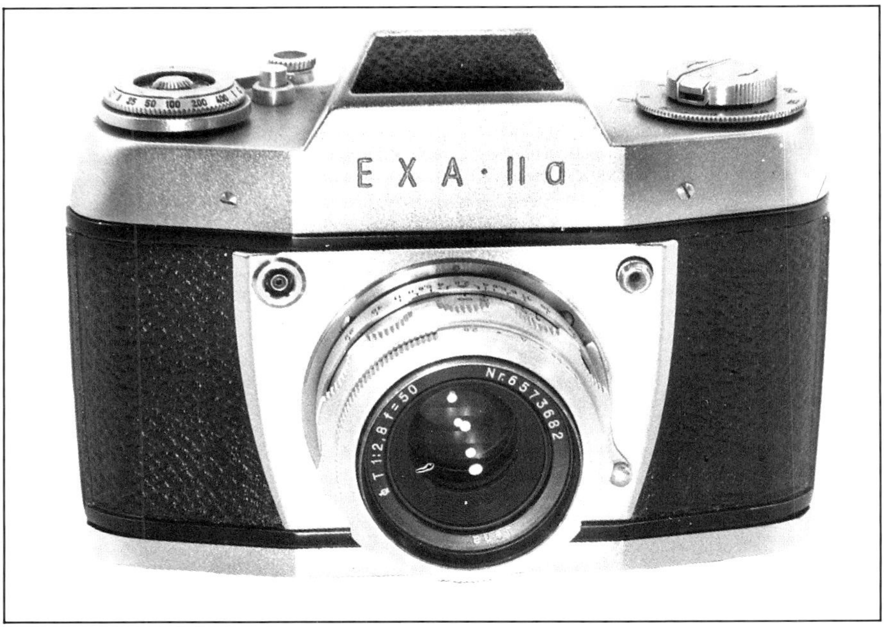

Exa IIa, No.146094, with 50mm f/2.8 Jena len No.6573682.

Approximate range of serial numbers: 140000 to 160000.

The Exa IIa, which was similar to the Exa I in appearance, was part of the Exa II range with its fixed viewing system. It had the same camera body as the Exa I but with a different upper housing. In order to reduce production costs, Ihagee had decided to standardise the components of these two models. The main features were:-

- "Exa IIa" was engraved on the front of the upper housing.
- The stroke of the wind-on lever was reduced to 135°.
- The exposure counter above the wind-on lever showed the number of exposures left in the camera, whereas on the Exa II it had shown the number of exposures made. A dial acting as film speed reminder was concentric with the counter.
- On the left, the shutter speed dial remained the same, but the rewind knob was replaced with a collapsible crank.
- As the camera body was is similar to that of the Exa I, the back was of the slide-on type instead of the hinge type.
- The shutter and speed range were the same as on the Exa II. However, the shutter-release locking system was not lever-operated, as on the Exa II, but was set by a small milled button with a red index mark.
- As with the first version of the EXA I, this model did not have strap eyelets.

EXA IIa, Version 2 1964 ★★

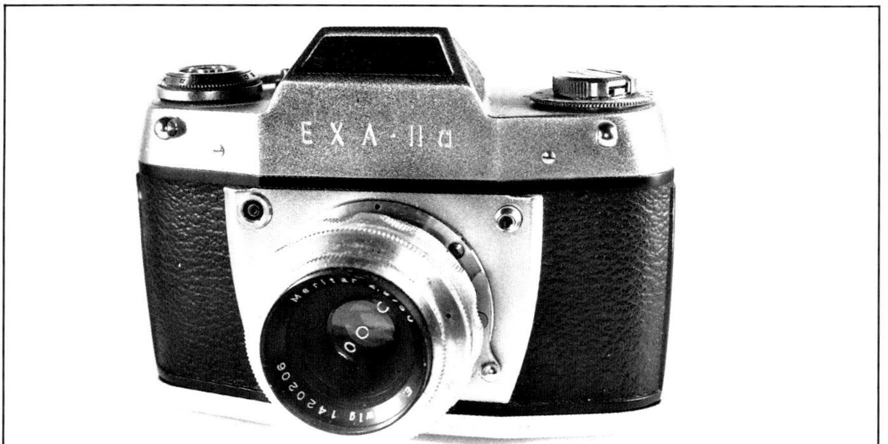

Exa IIa, No.170326, with 50mm f/2.9 Ludwig Meritar lens No.1420206.

Approximate range of serial numbers: 160000 to 190000.

The main difference compared with the Exa IIa was that strap eyelets were now provided on the front of the top plate. Other minor changes were that the milled button for resetting the counter to zero was now chrome and black, whereas before it had been entirely chrome; there was only one arrow instead of two engraved on the rewind crank; the shutter release locking button to the left of the eyepiece was replaced by a lever; and the letters "A" (open) and "Z" (closed) were engraved on the base by the locking catch for the back, whereas before there had been a red dot to indicate the open position. As with the first version, the take-up spool could be replaced with an empty cassette.

The viewfinder prism was not detachable but the camera was available with one of the following screens:-

1 - Plain ground-glass screen (particularly with the first version).
2 - Fresnel lens with central split-image rangefinder and frosted surround.

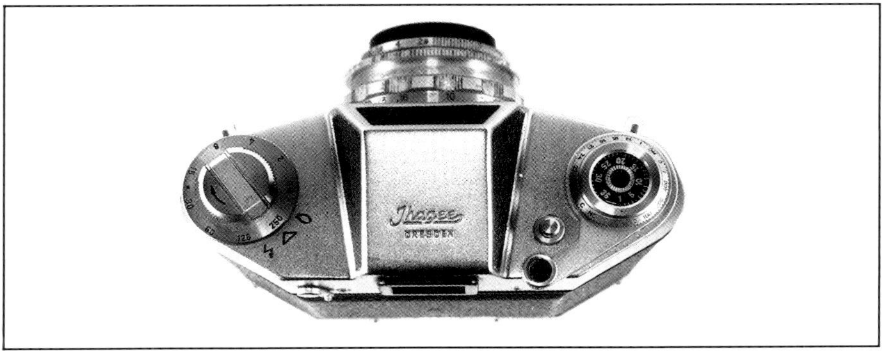

Exa IIa, top view.

EXA IIb 1965 ★

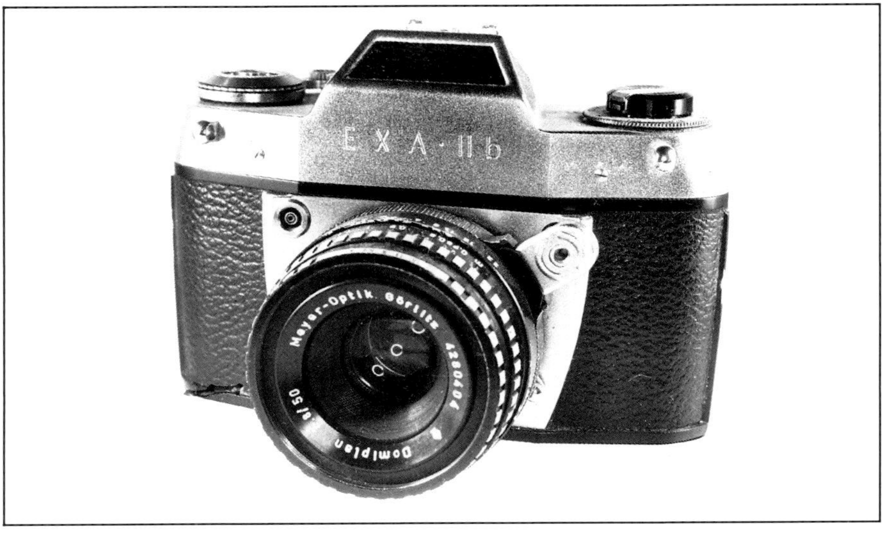

Exa IIb, No.220728 with 50mm f/2.8 Meyer Domiplan lens No.4280404.

Approximate range of serial numbers: 200000 to 270000.

This model was almost identical to the Exa IIa except that it had one modification of considerable importance. For the very first time, Ihagee introduced an automatic return mirror. This was to appear only after 1967 on the Exakta VX 1000. After picture-taking, a red index, located on the left-hand side of the eyepiece, indicated that the shutter was not cocked.

The following minor modifications were also made:-

- The wind-on lever was shortened and of the same type as on the Exa Ia.
- The shape of the film speed reminder was altered. The speed value was now shown through a small window.
- The rewind knob was black with a chrome-plated crank.

The speed range remained the same. The focusing screen was a Fresnel type lens with a central split-image rangefinder and a frosted surround.

EXA 500 1966 ★

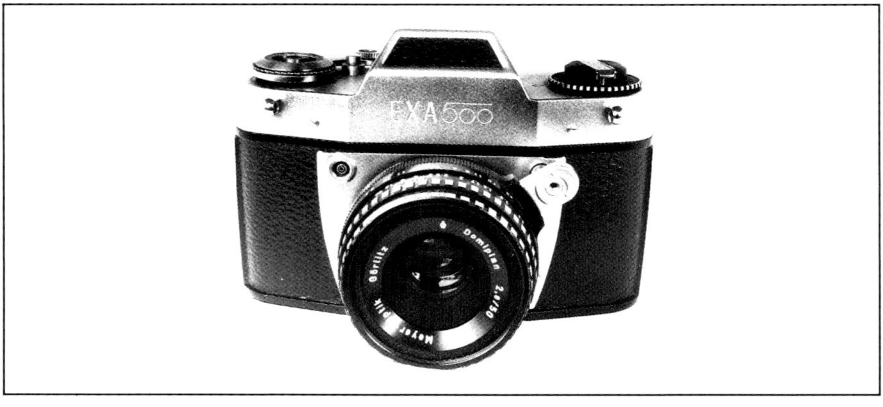

Exa 500, No.289756, with 50mm f/2.8 Meyer Domiplan lens No.4333132.

Approximate range of serial numbers: 280000 to 380000.

This was another model in the Exa II range, therefore with a fixed viewfinder system. It was to be the last model before Ihagee parted from Pentacon.

The external appearance of the Exa 500 was almost identical to the Exa IIb, the only noticeable differences being the shutter speed-ring, which became black, and of course the engraving "Exa 500" which appeared on the front of the prism roof.

The fastest shutter speed was now $1/500$ and the electronic synchronisation speed became $1/60$. In most cases the camera was available with a Fresnel lens focusing screen with microprism central area. On rare occasions it was delivered with a plain ground-glass screen.

The very last cameras to be manufactured were distributed under the name of VX 200, but the writers have not yet seen this model.

Chapter 8

Lenses for the 35mm EXAKTA Cameras

If we had to go through all the Exakta lenses and make a comprehensive list, the subject would need a whole book. Therefore we will only give you a general idea of the main lenses which were manufactured for these cameras from 1936 to 1976.

The lenses will be classified by makers and by dates. Ihagee did not produce lenses themselves, although some cameras were equipped with lenses carrying the Ihagee name. The Company arranged for several German manufacturers to produce lenses for them. In time other German makers, as well as makers in France, the U.S.A., England and Japan, also produced lenses with the Exakta bayonet mount.

The three makers associated with the 35mm Exakta from the beginning were Zeiss, Meyer and Schneider. We will deal with their Exakta lenses first, and then go on to describe the wide variety of lenses offered by other makers at various times.

There was one lens for the Kine Exakta that carried the Ihagee name. That was the 50mm f/3.5 Exaktar, a three element lens with a 28.5x0.5 filter thread.

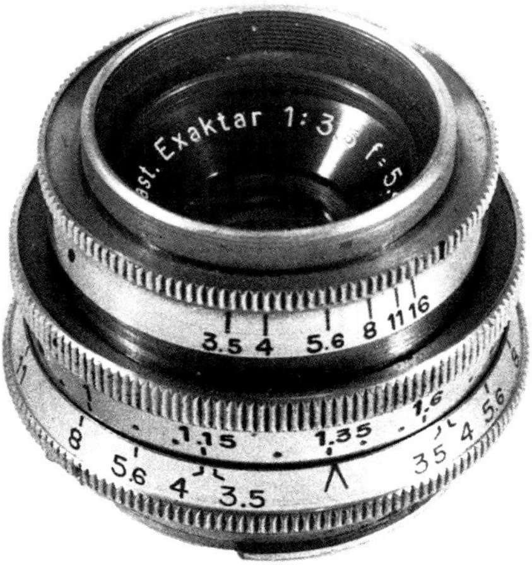

Ihagee Exaktar 50mm f/3.5 No.764827

CARL ZEISS, Jena

Zeiss was founded around 1902 in Jena. For about half a century the Company manufactured thousands of lenses for most of the German camera makers. At the end of the war in 1945, Zeiss at Jena in East Germany was separated from its head office located in the West. As a result of legal action regarding the use of the trade mark, the name 'Carl Zeiss' gradually disappeared from the lens mounts.

Lenses from 1936 to 1960

Lens	*Year Intro.*	*Focal length*	*Max. f/*	*Diaphragm*	*No. of elements*	*Filter thread (mm)*
Flektogon	1952	35	2.8	preselect		
Flektogon	1956	35	2.8	semi-auto*		
Tessar	pre 1940	40	4.5	manual		
Tessar	1936	50	2.8	manual	4	30.5x0.5
Tessar	1939	50	2.8	manual	4	28.5x0.5
Tessar	1949	50	2.8	manual	4	35.5x0.5
Tessar	1951	50	2.8	preselect	4	49x0.75
Tessar	1954	50	2.8	semi-auto*	4	49x0.75
Tessar	1961	50	2.8	semi-auto*	4	49x0.75
Tessar	1936	50	3.5	manual	4	30.5x0.5
Tessar	1939	50	3.5	manual	4	30.5x0.5
Boitar	1939	58	2	manual	6	40.5x0.5
Biotar	1951	58	2	preselect	6	40.5x0.5
Biotar	1955	58	2	semi-auto*	6	49x0.75
Biotar	1947	75	1.5	manual	6	58x0.75
Biotar	1950	75	1.5	preselect	6	58x0.75
Tessar	1950	80	2.8	preselect		
Miometar	1954	80	2.8	preselect		
Triotar	pre 1940	85	4	manual		
Tessar	pre 1940	105	3.5	manual		
Triotar	pre 1940	135	4	manual		
Triotar	1955	135	4	preselect		
Tessar	1949	165	3.5	manual		
Tele-Tessar	pre 1940	180	6.3	manual		
Sonnar	1952	180	2.8	preselect		
Tele-Tessar	pre 1940	250	6.3	manual		
Sonnar	1952	300	4	preselect		

* Semi-auto means manual setting with automatic stop-down

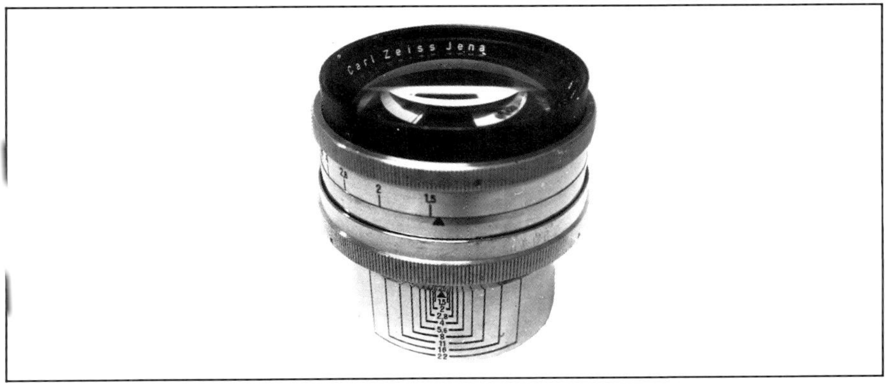

The 75mm f/1.5 Biotar

Standard Lenses for the 35mm Exakta

Some of the various Zeiss standard lenses that were usually available for the Exakta range are illustrated below. One can see the changes involved for each of them from its appearance. Not all the models can be described here, but we hope the reader will be delighted to find them out for himself. Generally speaking, the standard lenses fitted were:-

Kine Exakta (1936)	to	Exakta II (1949)	50mm f/3.5	Zeiss Tessar
Kine Exakta (1936)	to	VX 1000 (1970)	50mm f/2.8	Zeiss Tessar
Exakta II (1939)	to	VX IIa (1960)	58mm f/2	Zeiss Biotar
Exakta VX IIa (1961)	to	VX 1000 (1970)	50mm f/2	Zeiss Pancolar
Exakta Real			50mm f/2	Zeiss Pancolar

50mm f/3.5 Tessar

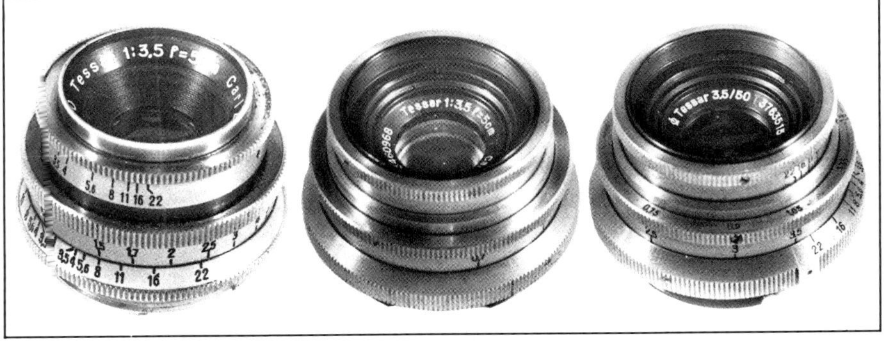

Left: The 1936 Kine Exakta; the engraving is in heavy characters.
Middle: 1939 Kine Exakta to 1948-49 Exakta II.
Right: 1947 Kine Exakta to 1948-49 Exakta II; similar to the previous model but here the letter "T" is engraved in red between the focal length and the serial number to show that the lenses have been coated.

This was one of the most widely-known lenses. There were of course versions with manual diaphragm presetting which were distributed at the same time as the versions with automatic diaphragm (4).

From (3) onwards, it is possible to find the same lenses engraved with either "50mm f/2.8 Carl Zeiss Jena Tessar" or "50mm f/2.8 Aus Jena". Letter "T" appears in white; (7) and (8) are examples.

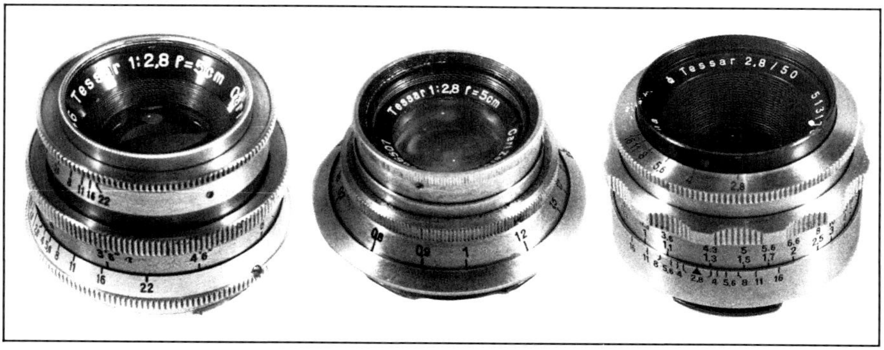

(1) Kine Exakta period (1936). Engraving in heavy characters, filter diameter 30.5x0.5, apertures from f/2.8 to f/22.
(2) Kine Exakta (1939) to Exakta II (1948-49). Filter diameter 28.5x0.5, apertures from f/2.8 to f/22.
(3) Exakta II (1949) to Varex (1954). Filter diameter 35.5x0.5, apertures from f/2.8 to f/16.

From this period onwards the letter "T" engraved in red on some models disappeared as all the lenses were then coated. The same lens can be found engraved with "Jena".

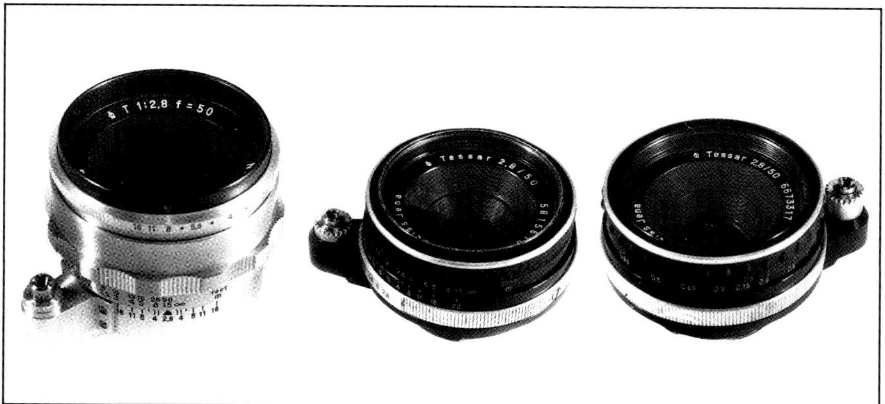

(4) Exakta Varex VX (1954). From this version onwards all the lenses featured an automatic presetting device. Filter diameter 49x0.75, apertures from f/2.8 to f/16. The version pictured here is engraved "Aus Jena", others were engraved "Carl Zeiss Jena".
(5) From Varex IIa (7th Version 1961) onwards. Filter diameter 49x0.75, apertures from f/2.8 to f/22. There is a version which is engraved "Aus Jena".
(6) From Varex IIb (1963) onwards. Filter diameter 49x0.75, apertures from f/2.8 to f/22. There is a version which is engraved "Aus Jena".

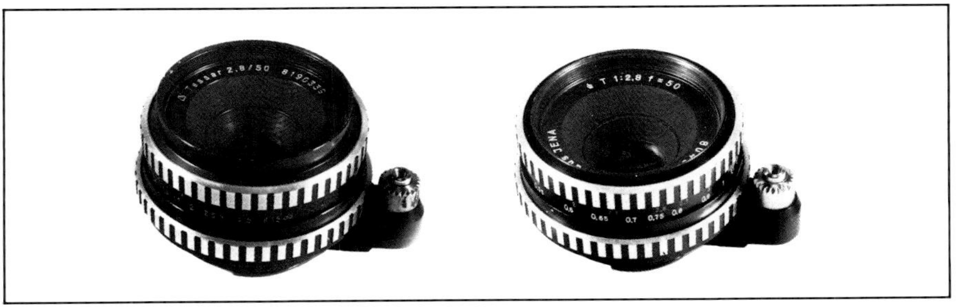

(7) From Varex 1000 (1967) onwards. Filter diameter 49x0.75, apertures from f/2.8 to f/22, Engraved "Aus Jena".
(8) Same model engraved "Carl Zeiss Jena".

58mm f/2 Biotar

The optical design of this lens was similar to that of the 58mm f/2 Biotar for the Contax (6 symmetrical elements). Before 1940, there was a 80mm version for the V.P. Exakta.

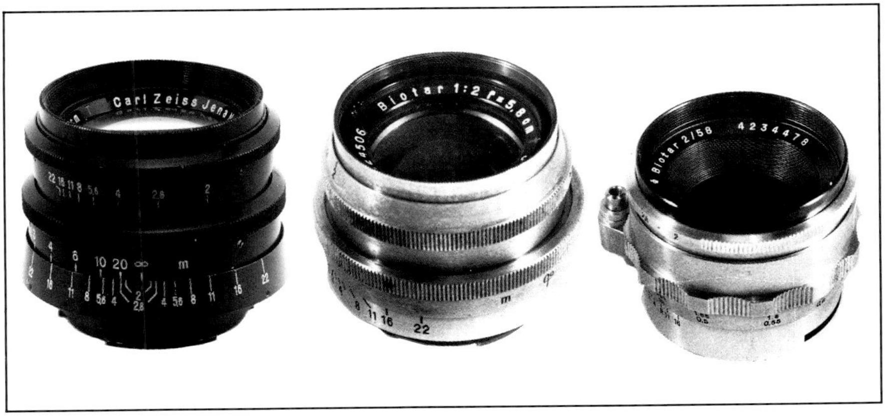

Left: Exakta II (1948-49). Filter diameter 40.5x0.5, apertures from f/2 to f/22, black-enamelled, letter "T" engraved in red.
Middle: Exakta Varex (1950) onwards. Filter diameter 40.5x0.5, apertures from f/2 to f/22, letter "T" engraved in red.
Right: Exakta VX 1954 to VX IIa 1959. Filter diameter 49x0.75, apertures from f/2 to f/16, automatic presetting diaphragm, letter "T" no longer present.

50mm f/2 Pancolar

A wide-aperture lens with 6 elements. From 1961 onwards, this model replaced the 58mm f/2 Biotar. There were 3 different models with the same presentation as versions (5) to (8) of the 50mm f/2.8 Tessar.

For each version, one can find lenses which are engraved "Carl Zeiss Jena" or "Aus Jena". There was also a version with internal coupling for the Exakta Real, and later the speed was increased to f/1.8 for a lens with internal coupling for the Exakta RTL 1000.

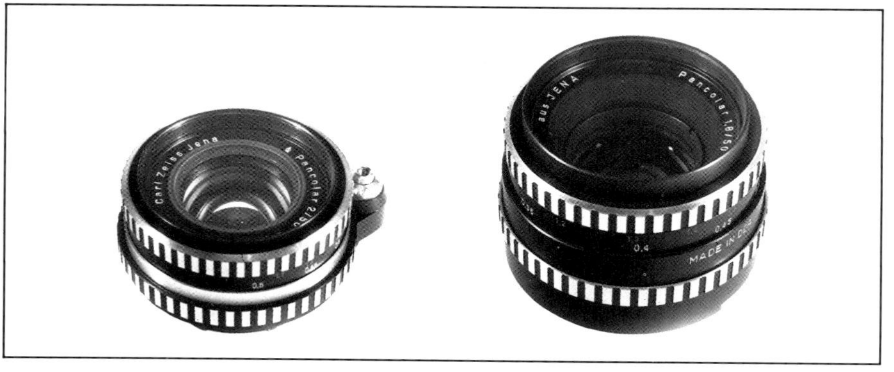

Left: Pancolar for VX 1000 (1967). Right: Pancolar f/1.8 for Exakta RTL 1000.

Automatic Lenses from 1960

Lens	*Year Intro.*	*Focal length*	*Max. f/*	*Diaphragm*	*No. of elements*	*Closest focusing distance (m)*	*Filter thread (mm)*
Flektogon	1963	20	4	auto	10	0.16	77x0.75
Flektogon	1961	25	4	auto	7	0.2	77x0.75
Flektogon	1961	35	2.8	auto	6	0.18	49x0.75
Jena T	1961	50	2.8	auto	4	0.5	49x0.75
Pancolor	1961	50	2	auto	6	0.5	49x0.75
Pancolor for RTL	1970	50	1.8	auto	6	0.35	49x0.75
Jena Bm	1961	80	2.8	auto	5	0.8	49x0.75
Jena Bm	1961	120	2.8	auto	5	1.3	67x0.75
Jena S	1961	135	4	auto	4	1.0	49x0.75
Jena S	1961	180	2.8	auto	5	1.7	86x1.0

There were also two mirror lenses introduced in the 1960's. These were the: 500mm f/4 (1966) with built-in filters, length 320mm, weight 7.3 Kg. 1000mm f/5.6 (1968) with built-in filters, length 510mm, weight 14 Kg.

MEYER, Gorlitz

Together with Zeiss Jena, and Schneider, Meyer had always been one of the main lens manufacturers for the Exakta. Although Meyer's lenses were not among the most expensive, the quality was often better than average. The 30mm f/3.5 Lydith wide-angle and 200mm f/4 Tele-Crestegor both had high resolution and strong contrast.

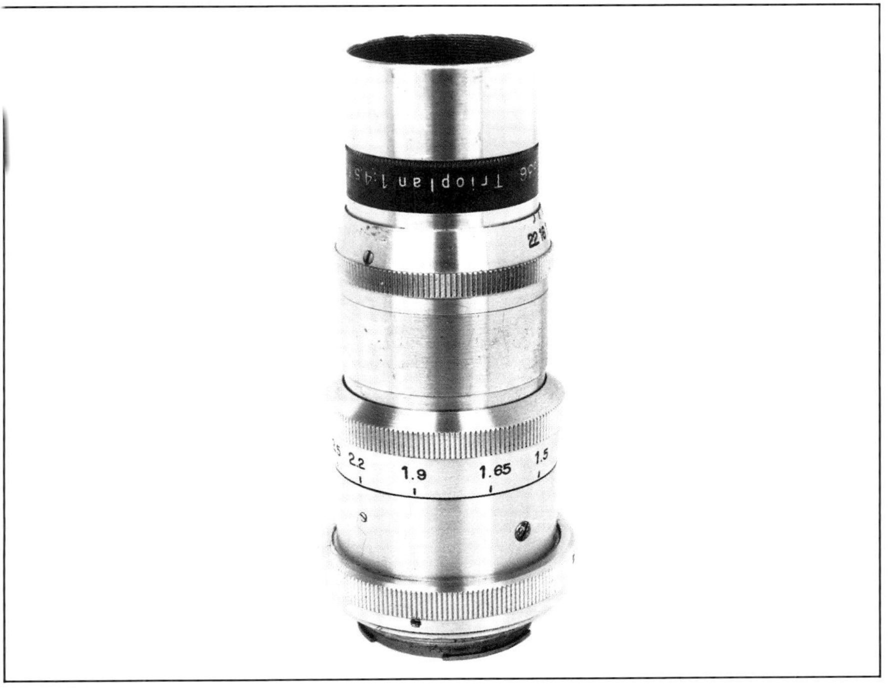

120mm f/4.5 Meyer Trioplan No.965636 (around 1939)

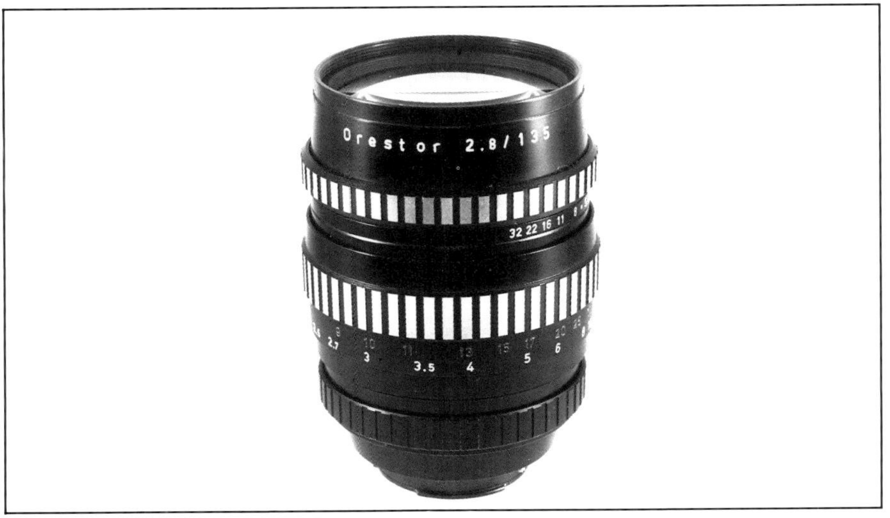

135mm f/2.8 Meyer Crestor No.4171974 (around 1969). Comparing this with the 120mm f/4.5 one can see the development over a period of about 30 years.

The Leading Meyer Lenses

Lens	*Year Intro.*	*Focal length*	*Max. f/*	*Diaphragm*	*No. of elements*	*Closest focusing distance (m)*	*Filter thread (mm)*
Lydith	1964	30	3.5	preset	5	0.3	49x0.75
Primagon	1957	35	4.5	preset	4	0.4	49x0.75
Trioplan	1952	50	2.9	manual	3	0.6	35.5x0.5
Primotar	1957	50	3.5	auto	4	0.5	40.5x0.5
Primotar	1960	50	2.8	preset	4	0.5	46.5x0.5
Domiplan	1962	50	2.8	auto	4	0.75	40.5x0.5
Domiron	1960	50	2	auto	6	0.34	55x0.75
Primoplan	1953	58	1.9	preset	5	0.6	49x0.75
Primoplan	1937	58	1.9	manual	5	0.7	38.5x0.7
Primoplan	1937	75	1.9	manual	-	-	-
Triplan	1959	100	2.8	auto	3	1.1	55x0.75
Telemegor	1937	105	5.5	manual	-	-	-
Triplan	1939	120	4.5	manual	3	1.5	33.5x0.5
Orestor	1969	135	2.8	preset	-	1.5	55x0.75
Primotar	1953	135	3.5	preset	4	1.6	55x0.75
Primotar	1957	180	3.5	preset	4	2.2	67x0.75
Telemegor	1957	180	5.5	preset	4	2.0	49x0.75
Telemegor	1937	180	5.5	manual	4	-	-
Orestegor	1963	200	4	preset	5	2.5	58x0.75
Telemegor	1957	250	5.5	preset	4	3.3	58x0.75
Telemegor	1937	250	5.5	-	4	-	-
Telemegor	1957	300	4.5	preset	4	3.3	82x0.75
Orestegor	1968	300	4	preset	5	3.0	95x1
Telemegor	1957	400	5.5	preset	4	6.0	82x0.75
Orestegor	1965	500	5.6	manual	4	6.0	118x1

Lenses for RTL 1000

Lens	*Year Intro.*	*Focal length*	*Max. f/*	*Diaphragm*	*No. of elements*	*Closest focusing distance (m)*	*Filter thread (mm)*
Orestegon	1970	29	2.8	auto		0.3	
Oreston	1970	50	1.8	auto		0.25	49x0.75
Orestor	1970	100	2.8	auto		1.1	
Orestor	1971	135	2.8	auto		1.5	

We have given the date of introduction for each lens, but some of them which were manufactured over a period of 20 years, exist in several different forms.

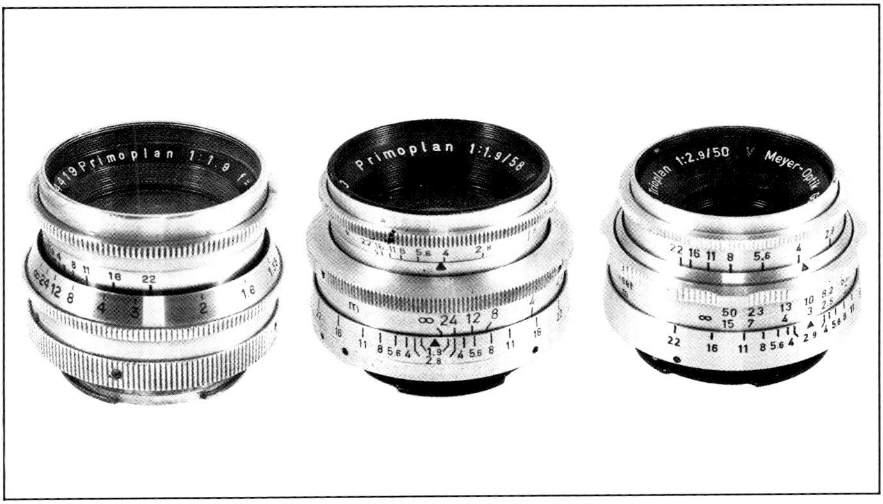

Left: 58mm f/1.9 Meyer Primoplan No.754419 (around 1939)
Middle: 58mm f/1.9 Meyer Primoplan No.1155183 (around 1950)
Right: 50mm f/2.9 Meyer Trioplan No.1512441 (around 1952)

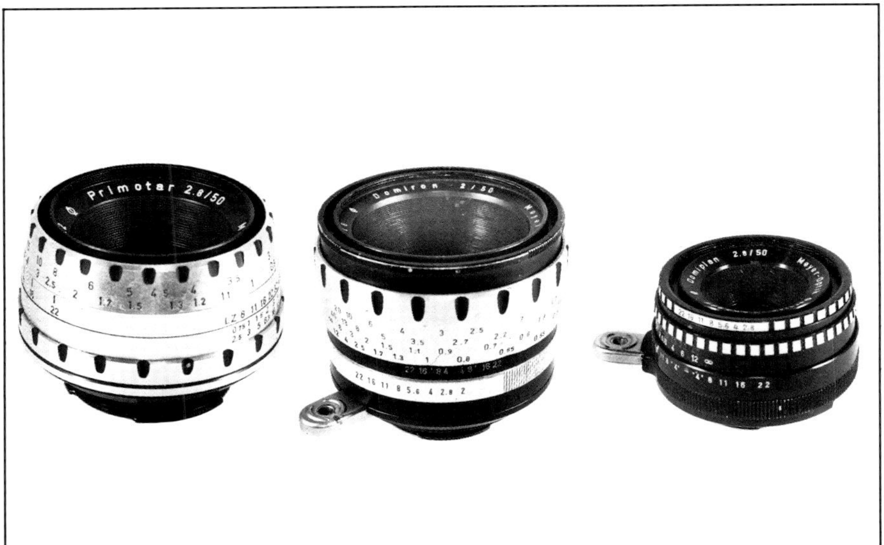

Left: 50mm f/2.8 Meyer Primotar No.2269022 (around 1960)
Middle: 50mm f/2 Meyer Domiron No.2741328 (around 1961)
Right: 50mm f/2.8 Meyer Domiplan No.4331717. A second version appeared in 1968 with the serial number engraved on the body whereas the first version had it engraved on the front barrel.

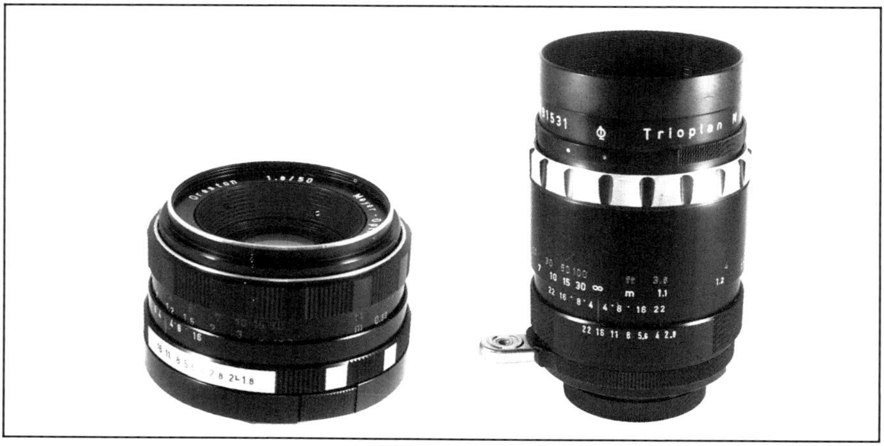

Left: 50mm f/1.8 Meyer Oreston No.5394074 (around 1970). Designed for the Exakta RTL 1000, this lens had an automatic diaphrapm and internal control system.
Right: 100mm f/2.8 Meyer Trioplan No.3791531 (around 1960)

SCHNEIDER, Kreuznach

Together with Zeiss and Meyer, Schneider was one of the first makers of lenses for the Exakta. Schneider was already equipping the 4x6.5 models and when the Kine was introduced in 1936, they started the production of the lenses with bayonet mount. Hence the production range of this manufacturer is very important. The list below will not be exhaustive. However, it will give an idea of the existing models with their respective dates of introduction.

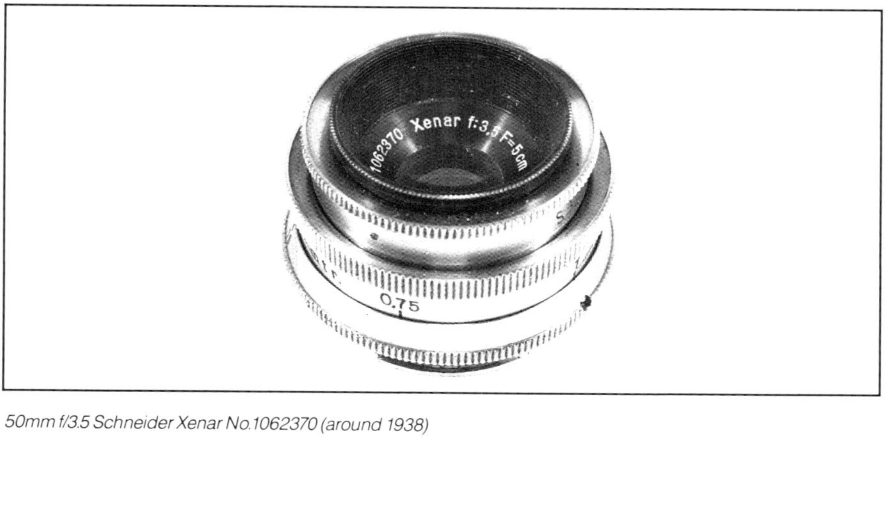

50mm f/3.5 Schneider Xenar No.1062370 (around 1938)

Schneider lenses for 35mm Exakta cameras

Lens	*Year Intro.*	*Focal length*	*Max. f/*	*Diaphragm*	*No. of elements*	*Closest focusing distance (m)*	*Filter thread (mm)*
Lenses from 1936 - 1957							
Isogon	1951	40	4.5	manual			
Xenon	1954	50	1.9	preselect			
Xenar	pre 1940	50	2	manual			
Xenar	pre 1940	50	2.8	manual			
Xenar	pre 1940	50	3.5	manual			
Xenon	1953	80	2	manual			
Tele-Xenar	1957	90	3.5	preselect			
Xenar	1953	105	3.5	manual			
Xenar	1951	105	4.5	manual			
Xenon	1948	125	2	manual			
Xenar	1949	135	3.5	manual			
Xenar	pre 1940	135	4.5	manual			
Tele-Xenar	1950	150	5.5	manual			
Tele-Xenar	1950	180	5.5	manual			
Tele-Xenar	1950	240	4.5	manual			
Tele-Xenar	1951	240	5.5	manual			
Tele-Xenar	1950	300	5.5	manual			
Tele-Xenar	1950	360	5.5	manual			
Lenses from 1958							
Curtagon	1959	28	4	auto	7	0.15	49x0.75
Curtagon	1958	35	2.8	auto	6	0.3	49x0.75
P.A.Curtagn shift lens	1966	35	4	manual	7	0.3	49x0.75
Xenon	1960	50	1.9	auto	6	0.5	49x0.75
Tele-Xenar	1957	135	3.5	auto	5	2.0	49x0.75
Tele-Xenar	1957	200	5.5	preselect	4	2.0	49x0.75
Tele-Xenar	1957	360	5.5	preselect	4	4.5	72x0.75
Variogon	1966	45-100	2.8	auto	14	1.2	67x0.75
Tele-Variogon	1963	80-240	4	auto	14	1.8	82x1.00

There were also lenses in appropriate mounts for the Exakta Real. These have been listed in the section relating to the Real camera.

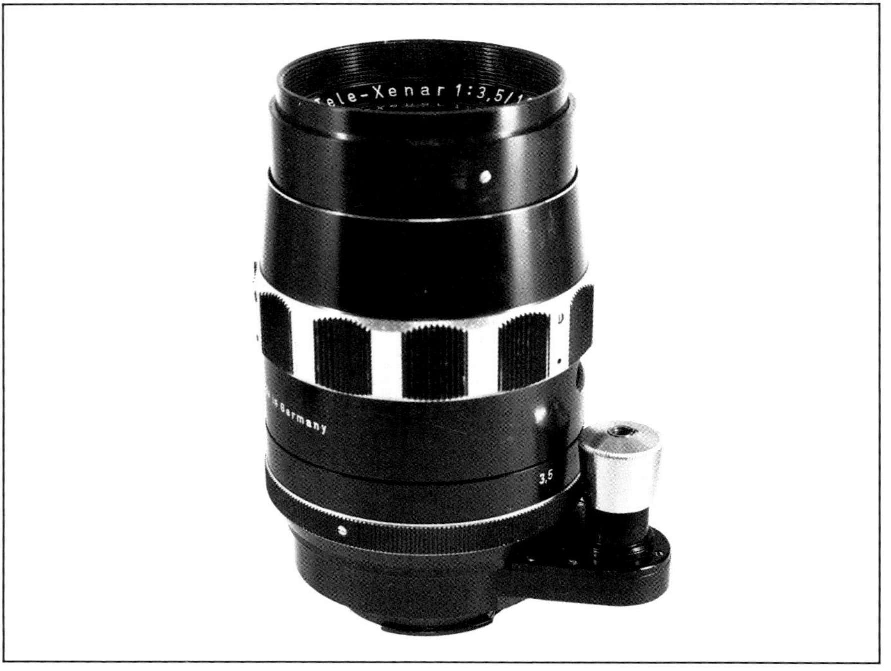

135mm f/3.5 Tele-Xenar lens No.5786708 with automatic diaphragm

Cell-Lenses (from 1961 onwards)

Lens	*Year Intro.*	*Focal length*	*Max. f/*	*Diaphragm*	*No. of elements*	*Closest focusing distance (m)*	*Filter thread (mm)*
Curtagon	1961	35	2.8	auto	6	0.35	49x0.75
Xenon	1961	50	1.9	auto	6	0.5	49x0.75
Tele-Xenar	1961	135	3.5	auto	4	2.0	49x0.75

These lenses were equipped with a detachable photo-cell exposure meter, adapted to each lens and coupling automatically with the diaphragm. The diaphragm could be either manual or with automatic presetting (depending on the operator's choice). The diaphragm allowed for wide aperture focusing and shut automatically to the aperture selected by the meter after release.

Thanks to a very ingenious system, the shutter speed could be selected according to the aperture or visa versa. Each lens featureed an automatic depth-of-field table. The sensitivity ranged from 12 to 800 ASA.

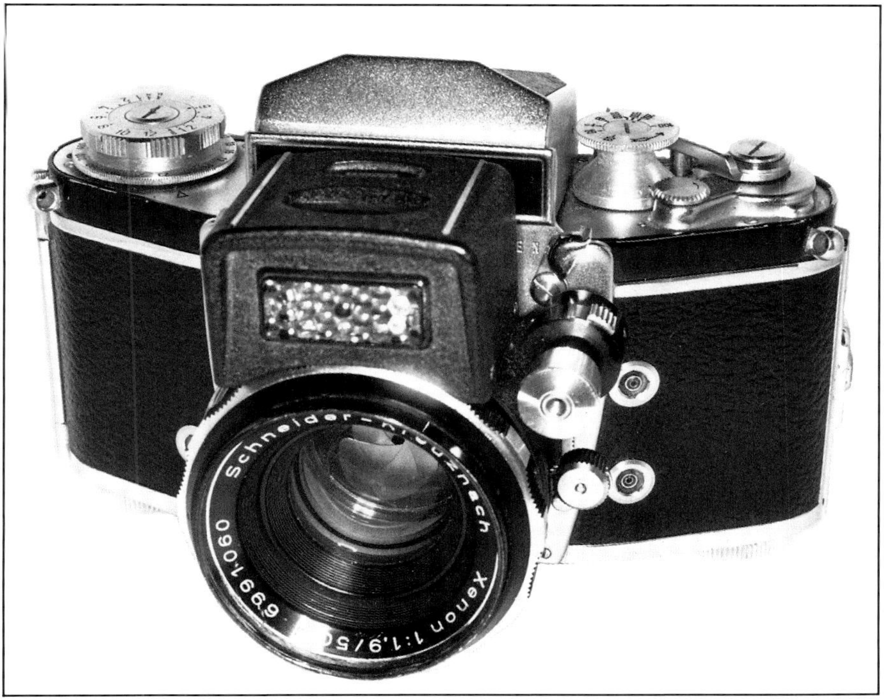

50mm f/1.9 Schneider Xenon lens, No.6991060 equipped with a cell and adapted to the Exakta Varex IIa (new plate)

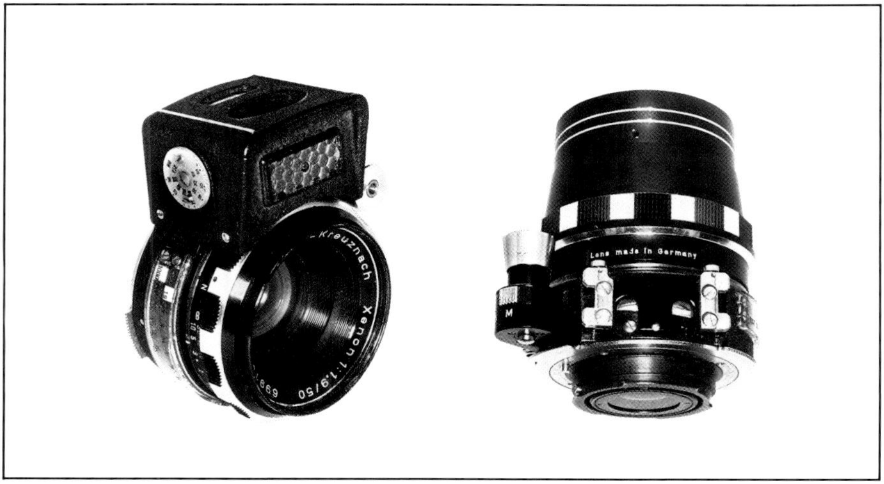

Left: 50mm f/1.9 Xenon, No.6991060 with cell
Right: 135mm f/3.5 Tele Xenar No.7375708 with cell removed

LENSES FROM OTHER MAKERS

Many other makers also offered lenses with the Exakta bayonet. These are given below in alphabetical order. The list is by no means exhaustive and no doubt collectors will be aware of many more.

ANGENIEUX, Paris

We will give you a complete panoramic view of the lenses manufactured by this Company for the Exakta. A few models were available in 42mm screw mounts for Praktica, Edixa and Pentax and in special mounts for Rectaflex, Alpa and Leica. The very first Angenieux lenses for the Exakta came out in 1950. The automatic models were still listed in the 1970 catalogues.

In 1950, Angenieux introduced the very first "retrofocus" wide-angle lenses. Specially designed for reflex cameras, with these lenses the distance between the rear element and the film plane is greater than the focal length. This enables the mirror to clear the rear of very short focal length lenses.

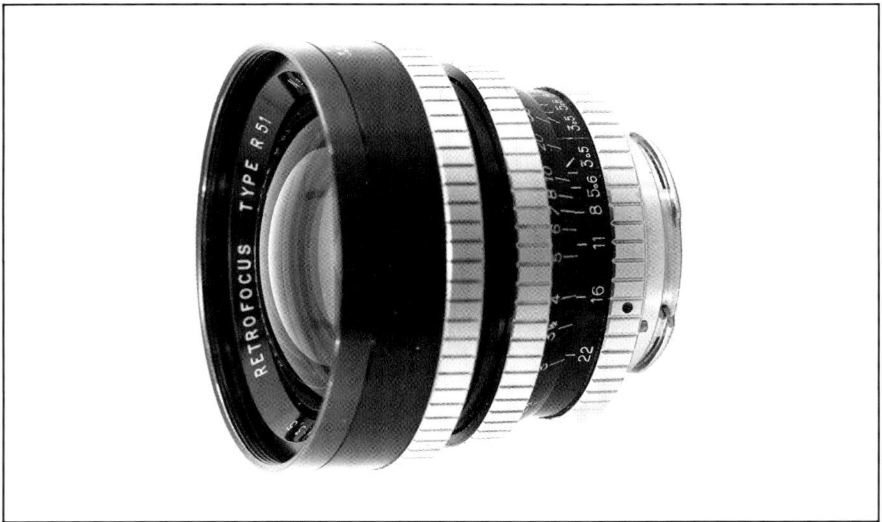

Type R51. 24mm f/3.5, retrofocus lens introduced 1957

From the very beginning Angenieux had a very good reputation. They made cine lenses for the professional and the general public, and NASA used Angenieux lenses for its space programmes. In 1970 a new Zoom for the Leicaflex was introduced and in 1983, other lenses for 35mm photography re-appeared. These were two zooms (35-70mm and 70-210mm), available in different mounts.

The Exakta lenses are listed in the table

In the SCOP catalogues of the 60's, one can find two special lenses for macrophotography with bellows, focusing mount and macro rings. These were:-

- Type Z1 12.5mm f/1.8, magnification ratio X21.
- Type Z7 50mm f/2.9, magnification ratio X4.5.

Angenieux Lenses

Lens	*Year Intro.*	*Focal length*	*Max. f/*	*Diaphragm*	*No. of elements*	*Closest focusing distance (m)*	*Filter thread (mm)*
Type R 51	1957	24	3.5	manual	6	0.5	62.5x0.75
Type R 61							
chrome	1959	24	3.5	auto	6	0.4	58.5x0.75
black	1961	24	3.5	auto	6	0.4	58.5x0.75
Type R 11							
manual	1953	28	3.5	manual	6	0.5	58.5x0.75
auto chrome	1959	28	3.5	auto	6	0.5	58.5x0.75
auto black after	1961	28	3.5	auto	6	0.5	58.5x0.75
Type R 1							
manual	1950	35	2.5	manual	6	0.8	51.5x0.75
auto chrome	1959	35	2.5	auto	6	0.8	51.5x0.75
auto black after	1961	35	2.5	auto	6	0.8	51.5x0.75
Type S 1	1952	50	1.8	manual	6	1.0	?
Type S 21	1953	50	1.5	manual	6	0.8	51.5x0.75
Type P 1	1953	90	1.8	manual	5	1.0	56x0.75
Type Y 12							
manual	1953	90	2.5	manual	4	1.0	43.5x0.5
auto chrome	1959	90	2.5	auto	4	1.0	51.5x0.75
auto black after	1961	90	2.5	auto	4	1.0	51.5x0.75
Type P 2	1953	135	2.5	manual	5	1.5	58.5x0.75
Type Y 2	1952	135	3.5	manual	4	1.5	43.5x0.5
Type P 21							
manual	1954	180	4.5	manual	5	2.5	47x0.75
auto chrome	1959	180	4.5	auto	5	2.5	51.5x0.75
auto black	1961	180	4.5	auto	5	2.5	51.5x0.75

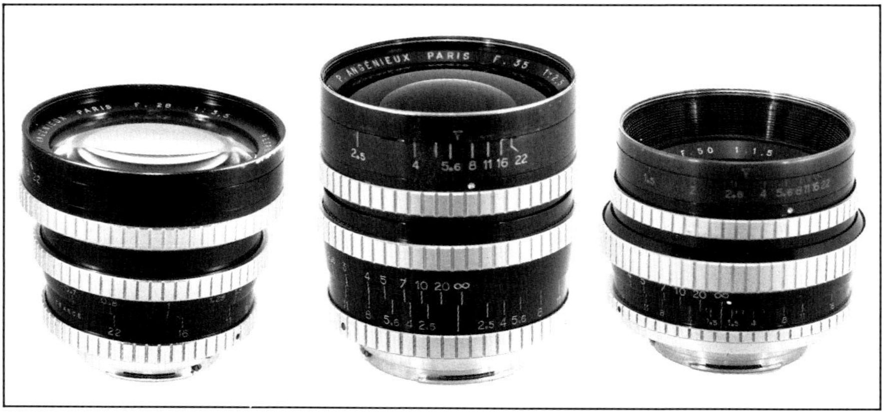

Three manual diaphragm lenses. Left: Type R11, 28mm f/3.5. Middle: Type R1, 35mm f/2.5. Right: Type S21, 50mm f/1.5

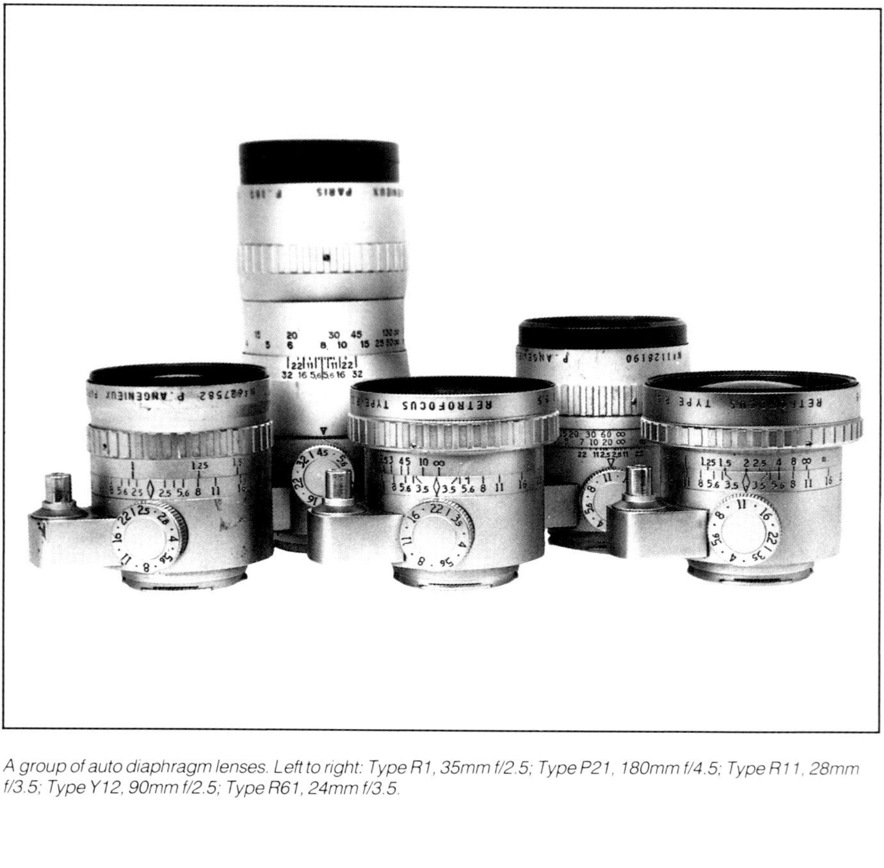

A group of auto diaphragm lenses. Left to right: Type R1, 35mm f/2.5; Type P21, 180mm f/4.5; Type R11, 28mm f/3.5; Type Y12, 90mm f/2.5; Type R61, 24mm f/3.5.

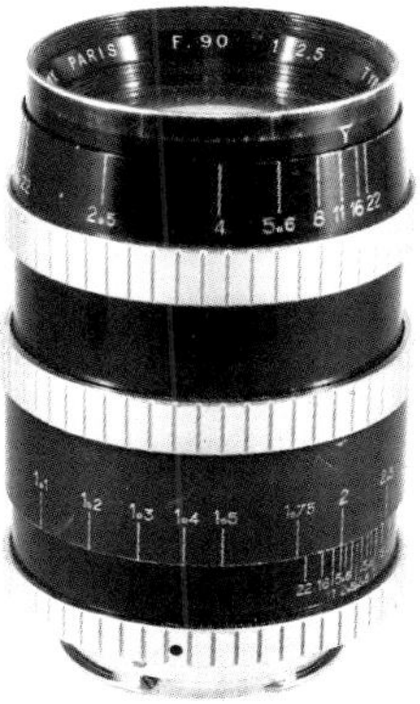

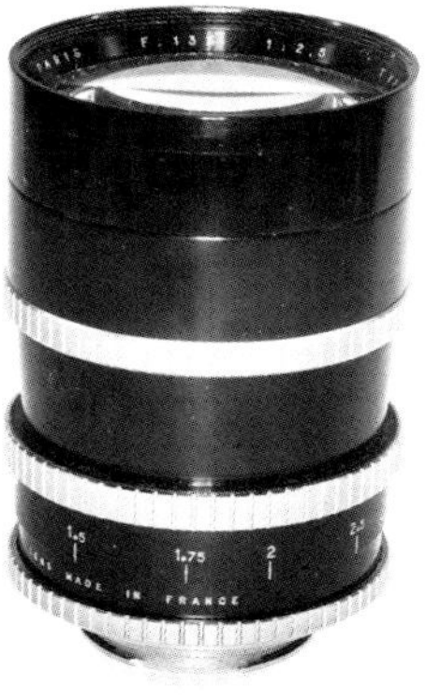

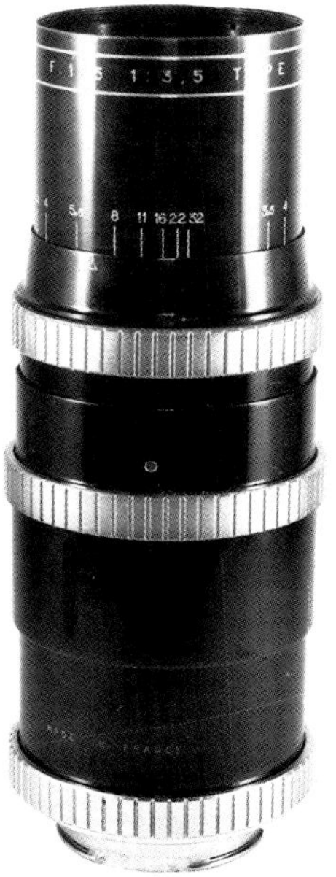

Left: Type Y, manual diaphragm, 90mm f/2.5.
Right: Contrast in 135mm lenses; Type P2 f/2.5 and Type Y2 f/3.5.

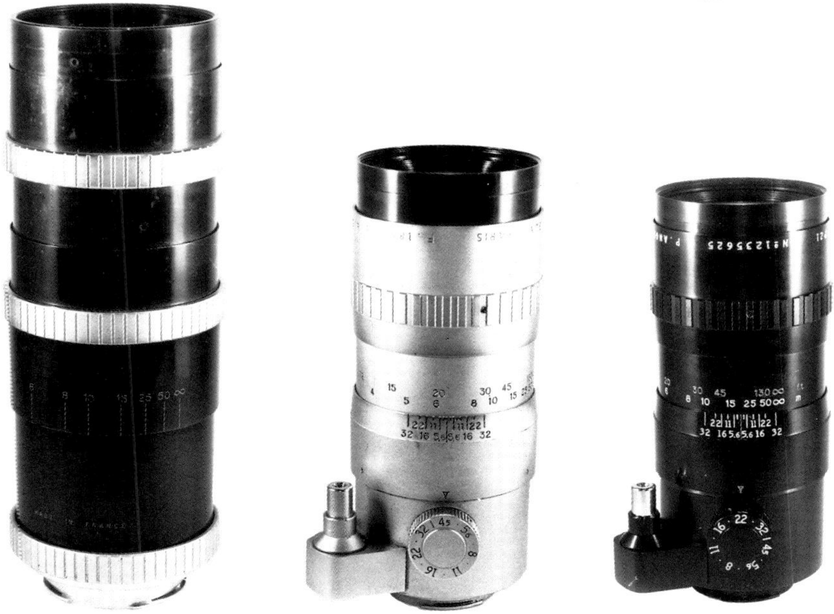

Three Type P21, 180mm f/4.5 lenses. Left to right: manual diaphragm of 1954; auto, chrome, of 1959; auto, black, of 1961.

ASTRO, Berlin

Astro is a German Opticial manufacturer specialising in the manufacture of long length focal lenses. They made the following lenses:

Type	Focal length	Aperture
Pantachar	125mm	f/2.3
Pantachar	150mm	f/1.8
Pantachar	150mm	f/2.3
Fernbild	300mm	f/5
Fernbild	400mm	f/5
Fernbild	500mm	f/5
Fernbild	640mm	f/5
Fernbild	800mm	f/5
Fernbild	1000mm	f/6.3
Astro-Telestan	2000mm	f/10

All lenses had a standard diaphragm without presetting.

BERTHIOT, Paris

According to our knowledge, there was only one lens designed by this French maker for the EXAKTA 24 x 36. This is the Olor 38mm f/5.7 with click stops without presetting. This wide-angle lens, which could be found until 1952, was not of a retrofocus type.

CORFIELD, Wolverhampton

This company was the U.K. distributor of the Exakta throughout the 1950's and early '60s. They also produced the Periflex camera and a range of lenses for it. In 1958 they offered their 100mm f/4 Lumar in an Exakta mount. This was a 3 element lens focusing down to 5 ft.

From 1960 other wide-angle and telephoto lenses were also offered in Exakta mounts. Enna Werk of Munich (below) made some lenses for Corfield, and from 1961 made them all.

DALLMEYER, London

By 1936 Dallmeyer was supplying their telephone lenses and a wide aperture standard lens for the V.P. Exakta. They were also later adapted for the Kine Exakta. The standard lens for the Kine Exakta was the 6 element Dallmeyer Super Six 58mm f/1.9.

There were two telephoto ranges:

Type	*Focal length (in)*	*Nearest metric equiv. (mm)*	*Type*	*Focal length (in)*	*Nearest metric equiv. (mm)*
Dallon			Adon		
f/5.6	4	100	f/4.5		
	6	150			
	9	230		9	230
	12	300		12	300
	14	350		14	350
	17	430		17	430
	20	500		20	500
	24	610		24	610
	40	1000			

Only the 4″ and 6″ Dallon lenses were regularly listed before the war, and the 9″ Dallon was added after the war. All the others were to special order. These lenses remained available until 1974.

ENNA, Munich

This maker had a strong reputation in Germany and some other European countries but was not well known in France. The 85-250mm zoom was the first of its type to be manufactured in Germany. It came on the market in 1963.

A few of their lenses available between 1961 and 1969 in Exakta mounts are listed in the table.

Lens	*Year Intro.*	*Focal length*	*Max. f/*	*Diaphragm*	*No. of elements*	*Closest focusing distance (m)*	*Filter thread (mm)*
Lithagon	1961	24	4	preselect	7	0.25	52x0.75
Lithogon	1961	28	3.5	preselect	6	0.3	52x0.75

Lens	*Year Intro.*	*Focal length*	*Max. f/*	*Diaphragm*	*No. of elements*	*Closest focusing distance (m)*	*Filter thread (mm)*
Lithogon	1961	35	2.8	preselect	6	0.5	52x0.75
Lithogon	1961	35	3.5	clickstop	4	0.5	52x0.75
Ennalyt	1961	85	1.5	clickstop	6	1.2	58x0.75
Ennalyt	1961	90	2.8	clickstop	5	1.5	52x0.75
Tele Ennalyt	1961	135	2.8	clickstop	5	1.5	52x0.75
Tele Ennalyt	1961	240	4.5	clickstop	5	3	52x0.75
Tele Zoom	1963	85-250	4	preselect	12	0.6-3.3	Water-house type
Tele Ennalyt	1961	400	4.5	clickstop	5	5.0	"
Tele Ennalyt	1961	600	5.6	clickstop	5	10.0	"

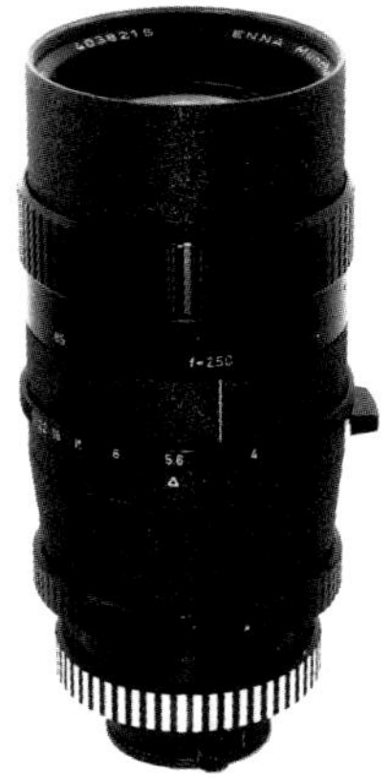

85-250mm f/4 Enna Zoom No.4038215.

'Sockel' Mounts and Lenses

This arrangement comprised a standard mount and the following seven focal length lens heads which fitted onto it: 24, 28, 35, 50, 95, 135 and 240mm. A 'Sockel' mount was produced for the Exakta, as well as for other makes such as Praktica, Edixa, Miranda and Alpa.

The Sockel standard mechanical mount was fixed on the camera and carried the helical focusing screw, the focusing scales corresponding to the focal lengths and the diaphragm presetting linkage. Each lens head had its own diaphragm and it was fixed to the 'Sockel' mount by a bayonet. The filter mount was the same for all lens heads: 52x0.75.

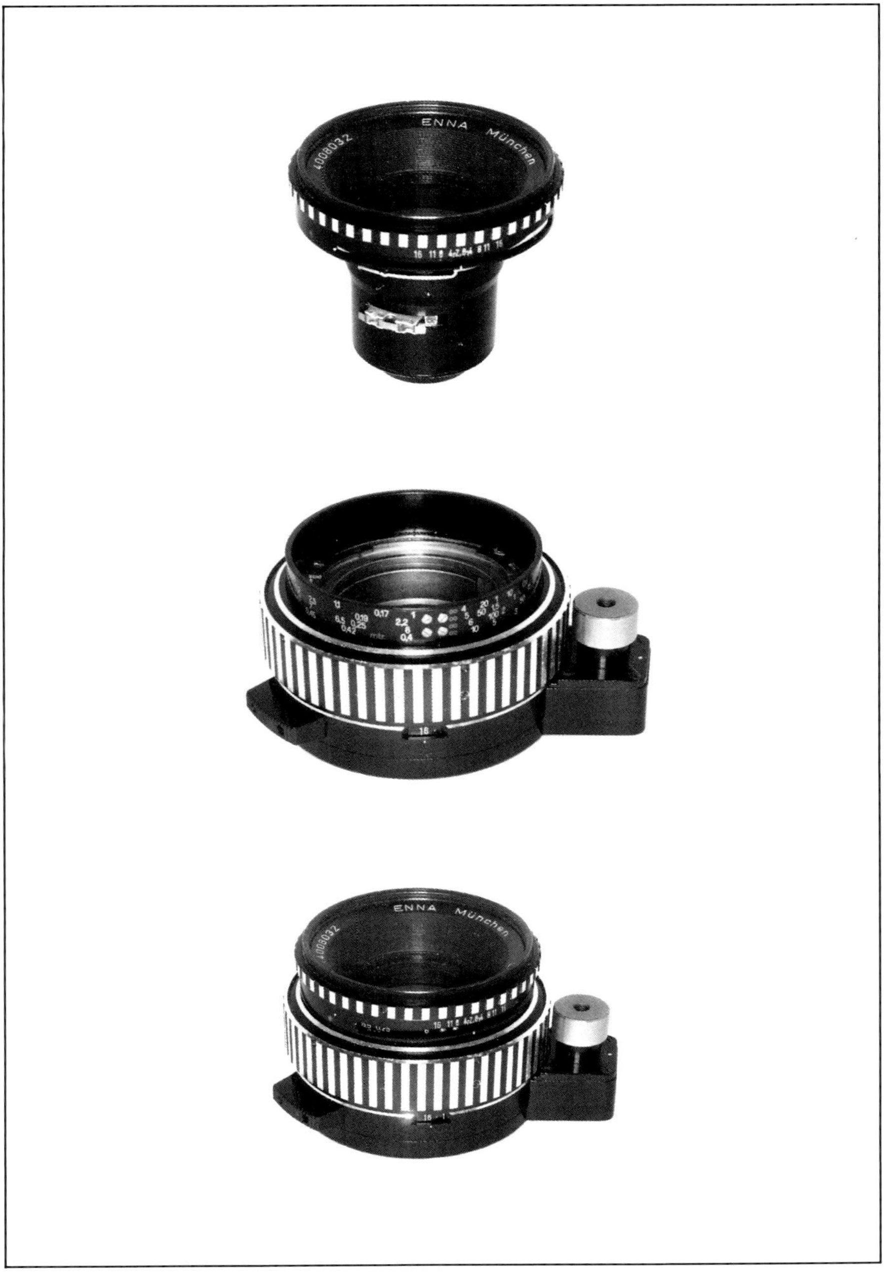

Top: Sockel mount. Middle: 35mm f/2.8 lens head. Bottom: the assembled lens

FEINMESS, Dresden

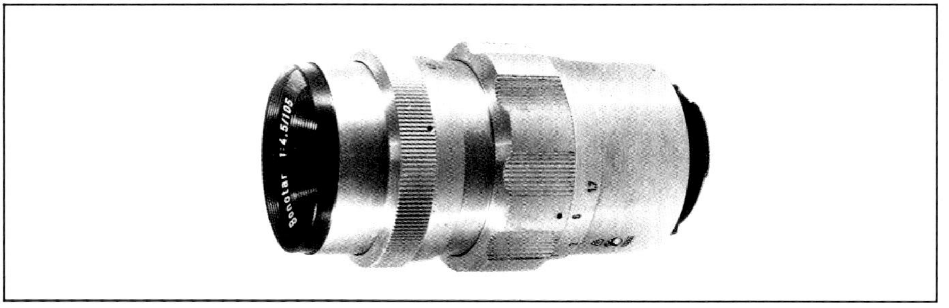

Feinmess Bonotar 105mm f/4.5 No.09265. A telephoto-lens with click stops and no presetting of around 1959. Closest focusing distance was 1.7m. To our knowledge, this lens was the only one from this manufacturer with an Exakta mount.

ISCO, Gottingen

Besides their conventional lenses, Isco also manufactured three lenses equipped with a detachable photo-cell coupled with the diaphragm. These lenses were similar to the Schneider models with cell. They also produced an anamorphic lens, the Iscorama, which is illustrated here.

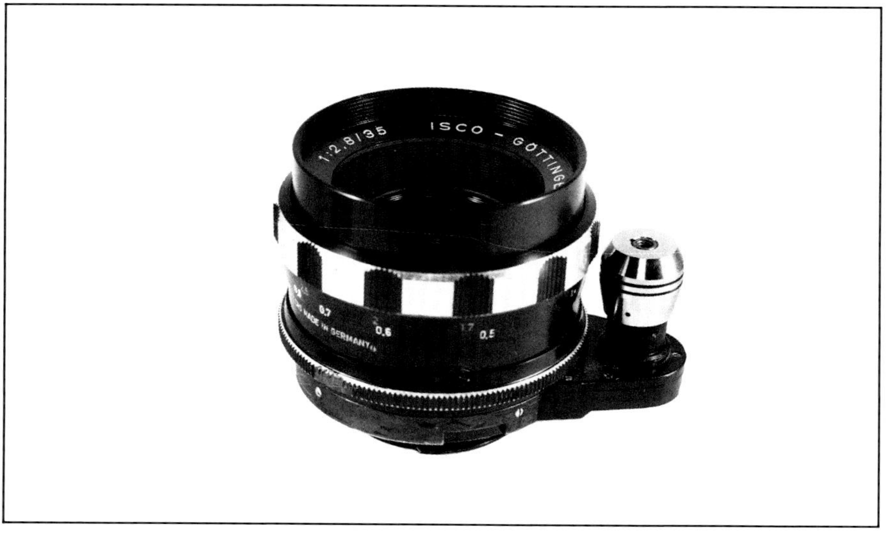

Westron 35mm f/2.8 No.773211, with automatic presetting

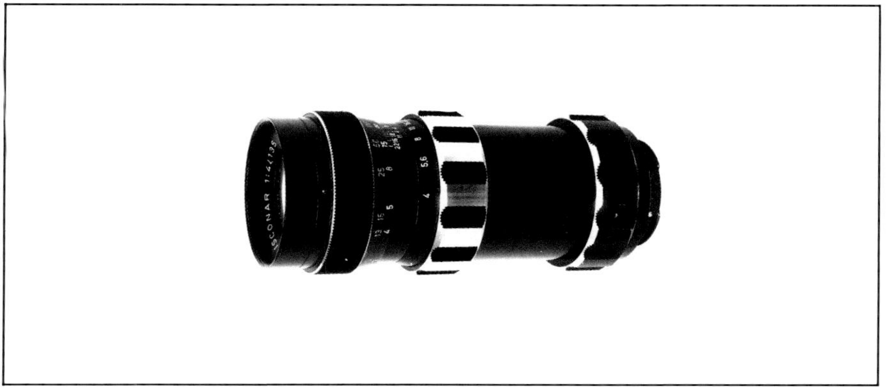

Isconar 135mm f/4 No.691069

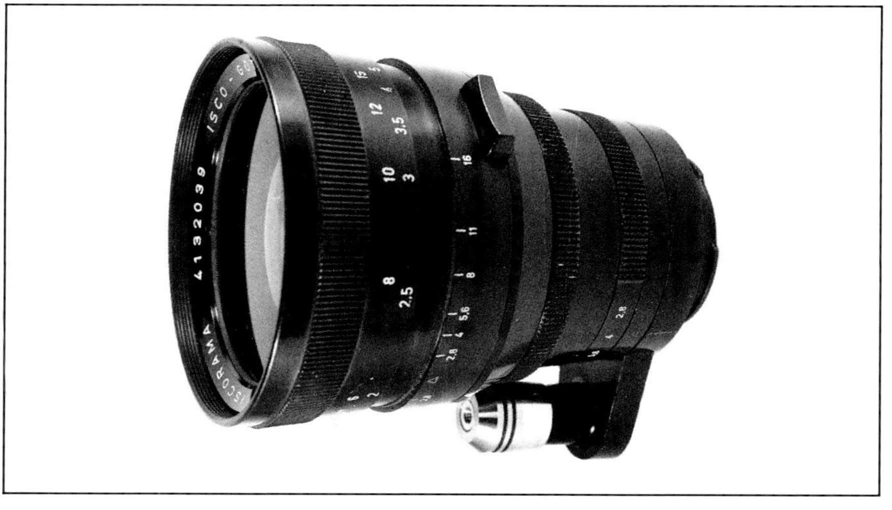

Iscorama 50mm f/2.8. This lens unit produced vertical or horizontal picture shrinkage during picture taking. The same picture was then restored to normal proportions in a ratio of 1 : 2.25 during projection, forming a panoramic image. This unit included the standard lens (50mm f/2.8) and the anamorphoser. A special reproduction lens with a 85 or 100mm focal length was also supplied according to the type of projector used.

KILFITT, Munich

This Company had built up its reputation on superb telephoto lenses and macro optics known as "Makro-Kilar". At the time these were the only ones to allow a 1:1 reproduction ratio with a 24x36mm reflex camera.

The specifications of the best known models are given in the table.

Lens	*Year Intro.*	*Focal length*	*Max. f/*	*Diaphragm*	*No. of elements*	*Closest focusing distance (m)*	*Filter thread (mm)*
Macro-Kilar Type D	1955	40	3.5	manual	4	0.05	special
Macro-Kilar Type E	1955	40	3.5	manual	4	0.1	special
Macro-Kilar Type D	1960	40	2.8	manaul	4	0.05	special
Macro-Kilar Type E	1960	40	2.8	manual	4	0.1	special
Macro-Kilar Type E	1960	90	2.8	manual	4	0.24	special
Tele-Kilar	1957	150	3.5	manual	4	?	?
Tele-Kilar	1957	300	5.6	manual	4	3.0	68x0.75
Pan-Tele-Kilar	?	300	4	manual	5	1.8	?
Fern-Kilar	1957	400	5.6	manual			
Fern-Kilar	1957	600	5.6	manual			

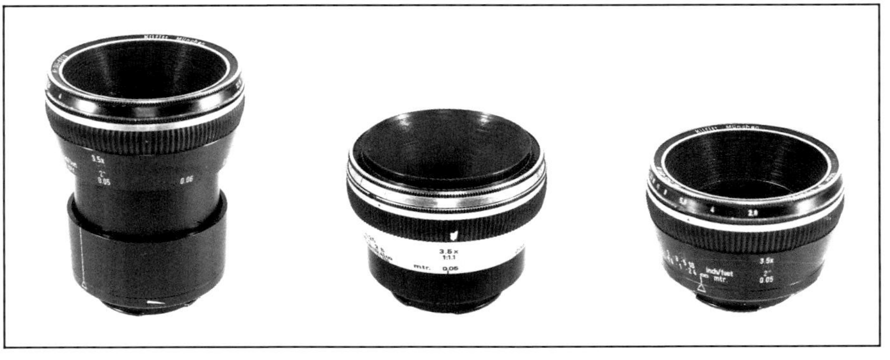

Left: 40mm f/2.8 Makro-Kilar, Type D, No.245-8910. Pictured here with its focusing sleeve on position 0.05m. Middle: 40mm f/2.8 Kilfitt Makro-Kilar, Type D, No.245-0206 with chrome-plated focusing ring. This model was manufactured by kamera Bau-Austalt in Vaduz, Liechtenstein. Right: 40mm f/2.8 Kilfitt Makro-Kilar, Type D, No.245-8910. Entirely black. Manufactured by Kilfitt in Munich.

The 300mm f/4 Kilfitt Pan-Tele-Kilar was a telephoto lens with 5 elements and twin focusing mechanism. One was of the rack-and-pinion type, focusing from 3m to infinity, the other at the front was a helical screw, focusing from 1.8m to 3m. If the helical ramp is drawn out, the rack can be used. The lens barrel had two sets of graduations. There was another version known as the 400mm f/4 Sport-Fern-Kilar.

These were 6x6 lenses which could be adapted to different camera bodies with interchangeable rings.

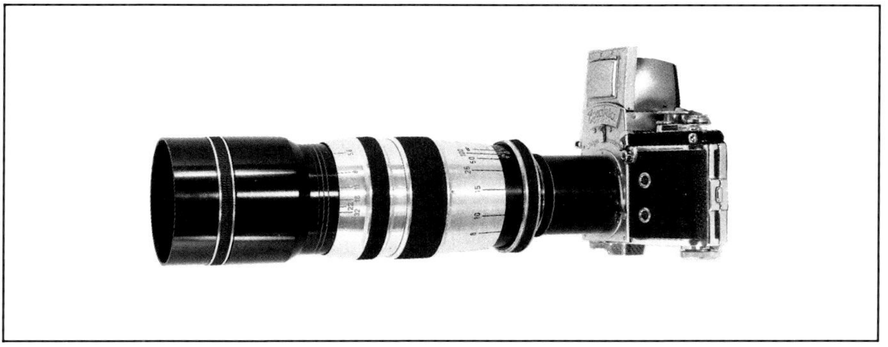

300mm f/5.6 Tele-Kilar on Exakta Varex IIa. This was a 6x6 lens, but it could be fitted with adapter rings and be mounted on camera bodies of various makes. Note the length of the adapter ring. There was also an adaptor ring for the 6x6 Exakta of 1950.

KINOPTIK, Paris

In the 60's this French manufacturer made a few lenses for the Exakta. We list below a few selected from the 1962 catalogue. Kinoptik also manufactured long focal length lenses which were used in the film industry.

Lens	*Year Intro.*	*Focal length*	*Max. f/*	*Diaphragm*	*No. of elements*	*Closest focusing distance (m)*	*Filter thread (mm)*
Apochromat	early 60's	210	2.8	manual	5	4.5	92bay
Special	60's	300	3.5	manual	3	6.0	92bay
Aplanat	60's	500	5.6	manual	2	8.0	92bay
Lenses for Bellows Focusing						*Magnification* *	
Apochromat	1960	75	2	manual	6	2.5x at 76mm	
Apochromat	1960	100	2	manual	6	1.6x at 125mm	
Apochromat	1960	150	2.5	manual	6	0.9x at 218mm	

* These are the magnifications given by an extension of 210mm when the lens is at the distance indicated from the chosen subject.

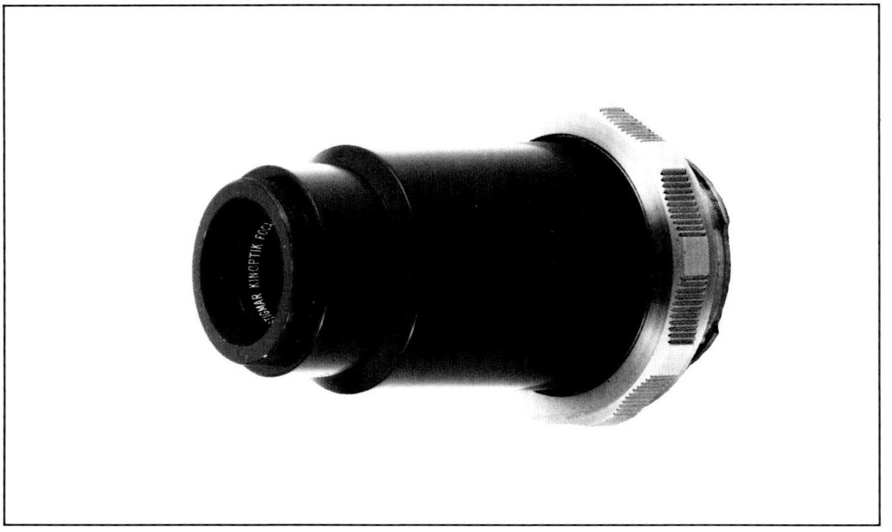

Kinoptik Stigmar 75mm lens No.53102. Optical specifications unknown.

LUDWIG, East Germany

There was only one well-known lens from this manufacturer, known as the 50mm f/2.9 Meritar. For many years, this simple and inexpensive lens was available as a standard lens for the Exa and Exa II. It had three elements, a manual diaphragm and focused down to 0.8m. There were two versions; the later one weighed 160g against the 120g of the earlier one. Filter size was 35.5x0.5mm.

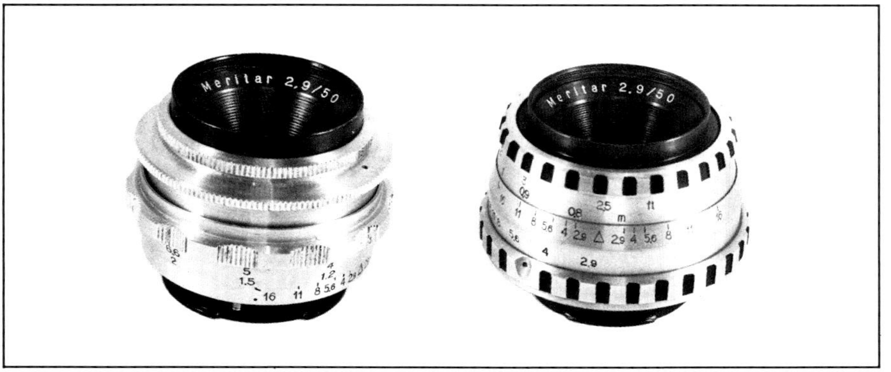

Left: Meritar, 1st version No.1420206, about 1952.
Right: Meritar, 2nd version No.1446487, about 1962.

NIPPON KOGAKU, Tokyo

Around 1950 Nikon started to distribute a lens for the Exakta. This was a version of Nikon's 135mm f/3.5 Nikkor-Q lens, originally made for the Nikon M and S rangefinder cameras. The rear of the lens was modified to be adapted to the bayonet of the Exakta. However, the lens in this version is very rare. Even more unique is the single known example of the 135mm f/4 Nikkor-Q with Exakta mount.

Full information on these lenses is given in: "Nikon Rangefinder Cameras" by Robert Rotoloni (Hove Foto Books) where the subject is fully discussed.

NOVOFLEX, Memmingen

Novoflex was particularly well-known for its long focal length lenses adaptable to various camera bodies, including the Exakta. Listed below are all the lenses which came out between 1955 and 1966. Some of these lenses were still available until 1972.

Lens	*Year Intro.*	*Focal length*	*Max. f/*	*No. of elements*	*Closest focusing distance (m)*
Macro					
Noflexar(1)	1964	35	3.5	4	0.07
Friedrich(6)	1960	60	4.5	3	
Corygon(6)	1960	75	4.5	3	
Noflexar(3)	1960	105	3.5	3	0.22
Noflexar(3)	1960	135	4.5	4	0.51
Xenar(2)	1966	135	4.5	4	1.7
Noflexar(3)	1960	240	4.5	3	1.7
Noflexar(4)	1955	240	4.5	3	2.75
Noflexar(4)	1966	280	5.6	3	3.0
Noflexar(4)	1955	300	5.6	3	4.45
Tele-lens(4)	1955	400	5.6	2	7.5
Tele-lens(5)	1960	640	9	2	10.0
Tele-lens(5)	1960	400	5.6	2	4.0
Tele-lens(4)	1958	640	9	2	18.0

(1) - This was the only lens of the range with a fixed mount for the Exakta.
(2) - On this particular lens, the fast focusing system was designed by Novoflex and the optics by Schneider.
(3) - There was no focusing mount on the lens head, it had to be mounted on bellows. Focusing on infinity is possible on this type of lens.
(4) - The lens head had to be fitted on the fast focusing grip.
(5) - This had a telescopic barrel with focusing mount and two lens heads (400mm and 640mm)
(6) - The lens head had to be mounted on bellows (for reproduction ratio of 1:1). Focusing to infinity is impossible on this type of lens.

RODENSTOCK, Munich

This Company did offer some lenses for the the Exakta Varex. We do not have much technical information but we cannot ignore this important make. The most important lenses are listed below. They are divided into two periods.

First period, until Exakta Varex IIa, 4th Version (with relief plate)
Second period, as from Varex IIa, 5th Version of 1961 (with new plate).

Lens	*Year Intro.*	*Focal length*	*Max. f/*	*Diaphragm*
Eurygon	pre 1961	30	2.8	preselect
	after 1961	30	2.8	auto
Heligon	pre 1961	50	1.9	preselect
	after 1961	50	1.9	auto
Rotelar	pre 1961	100	4	preselect
	after 1961	100	4	auto
Imagon	pre 1961	120	4.5	manual
Yronar	pre 1961	135	3.5	manual
Rotelar	pre 1961	135	4	preselect
	after 1961	135	4	auto
Rotelar	pre 1961	180	4.5	preselect

SCHACHT, Ulm-Donau

During the 60's, this manufacturer produced a range of lenses for the Exakta. They were also the first manufacturer to produce the pentaprism with through-lens metering.

The dates below are when they were introduced in France.

Lens	*Year Intro.*	*Focal length*	*Max. f/*	*Diaphragm*	*No. of elements*	*Closest focusing distance (m)*	*Filter thread (mm)*
Travegon	1959	35	3.5	auto	6	0.5	45x0.5
Travegon-S	1962	35	2.8	auto	7	0.5	49x0.75
Travenar	1963	50	2.8	auto	4	0.5	49x0.75
Macro-Travenar	1963	50	2.8	preselect	4	0.08	49x0.75
Travelon	1962	50	1.8	auto	6	0.5	49x0.75

Lens	*Year Intro.*	*Focal length*	*Max. f/*	*Diaphragm*	*No. of elements*	*Closest focusing distance (m)*	*Filter thread (mm)*
Travenar	1959	85	2.8	preselect	4	1.0	45x0.5
Travenar-R	1962	90	2.8	auto	4	1.0	49x0.75
Travegar	1963	100	3.3	preselect	3	0.9	49x0.75
Travenon	1959	135	4.5	manual	4	1.5	40.5×0.5
Travenar	1959	135	3.5	preselect	4	1.5	45x0.5
Travenar-R	1962	135	3.5	auto	4	1.5	49x0.75
Tele-Travelon	1968	200	4	preselect	4	2.0	58x0.75

STEINHEIL, Munich

Some of the lenses manufactured by Steinheil for the Exakta are given here. These lenses were distributed mainly between 1955 and 1965. Some of them could still be found in the 1970 catalogues.

Lens	*Year Intro.*	*Focal length*	*Max. f/*	*Diaphragm*	*No. of elements*	*Closest focusing distance (m)*	*Filter thread (mm)*
Culmigon	1949	35	4.5	manual	4	0.8	40x0.75
Auto-Quinaron	1957	35	2.8	auto	7	0.25	49x0.75
Auto-Culmigon	1961	35	3.5	auto	4	0.8	49x0.75
Macro-Quinaron	1965	35	2.8	auto	7	0.05[1]	54x0.75
Auto-Quinon	1957	55	1.9	auto	6	0.5	49x0.75
Macro-Quinon	1965	55	1.9	auto	6	0.22[2]	54x0.75
Auto-Cassarit	1961	100	3.5	auto	3	1.0	49x0.75
Macro-Quinar	1965	100	2.8	auto	4	0.5[3]	54x0.75
Auto-Tele-Quinar	1961	135	3.8	auto	4	1.2	49.0x75

Lens	*Year Intro.*	*Focal length*	*Max. f/*	*Diaphragm*	*No. of elements*	*Closest focusing distance (m)*	*Filter thread (mm)*
Auto-Tele-Quinar	1959	135	2.8	auto	5	1.7	54x0.75
Macro-Tele-Quinar	1965	135	2.8	auto	5	0.8[4]	54x0.75
Auto-Tele-Quinar	1961	200	3.5	auto	5	2.5	67x0.75

(1) To 10mm with second focusing screw
(2) To 40mm with second focusing screw
(3) To 240mm with second focusing screw
(4) To 460mm with second focusing screw

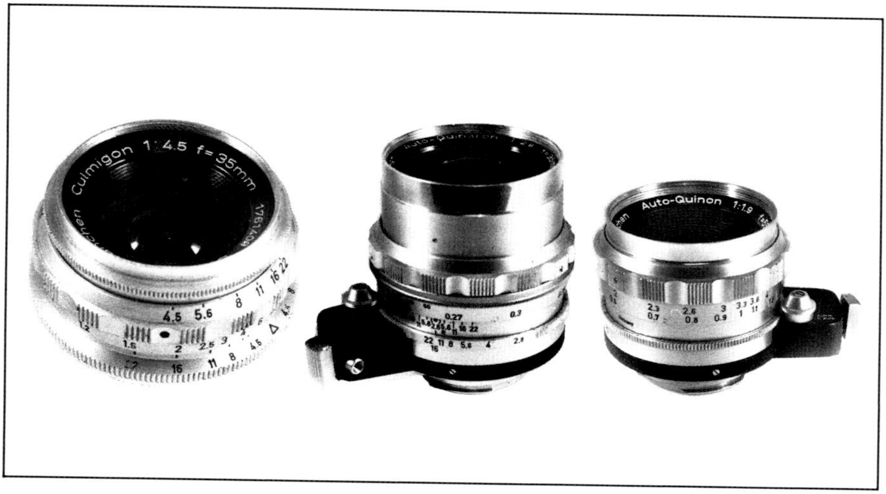

Left: 35mm f/4.5 Culmigon. Middle: 35mm f/2.8 Auto Quinaron. Right: 55mm f/1.9 Auto Quinon.

6x30 Monocular

Around 1961 Steinheil started the marketing of monoculars or binoculars specially designed for photographic picture-taking. These optics could be fixed onto the lens with an adaptating ring corresponding to the diameter of the filter mount. The focal length was equal to the product of the focal length of the lens and the binocular (or monocular) magnification. These binoculars were also used with twin-lens reflex cameras of the Rolleiflex type.

The 6x30 Monocular had an angle of view of 8.5°, field at 1000m of 150m, and brightness 28. Pupil diameter 5mm. Weight 230g.

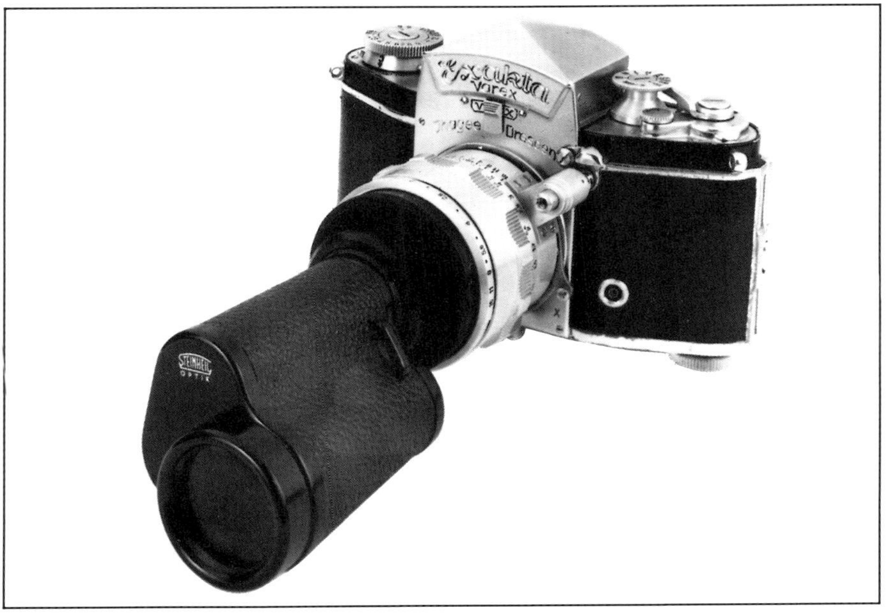

6x30 Monocular fitted on 58mm f/2 Biotar lens. Resulting focal length: 350mm.

TELEC, France

There was only one type of lens known from this maker. Unfortunately, we do not have any optical details. However, the compactness of the lens should be noted. It was 38mm long for a 90mm focal length. It was sold with the Exa range. It had a manual diaphragm, focused down to 1.5m, and was introduced around 1955.

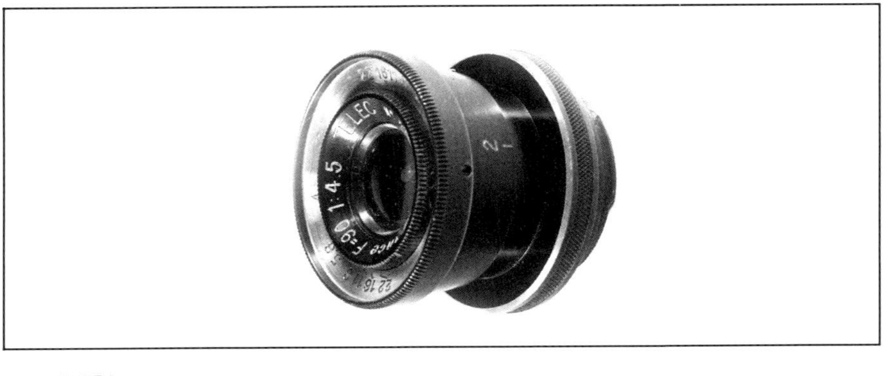

90mm f/4.5 Telec

TEWE, Berlin

Tewe specialised in long focal length lenses. They were adaptable to 33mm reflex cameras and 16 and 35mm cine-cameras. One could find these lenses in the SCOP catalogue until 1963.

Telon Type with 2 elements	*Telagon Type with 4 elements*
Telon 300mm f/5	Telagon 200mm f/3.2
Telon 400mm f/5	Telagon 300mm f/3.5
Telon 500mm f/5	Telagon 400mm f/4.5
Telon 600mm f/5	Telagon 500mm f/5
Telon 800mm f/6.3	Telagon 600mm f/5
Telon 1000mm f/6.3	

There was also a catadiptric lens, the 2000mm f/8.8 Tewe Shortygon.

VOIGTLANDER, Braunschweig

The 36-82mm f/2.8 Zoomar was developed as a result of a collaboration between Voigtlander and Zoomar in New York. It was the very first variable-focus zoom lens intended for 35mm cameras. Originally designed for Voigtland Bessamatic, it was also made available for other reflex cameras, including the Ihagee Exakta. It had 14 elements. Focusing was by a ring located at the lens-front. Change of focus was by motion of another ring which moved two groups of elements. The lens had an automatic diaphram, with minimum aperture f/22, focused down to 1.3m and had a 76x0.75mm filter thread.

LENSES MADE IN JAPAN

We do not have documentation on all the lenses made in Japan with an Exakta fitting. Japanese lenses were mainly distributed on the American market. However, Komura, Sun, Sigma, Soligor, Tamron and Vivitar were distributed in Europe. The Topcon lenses were of a bayonet type with an internal aperture interlinking device.
Many Japanese manufacturers fitted interchangeable mounts for their lenses, as indeed they still do, making them adapable for different makes of camera, including Exakta. Around 1951 Olympus manufactured a lens with an Exakta mount. This was the Zuiko 40mm f/4.5.

Chapter 9

Accessories for the 35mm Exakta and Exa Cameras

VIEWFINDERS AND VIEWING SCREENS

In this chapter we shall review the viewing systems used in all of the Exakta 24 × 36 range. We will start with the viewfinders of the Exakta Varex, from model VX to VX 1000, together with those of the Exa range. We will then look at the Exakta RTL 1000 which featured different viewing optics.

The viewing systems of the Exakta Varex and the Exa included the following viewfinders: –

- Hooded viewfinder
- Prismatic viewfinder
- Prismatic viewfinder with cell
- Viewfinder amplifier unit
- Stereo viewfinder

A range of ten focusing screens could be adapted to most of these viewfinders.

The viewing systems of the Exakta RTL 1000 included:-

- Hooded viewfinder
- Prismatic viewfinder
- Prismatic viewfinder with TTL cell
- Magnifying viewfinder.

A range of seven focusing screens completed this system. The Exakta Real system included only one hooded viewfinder, together with a prism without a cell. A model equipped with a cell was contemplated but to our knowledge it has never been distributed (refer to chapter on Exakta Real).

Hooded Viewfinder, Version 1, 1950

This first model of the hooded viewfinder was an exact replica of the viewfinder of the Exakta II. However, it was interchangeable on the 1950 Exakta Varex. The middle part of the cover hinged upwards to form a frame-finder. The magnifier, used to enlarge a portion of the image on the ground glass for precise focusing, retracted back into the cover to allow for a view of the whole screen.

When the viewfinder was placed in position, a small bar attached to it inserted itself into the upper part of the camera body and locked the shutter, which could then only be released when the cover was in the open position. Thus it was not possible to release the shutter when the viewfinder was closed.

The focusing screen was a thick glass block, finely ground on the focusing surface.

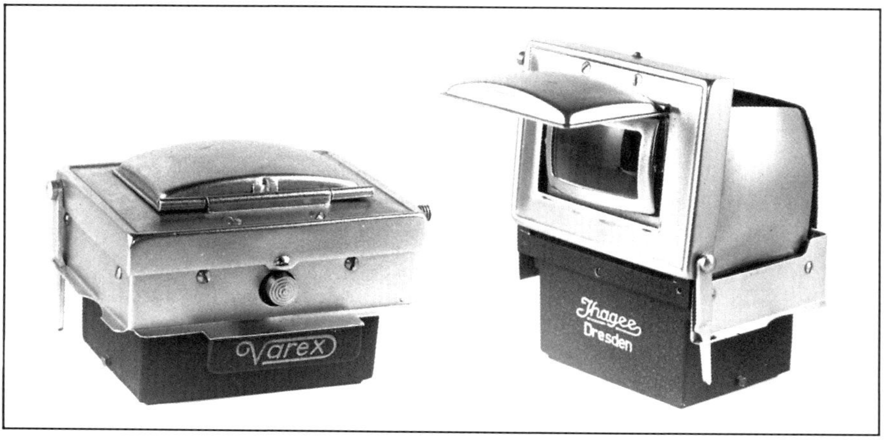

Left: Rear view of the collapsible viewfinder, marked "Varex". Right: Viewfinder open, with magnifier folded back against cover.

It was not removable. The viewfinder base was finished in black crackle paint, and the front was engraved "Ihagee Dresden". The rear, which was the only visible part when the viewfinder was attached to the camera body, was engraved "Varex". The upper part had a chrome-plated finish.

Hooded Viewfinder, Version 2, 1950

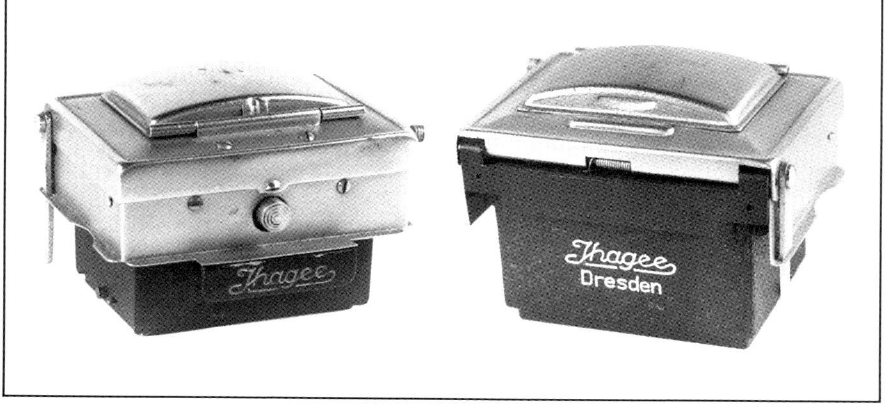

Rear view with the "Ihagee" engraving and front view of the folded hood.

The engraving made this model different from the first version. The rear was marked "Ihagee" instead of "Varex". It equipped the Exakta V and the 1951 Exakta VX distributed on the American market. The focusing screen was a thick glass block and not detachable.

Hooded Viewfinder, Version 3, 1954

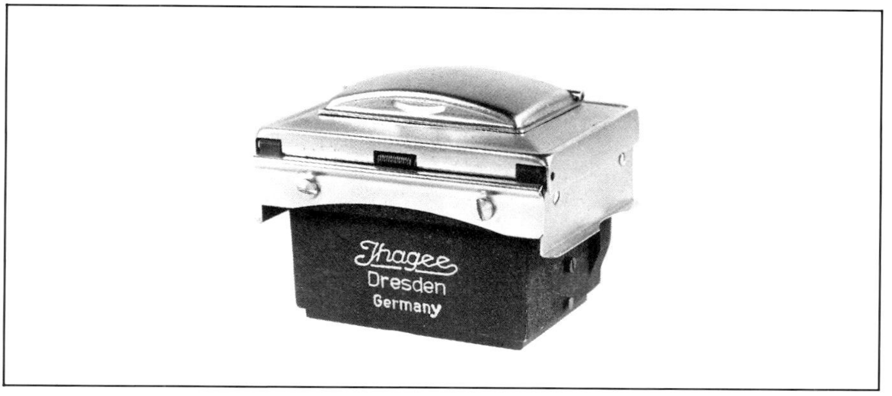

On this model the shutter-locking bar was absent. The reason was that from 1954 onwards the camera-bodies had an internal safety device. The finder was inscribed "Ihagee Dresden Germany". The important change was that the thick block focusing screen could be detached by unscrewing the two lateral screws.

Rheinmetall Hood, 1956

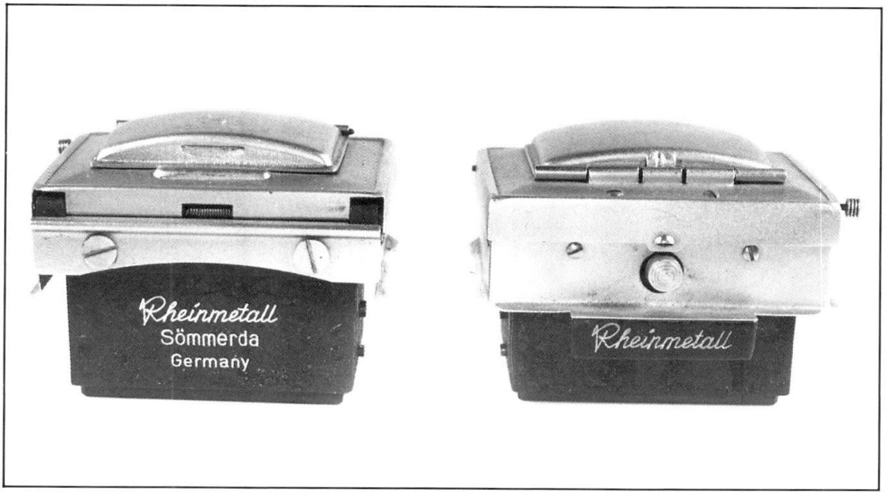

This model was similar to the third Version of the Ihagee hood, but was manufactured by Rheinmetall. The name appeared on front and back of the viewfinder. The focusing screen was detachable. This viewfinder was intended for the Exa Rheinmetall.

Hooded Viewfinder, Version 4, 1956

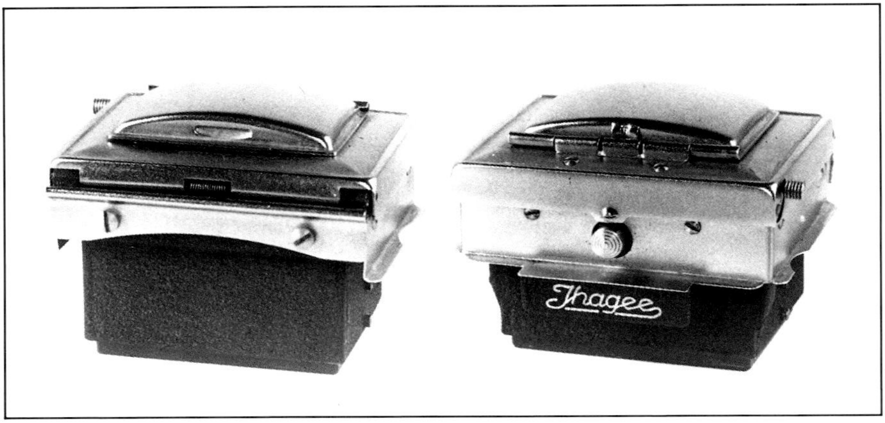

This model was of similar design to the previous one, but lacked the inscription on the front. "Ihagee" was engraved on the rear plate. The focusing screen was a thick block and could be detached by unscrewing the two screws. It also provided a frame finder for a 100mm lens.

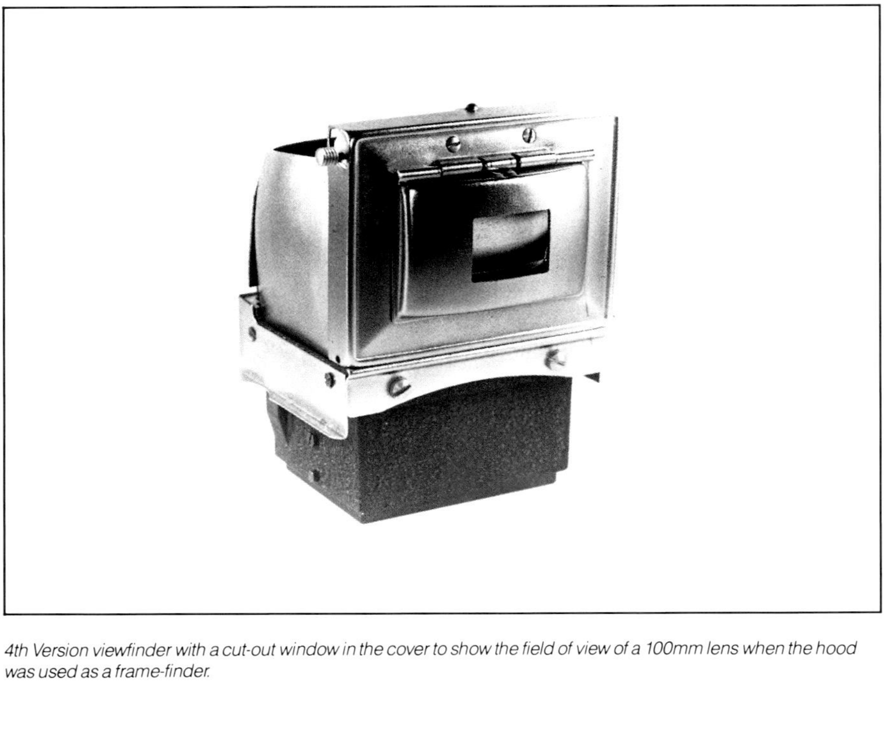

4th Version viewfinder with a cut-out window in the cover to show the field of view of a 100mm lens when the hood was used as a frame-finder.

Hooded Viewfinder, Version 5, 1960

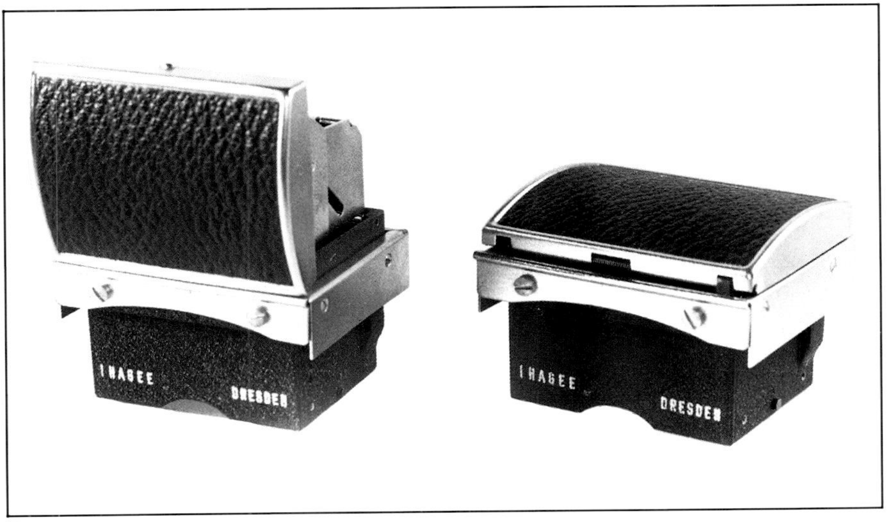

This model was quite different. The lid was covered with black imitation leather instead of being chromed, and the sports frame finder facility was absent. The viewfinder could be closed down instantly, even when the magnifier was in position. The focusing screen was thin, no longer the thick block, and interchangeable. "Ihagee Dresden" was engraved on the front.

Jubilee Hood, 1961

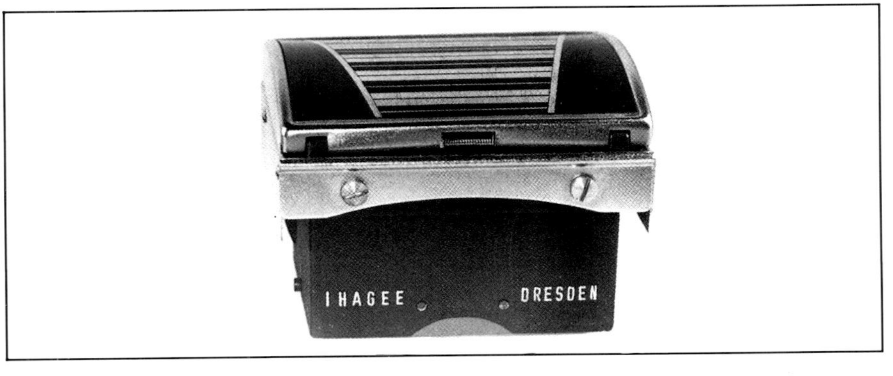

This model was similar to the previous one, except for the cover which featured white stripes on a black background. This viewfinder came out on the occasion of the 25th anniversary of the Kine Exakta.

Hooded viewfinder, Version 6, 1966

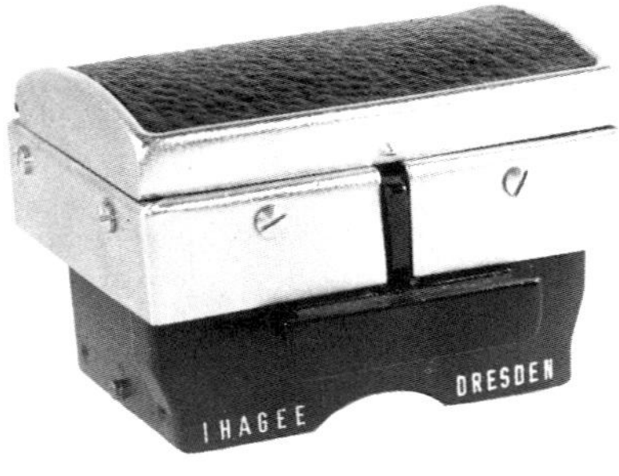

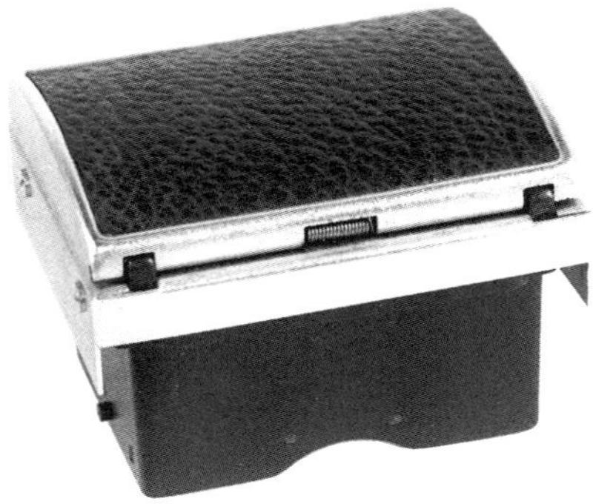

Several changes were made with this new model. The round metal push-button which opened the cover was replaced by an elongated plastic push-button. The base of the viewfinder, formerly crackle black, was changed to gloss black, and the metallic chrome frame surrounding the cover was made in a single piece. "Ihagee Dresden" was engraved on the rear of the hood, but a variant exists with no identification plate. This model was intended for the Exakta range from the VX 1000 onwards. The viewing optics remained the same.

Zeiss Prism, 1949

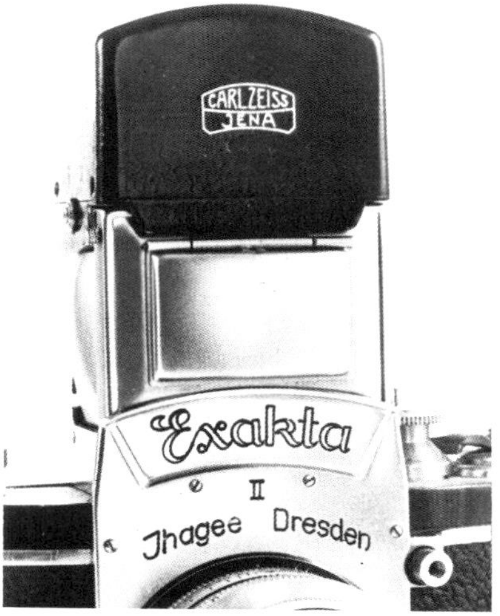

Zeiss prism on the Exakta II.

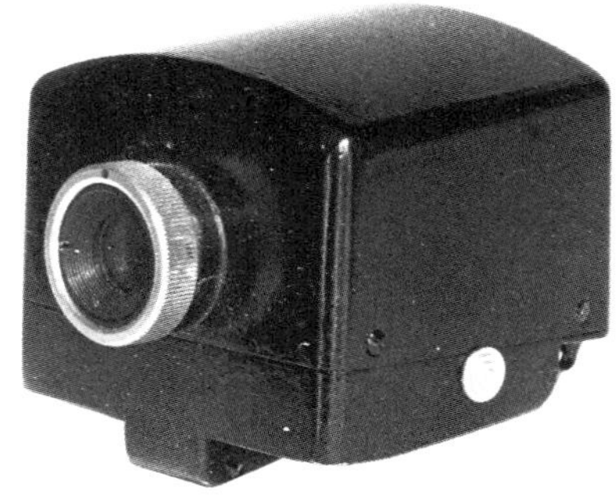

The prism shown here from the eyepiece side. (J. Dalbera collection).

Pentacon and Rectaflex were the first companies to use an inverting prism. Shortly afterwards Ihagee asked Zeiss to design an inverting prism suitable for the viewing hood of the Kine Exakta I and II. The prism fitted into the well of the viewfinder and inverted the image to the right-way-round aspect. The prism had a black painted metal body and was engraved on the front with "Carl Zeiss Jena".

Prism, Version 1, 1950

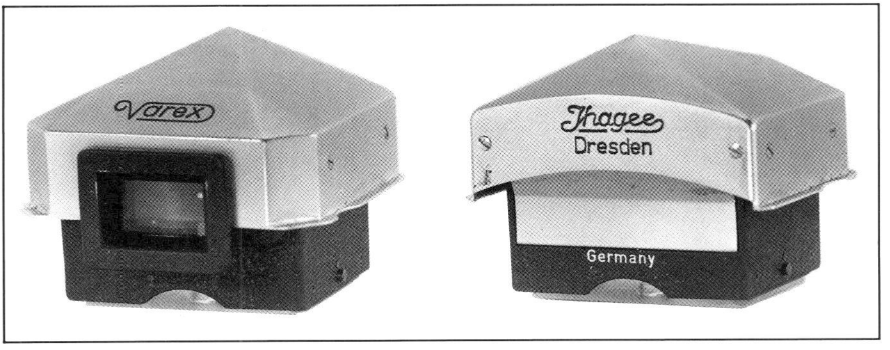

Left: Prism, 1st Version, eyepiece side. Right: Front of the prism

The first version of this viewfinder with an inverting prism, which was specially designed for the Exakta Varex, can be easily recognised by its hood which was entirely matt chromium-plated. "Varex" was engraved on top of the eyepiece and Ihagee Dresden on the front. The metal base was painted in crackled black and engraved "Germany". These models were not numbered and are not very common.

Prism, Version 2, 1950

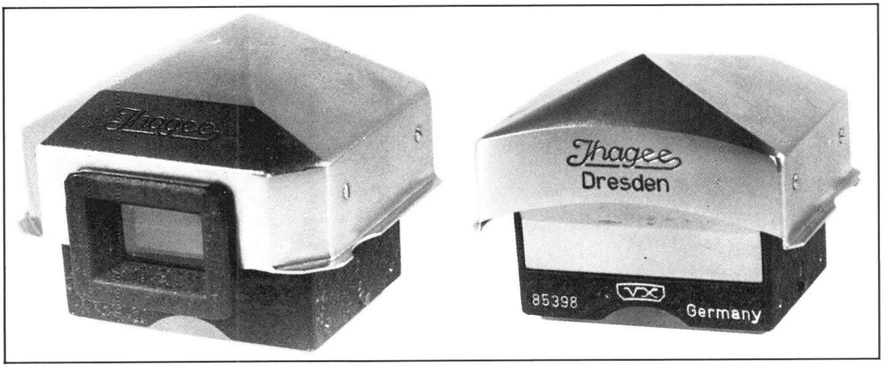

Specially designed for the Exakta V (US Market), VX and Exa, the external appearance was similar to that of the first version, except for the engraving which omitted the name Varex. "Ihagee" was engraved on top of the eyepiece and "Ihagee Dresden" on the front. The black-painted base was engraved "VX" and "Germany" and carried a serial number (known from 2600 to 85400).

Prism, Version 3, 1953

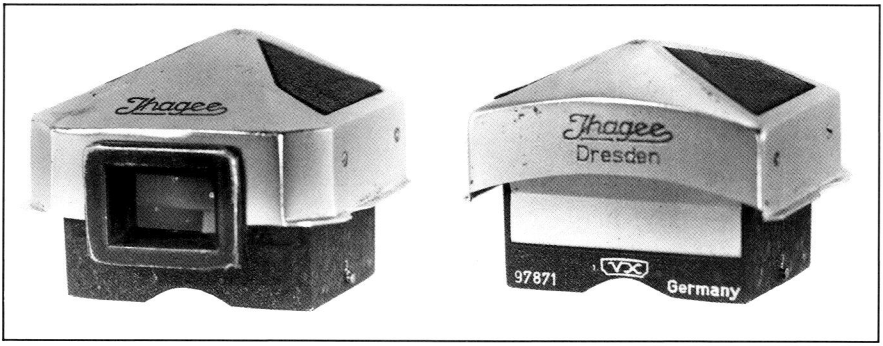

On this model the appearance of the hood was modified. Two black leather pieces of triangular shape were added to the roof. The engravings were similar to the previous version: "Ihagee" appeared on top of the eyepiece and "Ihagee Dresden" on the front. On the base one can find the inscription "VX" and "Germany" together with the serial number (at present there is only one number well-known to us: No. 97871).

Prism, Version 4, 1954

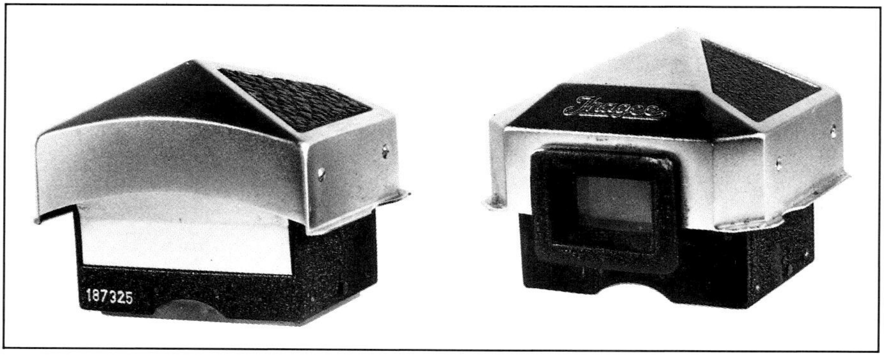

Prism, 4th Version, No. 187325.

On this model the hood was similar to that of the previous version, except for the rear identification plate where "Ihagee" was not engraved but set in relief instead. The front engraving was omitted. There were at least three different engravings on the base of the prism:-
- Serial Number and "Germany" (No. 151487).

- Serial Number only (Nos. 181370 and 187325).
- "Ihagee Dresden" with no serial number.

Prism, Version 5, 1960

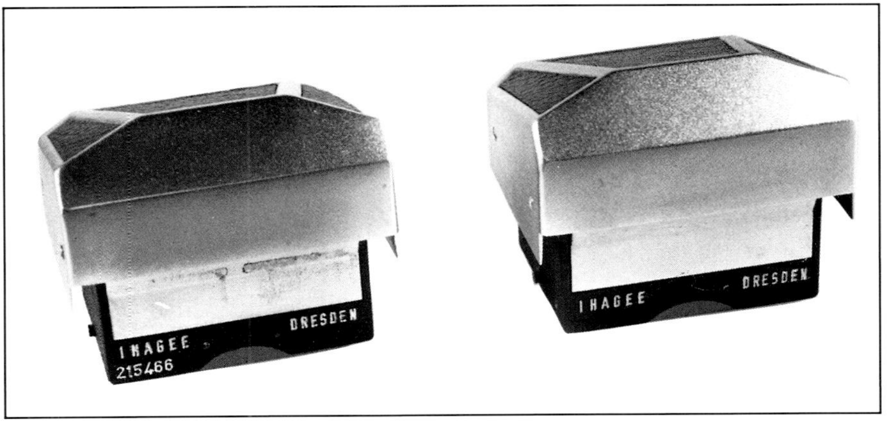

Two models of Prism, Version 5.

This model came out for the Varex II, which was equipped with a new screen. The shape of the housing was entirely different, being flatter and having three faces covered in leather panels. The base of the earliest models was finished in black crackle paint, but the later ones were in black gloss. All models were engraved "Ihagee Dresden". We know of only one numbered example, No.215466. There was also a slight modification to the small plate located on the base just above the identification plate. This had been smooth on previous models but was now embossed.

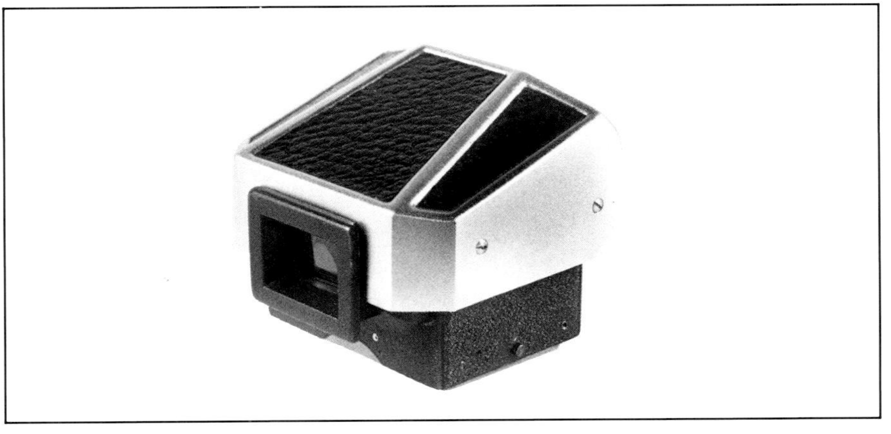

Prism, eyepiece side.

Jubilee Prism, 1961

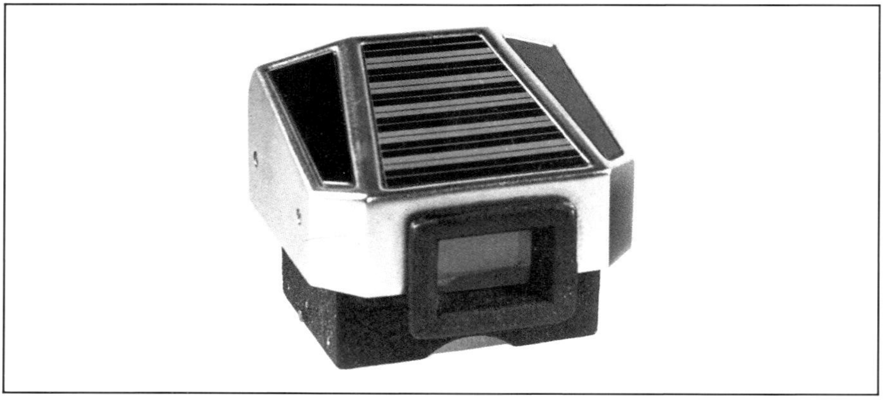

In 1961, on the occasion of the 25th anniversary of the Kine Exakta, Ihagee introduced a new inverting prism. The central part of the hood was covered with a black-painted plate with white stripes. The two lateral faces were in black plated metal. The general aspect was similar to that of the Jubilee Hood as previously described. These models were numbered and two are well-known to us: Nos. 187416 and 208222).

Prism, Version 6, 1967

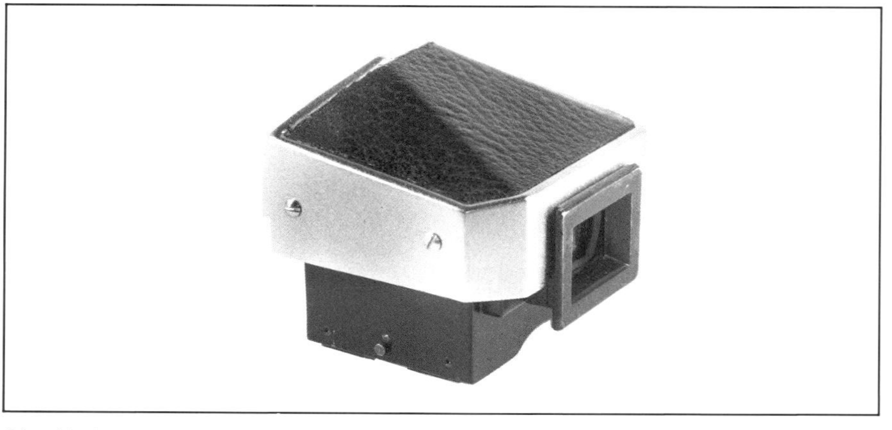

Prism, Version 6 designed for VX 1000.

This was the final version of prism designed for the Exakta Varex. It can be recognized on the VX 1000. The hood kept its general aspect except for the black covering which now entirely covered the roof in one single piece. The base of the prism was in gloss black and engraved "Ihagee Dresden" on the early models. For the VX 500 and the Elbaflex the identification plate was omitted.

Ihagee Cell-Prism, 1958

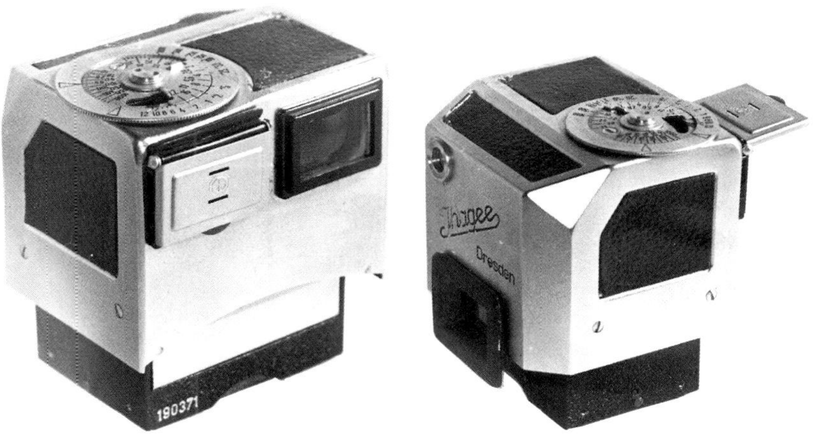

This cell-prism, which was the only one manufactured by Ihagee, was completely different from the later Travemat and Examat ones. The selenium cell, which was located on top of the prism, measured the external light. The film sensivity could be adjusted from 10 to 1000 ASA. The measurement was made when the galvanometer needle tallied with an indicator. The speeds and stops indicated on the disk were then transferred to the camera. There were two reading ranges:-

- Poor light with direct reading (red signal).
- Strong light, for which a slotted cover was swung down in front of the cell (black signal).

The body and hood were metallic. The hood was matt chrome with four leather panels and engraved "Ihagee Dresden" next to the eyepiece. This prism would have been of classical type if it were not accompanied by an optical viewfinder which determined the field of view with a 50mm lens. The focusing screen of the Varex could be adapted to this prism.

Travenat Cell-Prism, 1966

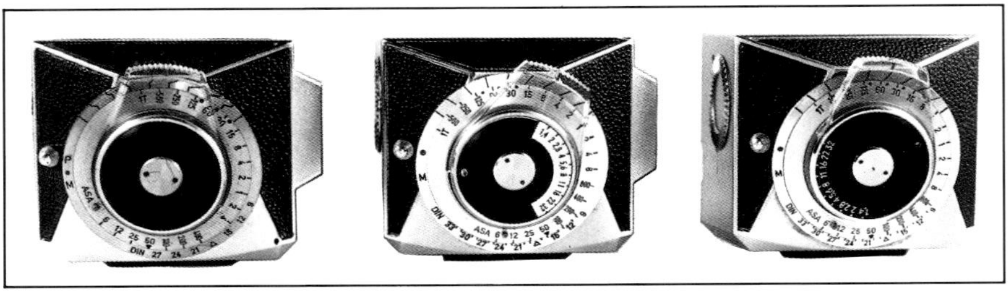

From left to right: the three versions of the Travemat which differed with respect to the measuring scales.

This was the very first model of cell-prism with reading from the rear of the lens. It was specially manufactured for Ihagee by Schacht in Ulm. To our knowledge there were three versions. The examples we have seen had the following serial numbers:-
- 1st Version, Nos. 400685, 403552 and 404080
- 2nd Version, Nos. 415449, 417293 and 420421
- 3rd Version, Nos. 421979

The sensitivity ranged from 6 to 400 ASA with the first version and from 6 to 800 ASA for the two other versions. The cell was of the CdS type. The reference of the battery was PX13 (Mallory) or PX625. The meter featured three types of reading:-
- Selection of the shutter speed on the camera-body with transfer on to the cell. Reading by turning the diaphragm ring to actual aperture.
- Selection of the aperture, followed by adjustment of the shutter speed on the cell and transfer to the camera body.
- Set to maximum aperture and read at maximum aperture. Read off indication of the stop/speed combination (did not apply to the 1st version).

The focusing screen was interchangeable. The body was black plastic and the hood was chrome-plated with three black covered faces on the top.

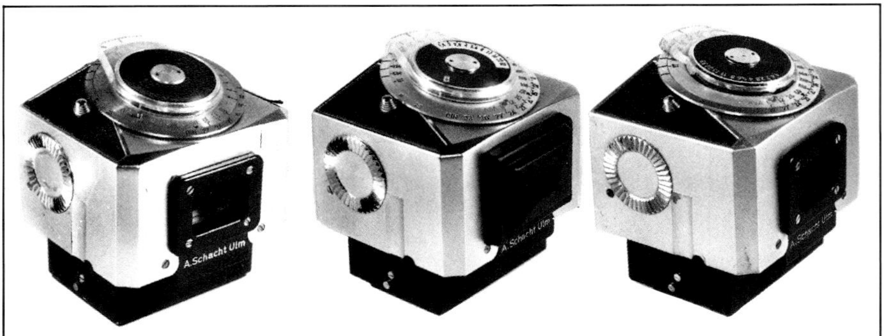

Left: Travemat 1st Version. No scale, allowing work at wide lens apertures. Sensitivity ranging from 6 to 400 ASA. Middle: Travemat 2nd Version. With scale allowing measuring at wide aperture. Sensitivity ranging from 6 to 800 ASA. Right: Travemat 3rd Version. Specification simialr to Version 2, except for the inner disk.

Examat Cell-Prism, 1967

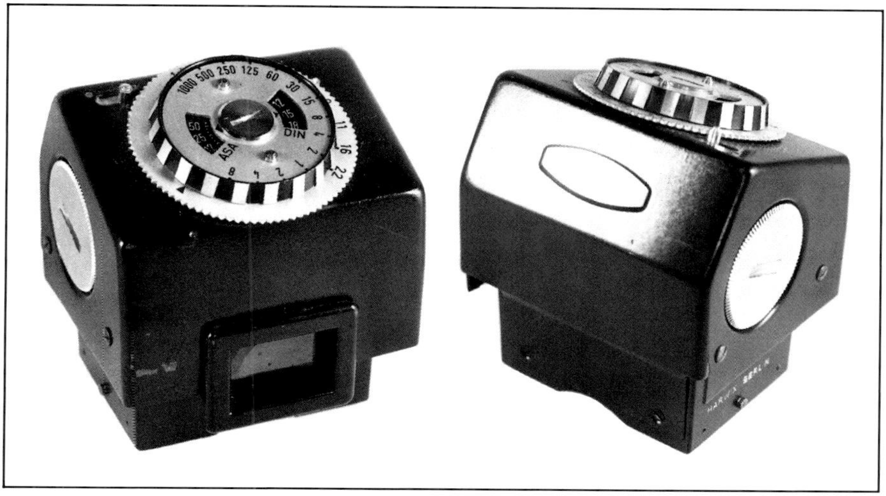

Examat prism. Left, the dials; right, the on-off switch.

This prism with a CdS built-in cell was manufactured by Harwix in Berlin. It allowed measurement of the light which passed through the lens and entered the viewfinder. The sensitivity range was from 6 to 1600 ASA. The reference of the battery was PX 13 (Mallory) or PX 625 mercury oxide. The reading range covered 13 exposure values. Each shutter speed could be combined with any aperture from f/1.4 to f/22. Like the TRAVEMAT previously described, there were three types of reading. The body and roof were metall with a black gloss finish. The prisms were numbered and two versions are known:-

- Prior to No. 3200 the printed circuit carried adjustable potentiometers for calibration.
- From No. 3200 to No. 15000, fixed resistors replaced the potentiometers.

Magnifying Unit, 1958

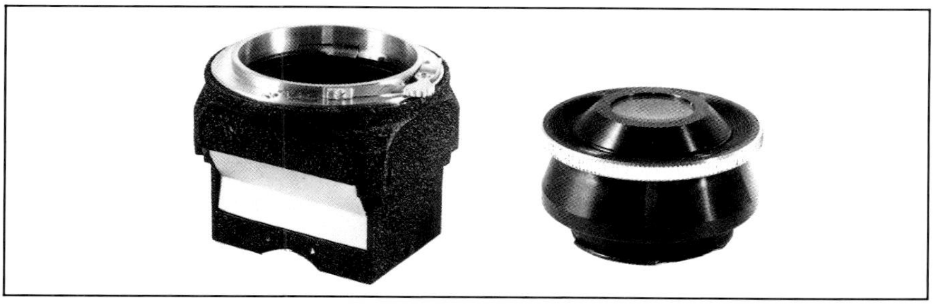

The magnifying unit with its magnifier.

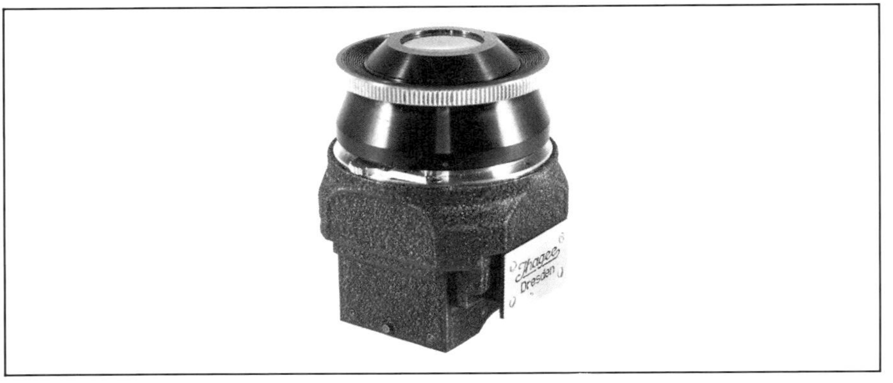

The assembled unit.

This viewfinder was required for macro- and microphotography. The body carried the focusing screen of the Varex, and a detachable magnifier fitted above it by means of an Exakta bayonet flange. The magnifier was needed in order to get a perfectly clear and sharp image. The body was finished in black crackle. A chrome-plated plate was engraved "Ihagee Dresden" and attached to the back with four screws. The body was usually supplied with a ground glass screen, but the magnifier was always sold separately.

RTL 1000 Hood, 1970

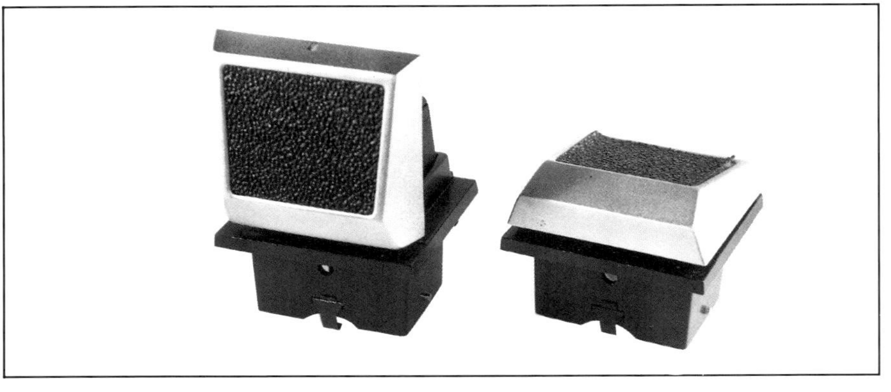

RTL 1000 Hood open and closed.

Opening and closing of this hood could be done in one movement. Like all the viewfinders of this type, the picture was laterally reversed. The magnifier was detachable: it afforded a 4.5x enlargement and allowed a complete view of the screen image. When closed, the magnifier folded back automatically. The focusing screen was interchangeable and well protected against stray light. This viewfinder had a matt chrome finish and the central part of the roof had a black covering. There was an all-black version which was specially designed for the Praktica VLC but, as mentioned previously, it could also be fitted to the RTL 1000.

RTL 1000 Prism Viewfinder, 1970

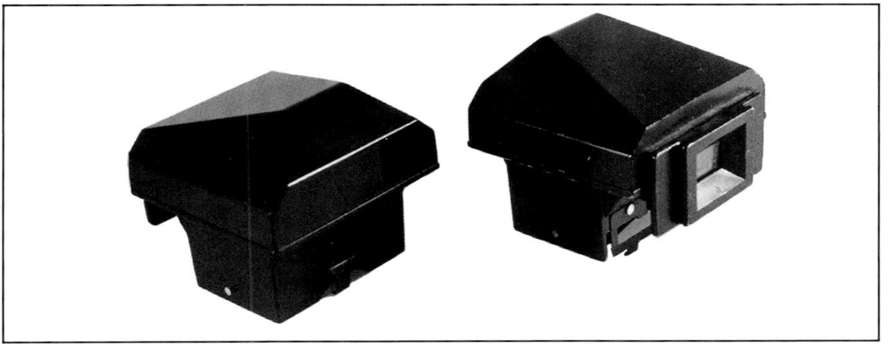

This viewfinder gave an exact right-way-round image. With a 50mm lens the image could be seen full-size. The eyepiece fitted was set to 0 dioptre. It had the same frame as the cell-prism and could be fitted to various viewing accessories (eyepiece, focusing magnifier, angle viewfinder). The finish was gloss black.

RTL 1000 Magnifying Viewfinder, 1970

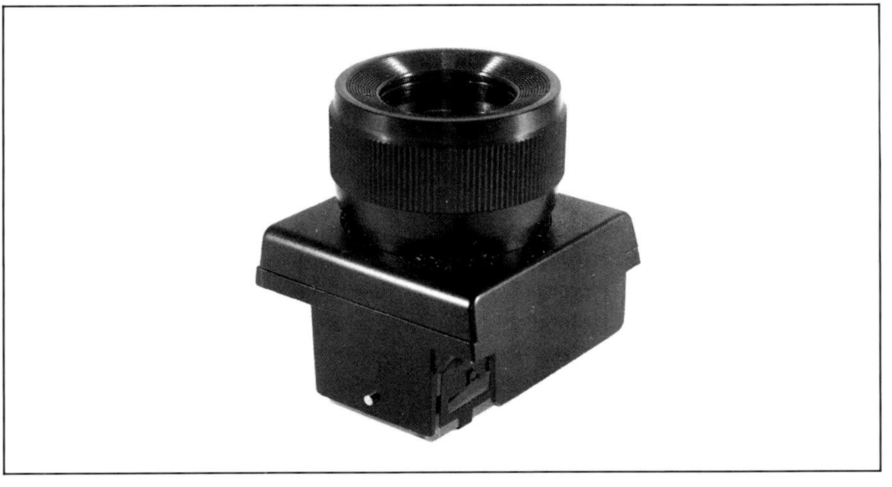

This gave a 5.3x magnification. The eyepiece could be adjusted from +2 to -4 dioptres, but the graduation marks were not numbered. The finish was gloss black. Like the other RTL 1000 viewfinders, the focusing screen was interchangeable.

RTL 1000 Cell-Prism, Version 1, 1970

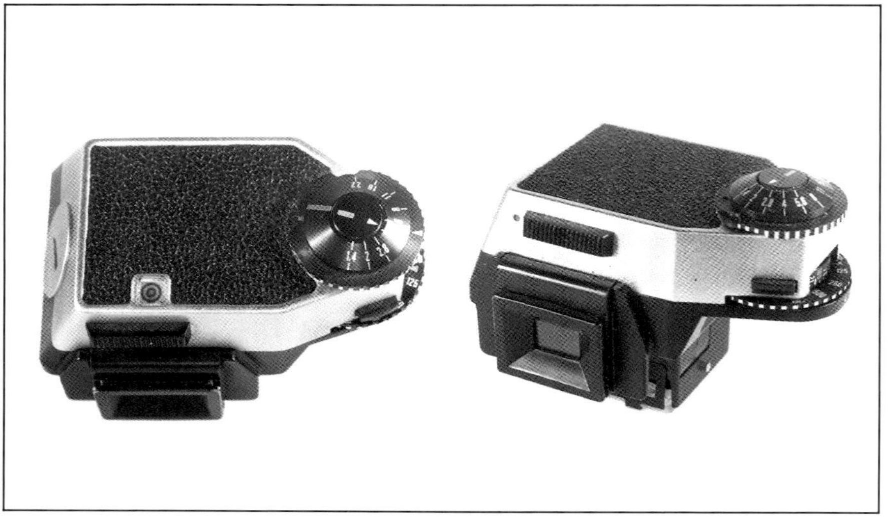

Earliest model of cell-prism with on-off switch on top. Serial numbers 3000 to 14000.

RTL 1000 cell-prism, 2nd version. Serial numbers 14000 to 46000.

This was an inverting prism which featured exposure reading through the lens (TTL). It operated on the principle of integrated light measurement and had provision for 13 exposure values. Readings were valid for a Fresnel lens with microprisms and ground annular field. With a fully ground screen the film sensitivity had to be set to a value 4 DIN higher. With a ground screen and a 6mm clear screen circle the sensitivity had to be set 3 DIN higher. The measuring range was from 9 to 30 DIN or 6 to 800 ASA. It required a mercury oxide battery (Mallory PX13 type). Two measuring modes were possible:-

- At taking aperture.
- At full aperture, provided the indications given by the cell were then transferred on to the lens because there was no coupling between the diaphragm and the prism.

RTL 1000 Cell-Prism, Version 2, 1971

On this second version, which was more common, the words "on - off" were replaced with two marks, one green one red, located on each side of the switch. All other characteristics remained the same.

Viewing Accessories for the RTL 1000

Magnifier could be fitted to the eyepiece frame and enlarged a 10mm diameter area in the middle of the field by 2.7 times. It was adjustable from -7 to +7 dioptres.

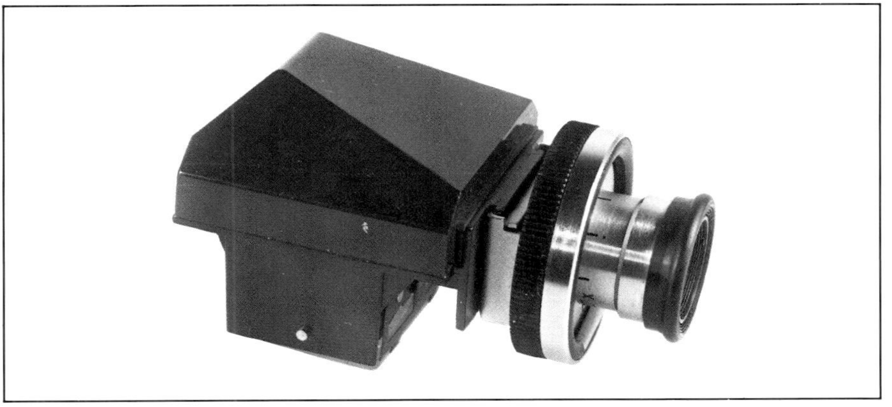

The Focusing Screens

There were three different ranges of viewing screens for the 35mm Exakta and 10 different types of viewing and focusing aids.

Series 1. Thick glass, Size 28x39mm.

These thick block glass screens could be fitted to the Varex hood viewfinders from Version 3 of 1954 onwards. They could be interchanged by unscrewing the two lateral screws on the viewfinder which engaged in a slot each side of the block. The following types were available:-
- Plain ground glass (not pictured here).
- Ground glass with engraved cross-hairs (No.6).
- Clear glass with engraved cross-hairs (No.7).
- Ground glass with a 3mm diameter reticulated clear screen circle (No.8).
- Ground glass, cross-ruled every 5mm (No.10).

Series 2. Thin glass, Size 26x38mm.

These screens were specially designed for the prisms from the 1950 Varex onwards, the version 5 viewing hood from 1960 onwards, and for the magnifying unit. They could also be fitted to the cell-prisms of the Travemat and Examat (No.1 in particular) together with the Exakta Real. The following types were available:-
- Plain ground glass (not pictured here).
- Ground glass with engraved cross-hairs (No.6).
- Clear glass with engraved cross-hairs (No.7).
- Ground glass with the 3mm diameter reticulated clear screen circle (No.8)
- Ground glass, cross-ruled every 5mm (No.10).
- Reticulated ground glass graduated in mm (No.5).
- Ground glass with rangefinding central spot (No.3).

- Fresnel lens with rangefinding central spot (No. 2).
- Fresnel lens with microprism spot and ground surround (No. 1).

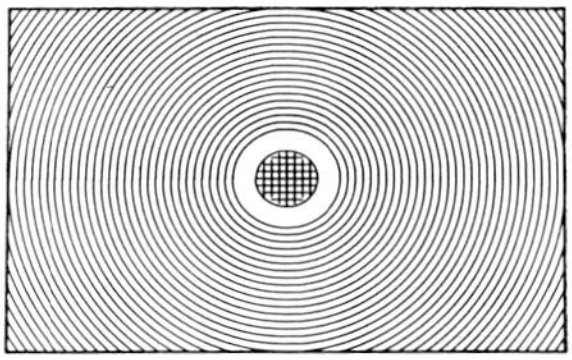
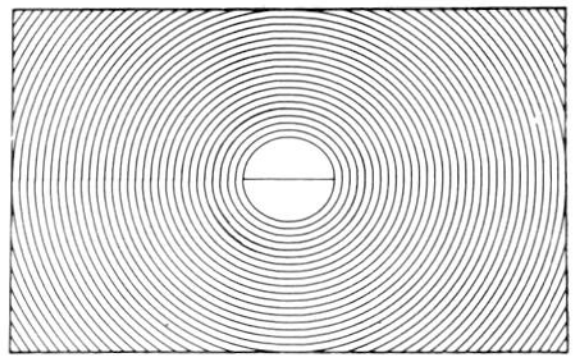
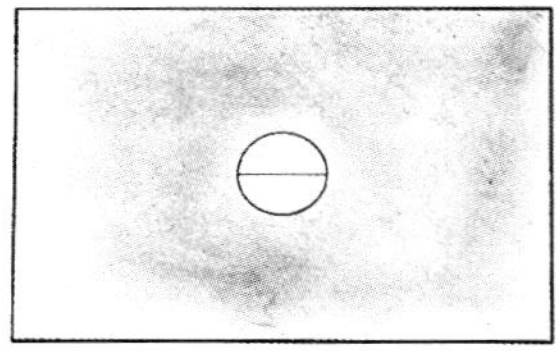
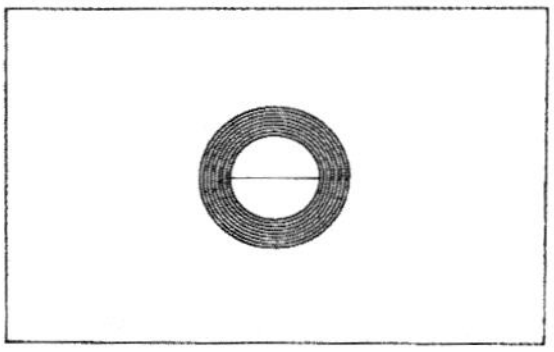
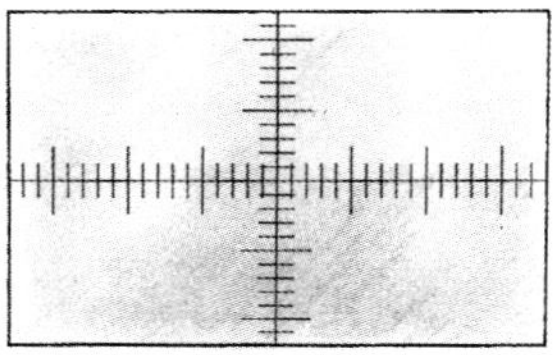

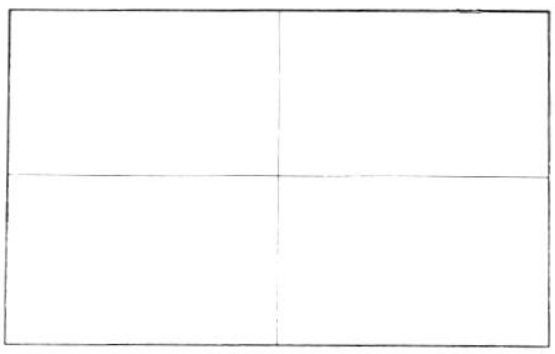
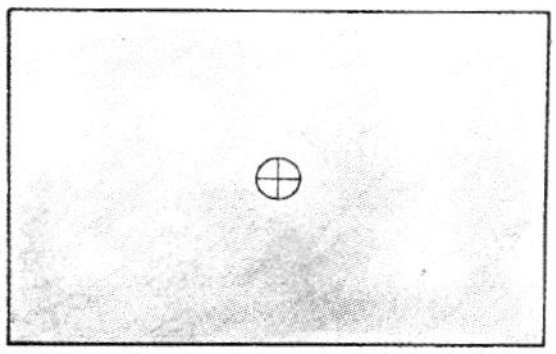
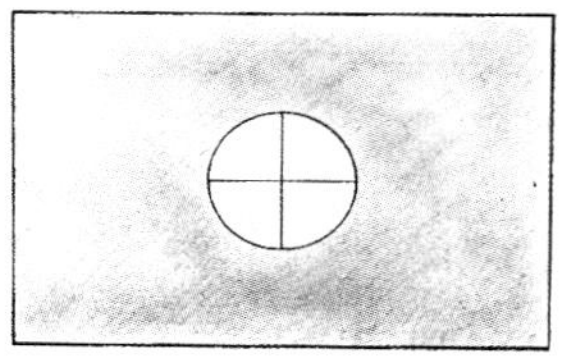
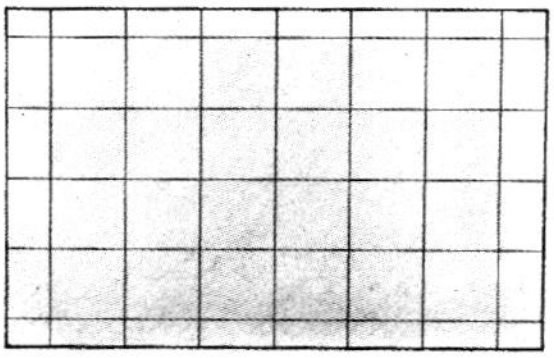

Series 3. Thin glass, Size 25x36mm.
These screens were only for Exakta RTL 1000 viewfinders and were made in the following types:-

- Plain ground glass (not illustrated).
- Fresnel lens with microprism spot and ground surround (No. 1).
- Ground glass with rangefinding central spot and Fresnel surround (No. 4).
- Ground glass with 6mm diameter reticulated clear screen circle (as for No. 8).
- Reticulated ground glass graduated in mm (No. 5).
- Reticulated clear glass graduated in mm (not pictured here but similar to No. 5).
- Ground glass, cross-ruled every 5mm (No. 10).

Pair of Rings with Extension Tubes

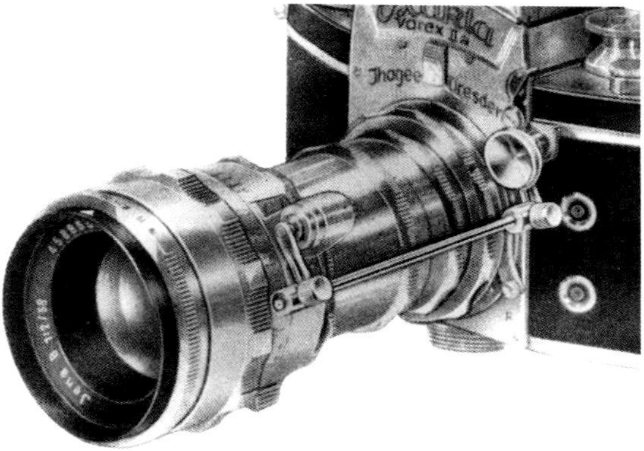

Range of rings and extension tubes for the Varex IIa, shown with the Release Transmission for operating the lens diaphragm (see below).

This unit comprised 5 parts, always sold complete, which were:-
- 1 rear ring, 5mm long
- 3 extension tubes 5, 15 and 30mm long
- 1 front ring 5mm long

The bayonet of the rear ring fitted the camera body and the bayonet of the front ring received the lens. The two rings screwed on top of each other (extension 10mm). One or several extension tubes could be inserted. The screw thread diameter was 42mm at a pitch of 0.75.

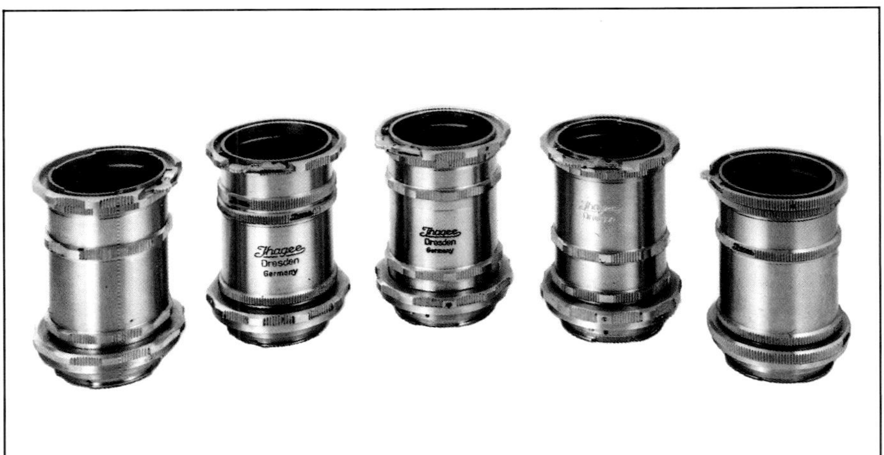

5 sets of extension rings of different patterns.

5mm Ring

This ring was made in a single part and allowed a fixed short extension of 5mm. The ring could be inserted between the lens and the camera body. With the set of extension rings and the 5mm ring the total extension could reach 65mm in steps of 5mm.

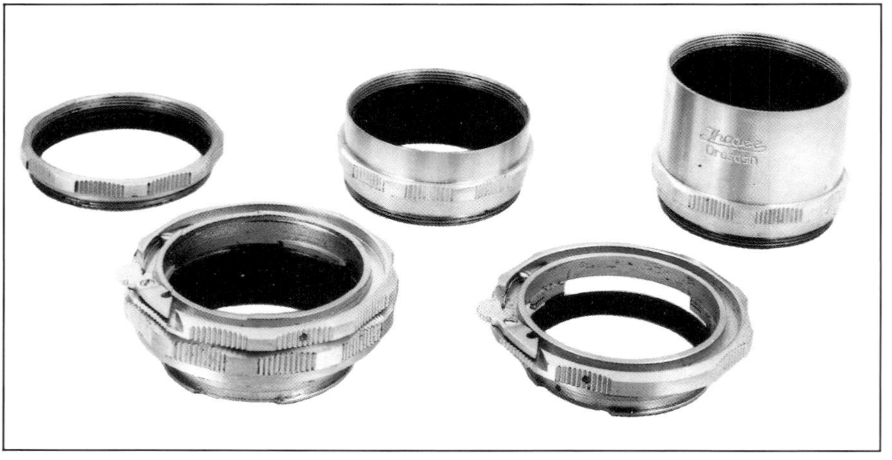

From left to right and from top to bottom: 5mm tube, 15mm tube, 30mm tube, pair of rings and the 5mm ring.

The Rings for the Exakta RTL 1000

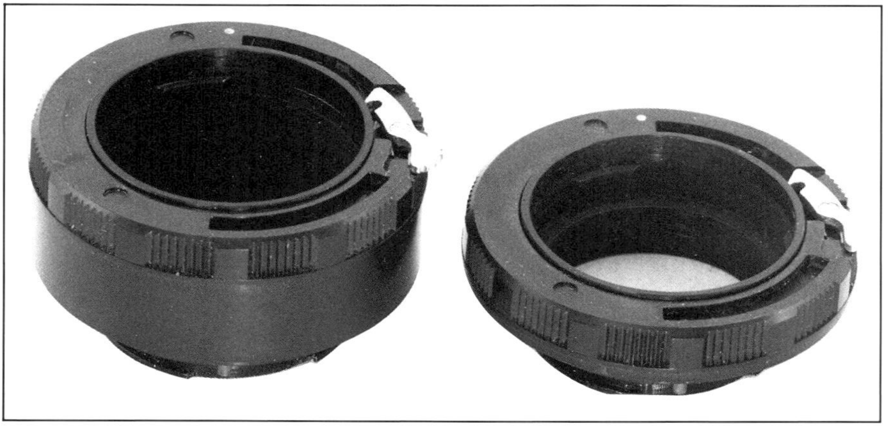

The rings of the Exakta Varex could be fitted to this model. However, a set of two rings was specially designed for the RTL 1000 which were 12.5 and 25mm long respectively. They controlled the aperture by an internal transmission. They could be used separately or together.

The Reversal Ring

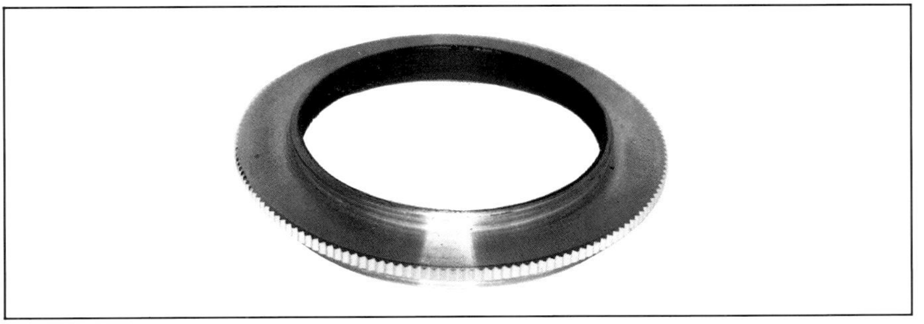

Reversal ring 49x0.75.

When the reproduction ratio reached or went beyond 1.5x, it was recommended that the lens be mounted the other way round. The reversed lens could be screwed onto the front tube with this ring. When mounted on the bellows focusing stage the rear ring included in the set of extension tubes had to be used between the bellows and the reversal ring.This accessory was supplied in the most commonly used lens diameters, such as 35.5x0.5, 40.5x0.5 and 49x0.75.

The Microscope Attachments

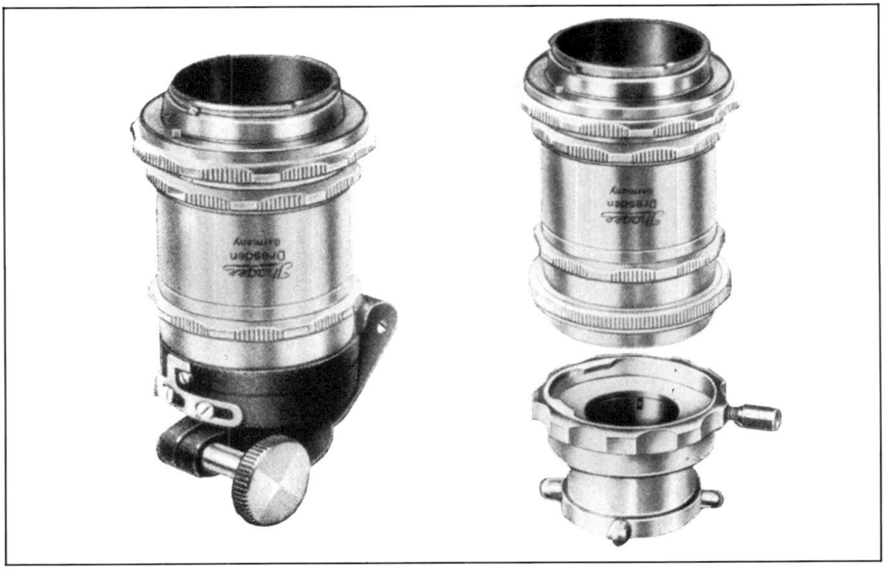

Left: Micro attachment type 1, equipped with a joint to swing the camera aside for observing through the microscope.
Right:Micro attachment type 2, equipped with a bayonet permitting rapid dismantling.

With these two microscope attachments, the Exakta Varex could be used with any microscope equipped with a 25mm diameter eyepiece tube. Fitting could be done in only a few seconds. The image could be found either through the lens and the microscope eyepiece, or through the microscope lens alone. Normal reflex viewing and focusing was with the frosted, clear, or frosted with clear centre circle screens. The magnifying unit was generally used as well.

Endoscope Attachments

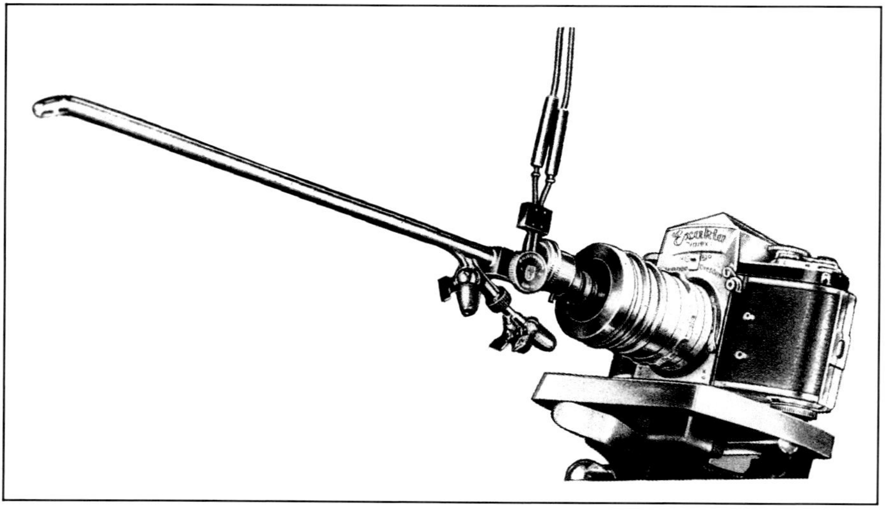

Endoscope adapted to Exakta Varex.

The cavities of the human body and the interiors of certain inaccessable organs can be observed by means of an endoscope. Not only can one observe through endoscopes but one can also take pictures using electronic flash or the built-in overrun lamps. The part of the endoscope where the eyepiece is normally attached could also be attached to the standard lens of the Exakta Varex. The image was visible by reflex focusing. In order to adapt the endoscope to the lens the attachment was supplied to special order to fit the size of the eyepiece. The attachment was made in two parts which suppored the eyepiece tube and were joined by a screw thread. The whole unit was screwed onto the Exakta lens.

Ihagee Exposure Meter

The Ihagee exposure measurement device, intended essentially for use in macro and microphotography, is to our knowledge unique in its working principle. It came out around 1958. It could be regarded as the ancestor of TTL exposure metering, but it was used exclusively for scientific photography.

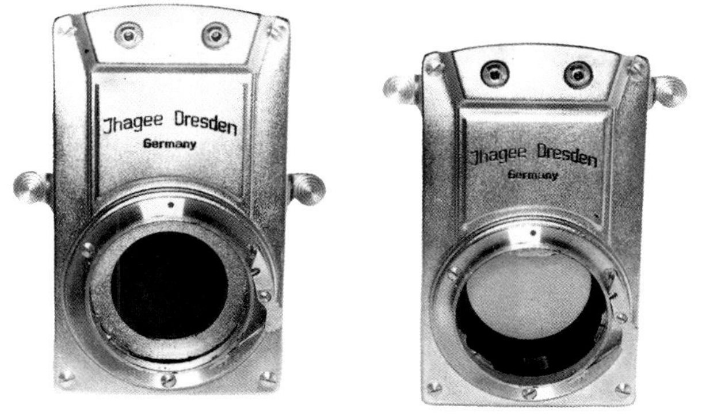

Left: Meter in Low position. The selenium cell (dark) is visible. The levers at the side, which move the cell down, also lock the shutter.
Right: Meter: High position. The side levers are raised to retract the selenium cell.

The body of the exposure meter was matt chrome-plated. It carried a male bayonet on one side for fitting to the camera body and a female bayonet on the other for fitting extension rings, lens, microscope, etc. It had a total thickness of 20mm interposed between the optical system and the camera body. The exposure meter was easy to operate. A selenium cell could be slid up or down in a guide. When set on its high position, the cell was ineffective, but when set in its low position it intercepted the light beam (the shutter was set at the same time). A lead from the two insulated terminals was connected to a standard micro-ampmeter (of internal resistance from 1000 to 1500 ohms for readings ranging from 5 to 100 microamperes) for reading the resulting current. It was necessary to calibrate the meter by first carrying out several trials. Needless to say, with the same film speed the same deviation of the pointer corresponded the same exposure time.

Macro Focusing Bellows 125

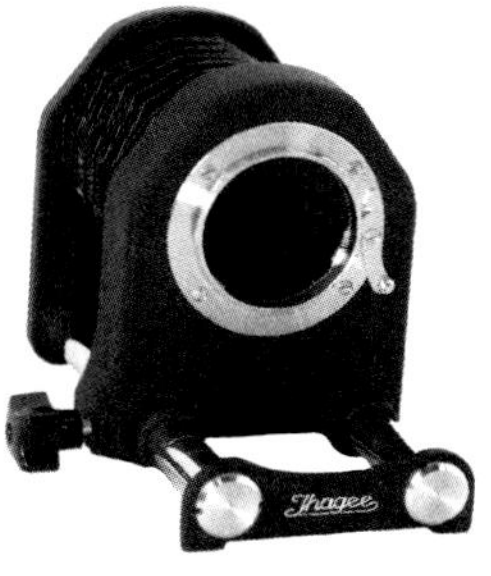

Macro Bellows

A continuous extension range from 35 to 125mm could be obtained with these bellows. The front and back plates had a crackle black finish. The guide bars were chrome-plated, but there was no rack as is often found with this type of accessory. "Ihagee" appeared on the front plate which connected the two slide bars. There was also a similar version of this accessory but with no identification plate. It was distributed for the latest VX 1000 and Exakta Real 1000 cameras.

Release Transmission

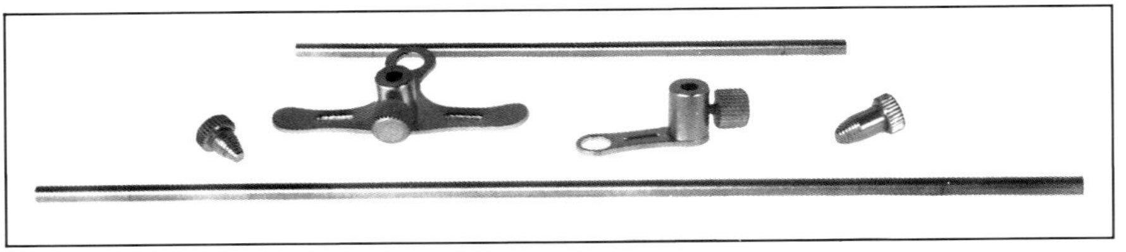

Release Transmission, 2nd version.

When extension rings or macro bellows were inserted between the lens and the camera body, the automatic preselection of the aperture was disconnected. This could be overcome by the transmission release device. The device consisted of:-

- Short coupling rod, length 90mm.
- Long coupling rod, length 150mm.
- Two sliding parts equipped with a locking device.

The short rod was used for extensions ranging from 5 to 60mm and the long one for extensions ranging from 35 to 125mm. The sliding parts could be adjusted according to the extension. The unit was sold complete. Two versions are known.
1st Version: the front sliding part had no screw for fixing on the lens but simply fitted in the release socket. **2nd Version**: a milled head screw fixed the sliding part inside the release socket.

Miscellaneous adapter rings and other accessories

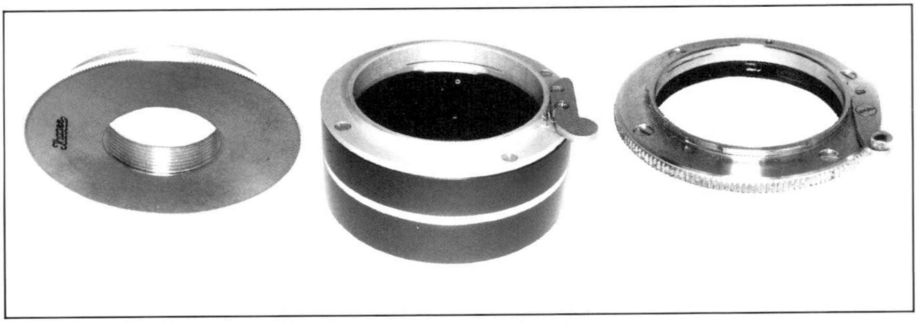

Left to right: ring for mounting microscope objectives, with type W0.8″x1/36 thread, to the Exakta extension tubes in order to obtain very large scales of reproduction; ring for attaching Exakta lenses to 16mm cine cameras with a type C mount; external bayonet ring to screw over the set of extension tubes so that Exakta lenses with an external bayonet could be fitted. There were also adapter rings for terrestrial and astronomical telescopes.

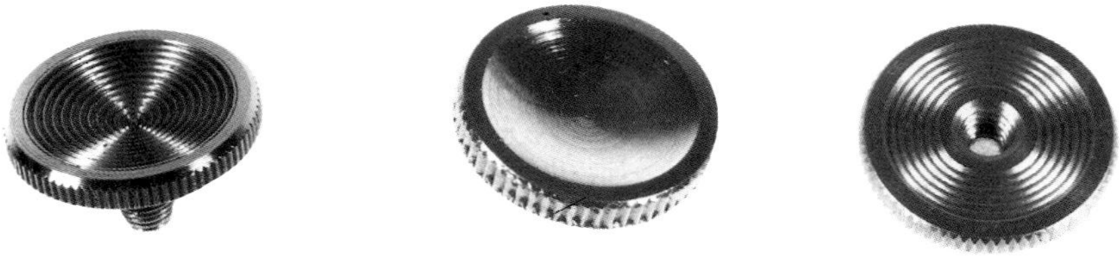

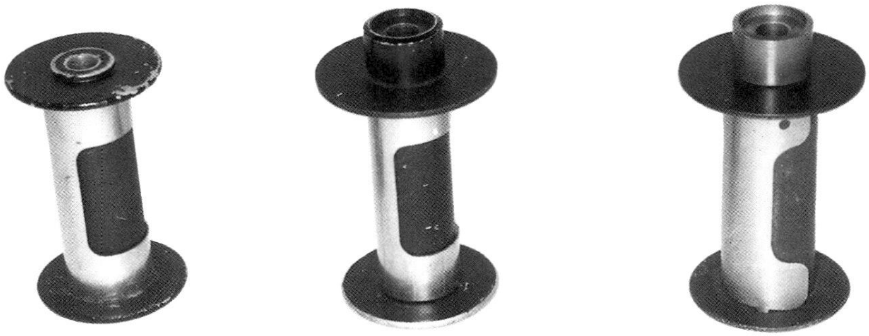

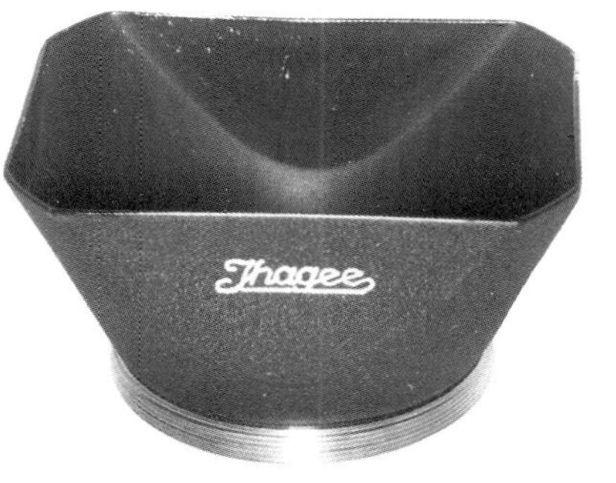

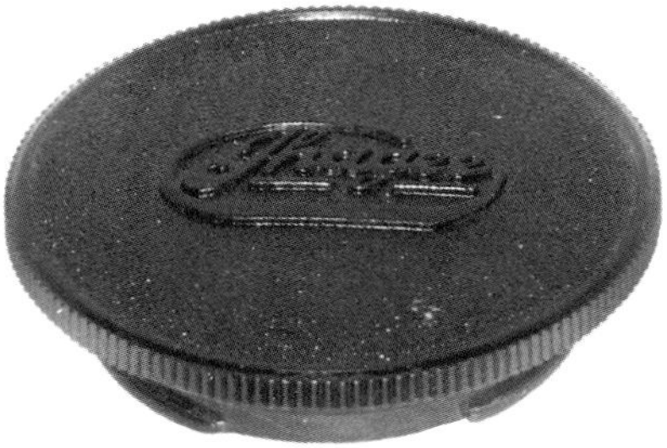

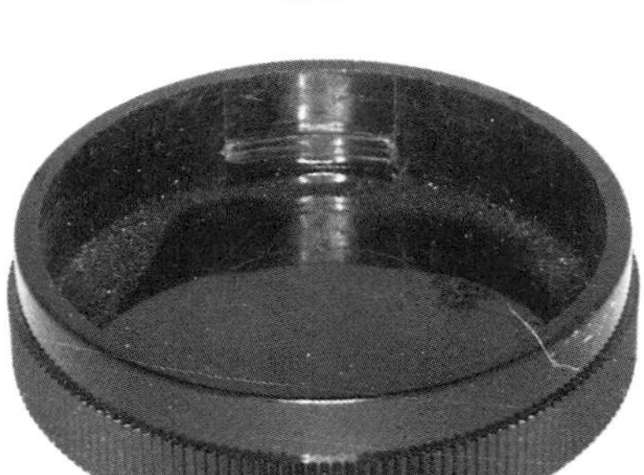

Top: Large knob, screwed over the shutter release to aid handling of the camera when wearing gloves or with the release transmision and extension tubes. There were three types.
Middle: Take-up spools: one was always supplied with the camera but they were also available separately. L to r: for Kine Exakta, Exakta II, Varex and V̂; with small hub for Varex VX and Exa models; with large hub for Varex IIa onwards.
Bottom: Ihagee lens hood, metal, for 50mm lens with 0.75 pitch thread; plastic body cap with bayonet and rear lens cap with bayonet. There were also slip-on lens caps.

Flash

As mentioned in the chapter on the VP Exakta, Ihagee was one of the first manufacturers to develop flash synchronisation.

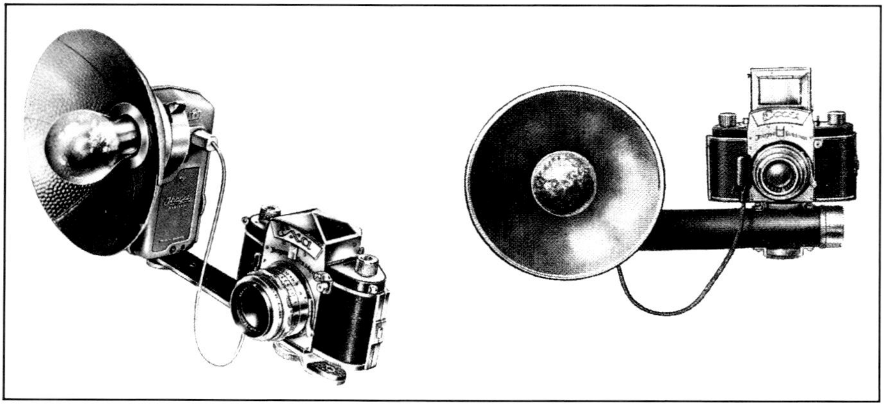

Left: Small Ihagee flashgun, about 1953. A capacitor flashgun for bulbs. The body was of a moulded synthetic material, the reflector was collapsible. Any type of bulb available at the time could be fitted in the spring-loaded socket. It was available with a bar to fix below the camera body and a synchronisation lead.
Right: Large flashgun, also about 1953. A capacitor gun with a universal socket for bulbs and an adjustable reflector. The body could be used as a handle and included a circuit controller together with a socket to plug in a second lamp. Both these models came out after the war and replaced the Vacublitz of 1939.

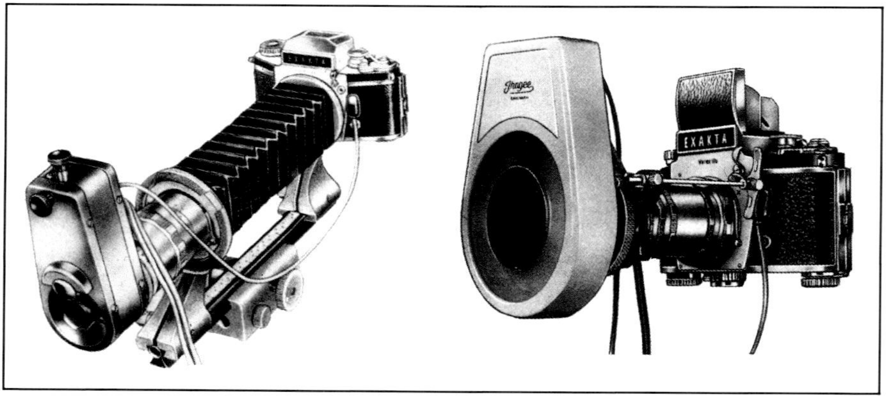

Ringflash for use in macrophotography. They had their own firing device and could be powered with any type of standard generator supplying up to 250 W/seconds at 500 volts. They were delivered with a lead but with no connecting plug (which depended on the power source).
Above: RB1 Model of about 1960, mounted on a Zeiss 135mm lens on the focusing bellows. It was equipped with a pilot lamp for focusing and framing (6v, 15w.). The small diameter of this ring-shaped tube only allowed the use of 100 to 135mm lenses giving an approximate magnification in the region of 0.5x. The end of the tube was threaded (M24 x 0.5) which made it possible to fit a filter This flash was generally used with the Ihagee Kolpofot.
Below: RB2 Model of about 1965, mounted on a Zeiss 50mm lens on the extension tubes. The diameter of this flash tube allowed the use of 50 to 80mm lenses giving a ratio 1:1 for 50 mm and 4:1 for 80 mm lenses. It also allowed the taking of stereoscopic pictures at short distances. A filter holder could be fitted to the front of the flash which was threaded (58 x 0.75mm).

Ihagee Universal Unit (Vielzweck)

This unit comprised the following components: bellows device, focusing rack, swing angle attachment (camera cradle with rotating head), baseboard and column, and lighting support. All the items were sold separately. They could be used in numerous applications such as macrophotography, microphotography, reproduction of documents, etc.

1. Focusing rack and swing angle attachment.

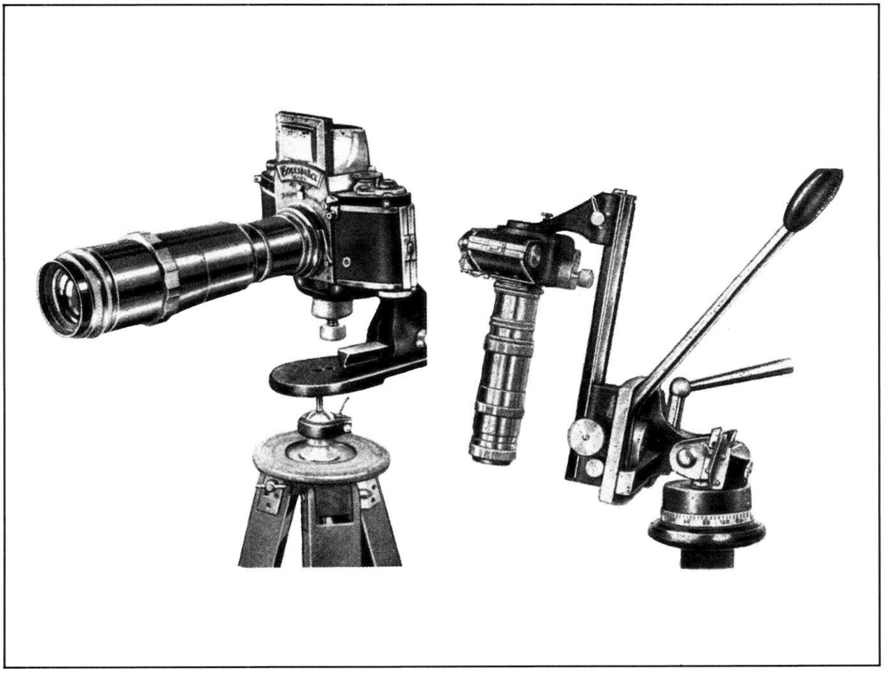

Left: Swing angle attachment mounted on tripod. Right: Focusing rack and swing angle attachment mounted on tripod.

These were used in conjunction with a set of extension tubes and a tripod. This arrangement allowed macrophotography with accurate focusing. By simple rotation the Exakta Varex could be placed vertically or horizontally, thanks to the swing angle attachment.

2. Focusing rack and bellows device.

This outfit was used for picture taking at very short distances and with high magnification. The bellows extension ranged from 35 to 200mm. All the lenses of the Exakta range could be fitted to the front plate. A special lens with a collapsible mount

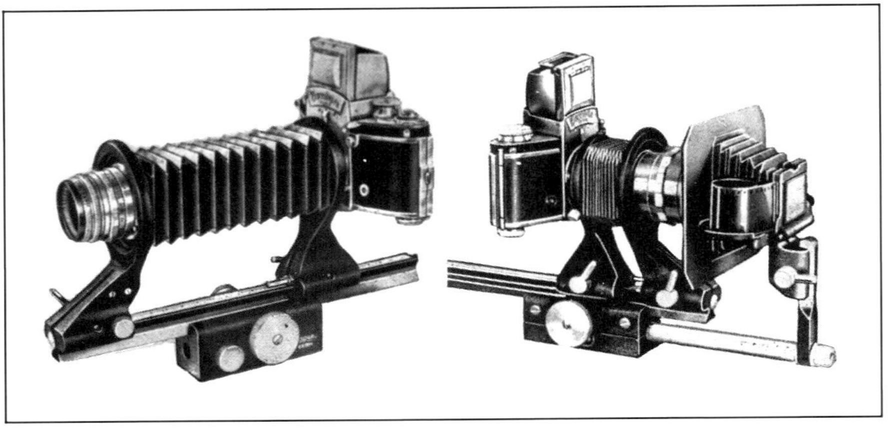

Top: Bellows device and focusing rack. Bottom: Bellows and focusing rack with negative copying device.

(50mm f/2.8 Zeiss Jena T) was used for a reproduction ratio of 1:1. A device for the reproduction of transparencies and negatives could be fitted to the focusing rack. The exposure frame held either film strips or single mounted slides.

3. Baseboard and column with bellows and focusing rack.

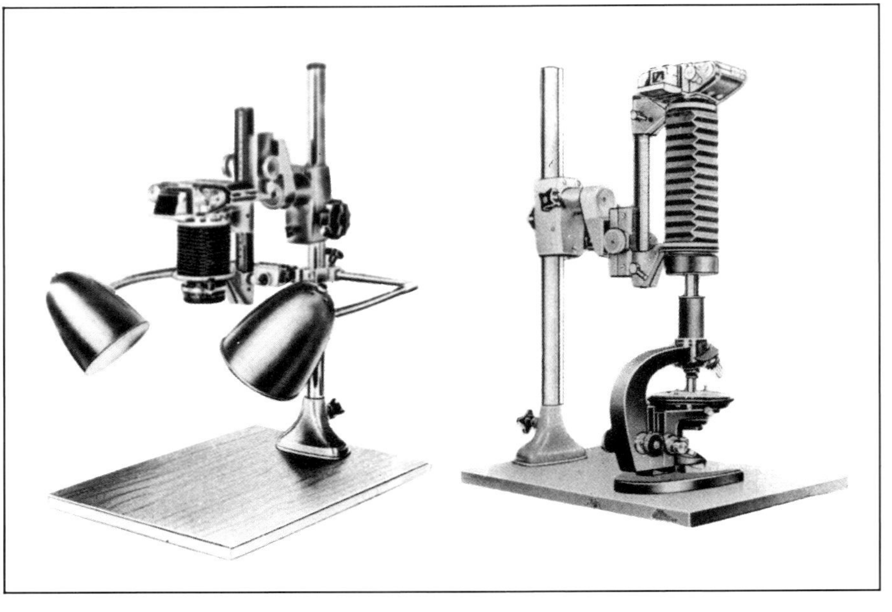

Left: Arrangement for copying. Right: Arrangement for microphotography.

This assembly, together with the lighting unit, could be used for the reproduction of documents. The baseboard was wood, 34x50cm, and the column carried a supporting bracket with a hand-wheel for adjusting its position. The lighting unit consisted of two lamps with reflectors mounted on a flexible arm. The set-up was also used for microphotography, avoiding the inflexible link with the microscope given by the Ihagee microscope attachment.

Other applications, not illustrated here, could be covered by combining the various components. The universal unit can be found in two versions. The early ones were crackle black painted and the stand column had a cylindrical base. The second version (from 1960 onwards) was hammered blue painted and the stand column had a splayed base, as in the illustrations.

Ihagee Kolpofot

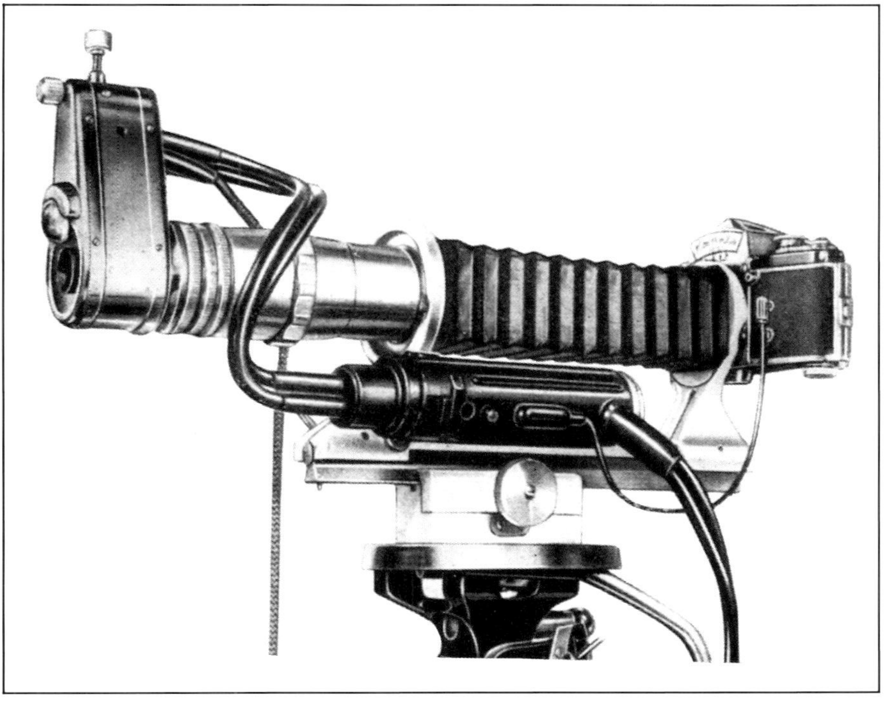

Kolpofot with ring flash, 135mm Zeiss lens and bellows.

The Kolpofot was used for medical macrophotography, of either the surface or the cavities of the human body. It included the following components: bellows, focusing rack, 135mm f/4 special Zeiss lens with a stop-down range to f/45, RB1 ring flash, necessary cables for connection to the power source, adjustable pilot lamp and necessary supply. The whole unit could be mounted on a special pillar equipped with a ball joint and a rack.

Stereoscopic Devices

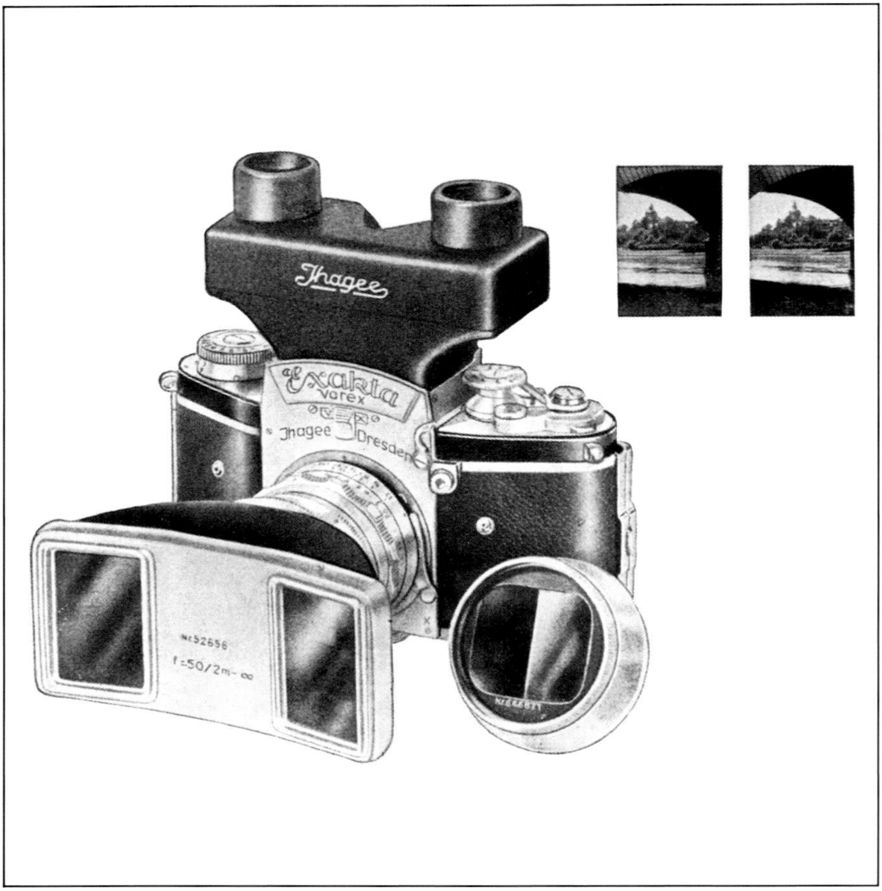

Stereo device, 1st version.

The stereo device for the Exakta consisted of a prism unit to be mounted on the lens, giving a pair of pictures 15x22mm, and a stereoscopic viewfinder, using the Varex viewing optics. The viewfinder could be used as a stereo viewing apparatus for examining the slides. There were two models of the prism:-

- Large base: 65mm for picture taking from 2m to infinity.
- Narrow base: 12mm for picture taking from 0.15m to 2m.

The device featured an adjustable mount with a 49 x 0.75mm thread. There were also reduction collars for the lenses of 40.5 x 0.5 and 35.5 x 0.5 threads. The system could only be used with 50mm lenses.

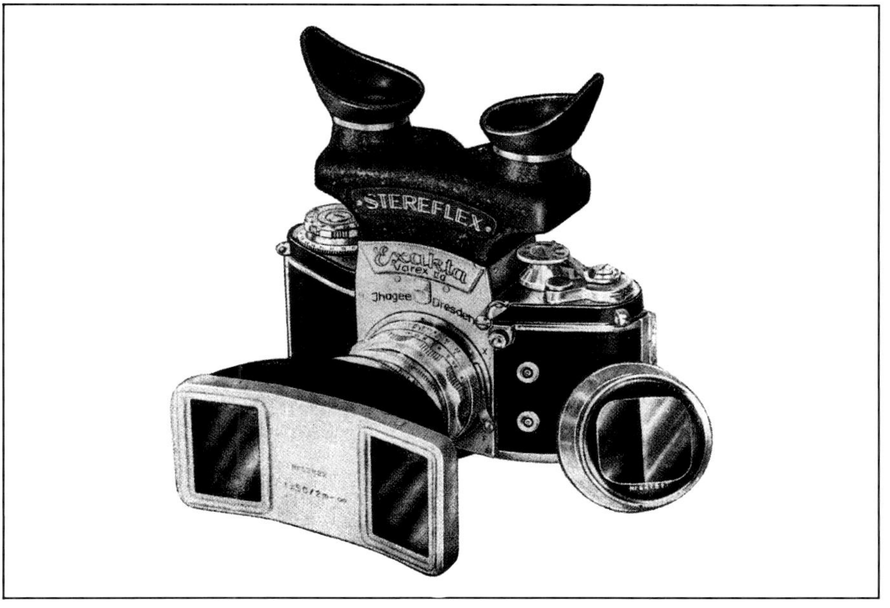

Stereo device, 2nd Version, 1955 onwards. In a 1965 advertisement the large base prism is marked "Aus Jena".

Chapter 10
The Exakta 66, Its Lenses and Accessories

EXAKTA 66 1938 ★★★★★

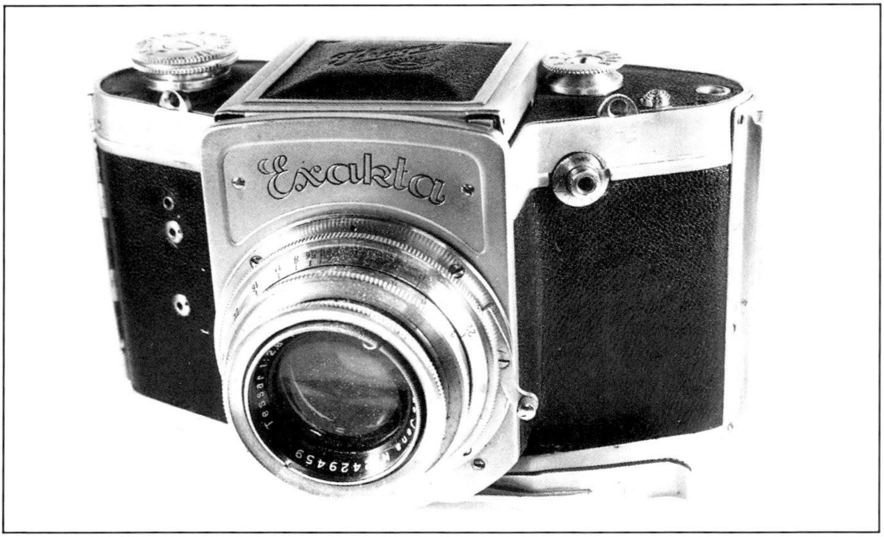

Exakta 66 No.553850, with 80mm f/2.8 Zeiss Tessar No.2429459.

It seems that Ihagee reserved the serial numbers from 550000 to 555000 for this model. The numbers we have discovered, and those known by other collectors or associations, fall between 553504 and 554676.

The production of this new 6x6cm single-lens reflex camera met with all the requirements of professionals and amateurs of the time. Ihagee used a similar specification to that of the Exakta B and Kine Exakta to design this new model, which was later to inspire others such as the Praktisix, Pentacon Six and, more recently, the Pentax 6x7.

By the end of 1938, from a technical point of view, the new Exakta 6x6 was way ahead of its competitors, such as the Reflex Korelle, Primarflex and Noviflex. Unfortunately 1938 was not a very good year to start and the model was on the market for only a short time.

One can recognize this third generation Exakta at a glance. The heavy aspect and impeccable matt chrome finish signal the Exakta 66 as a very strongly built camera of excellent quality. The camera body was a single die-casting of a rounded trapezoid shape. It measured 160x100x100mm and weighed 1300g. It had interchangeable lenses equipped with a fast locking bayonet.

The focal plane shutter had cloth blinds and horizontal motion similar to the Exakta

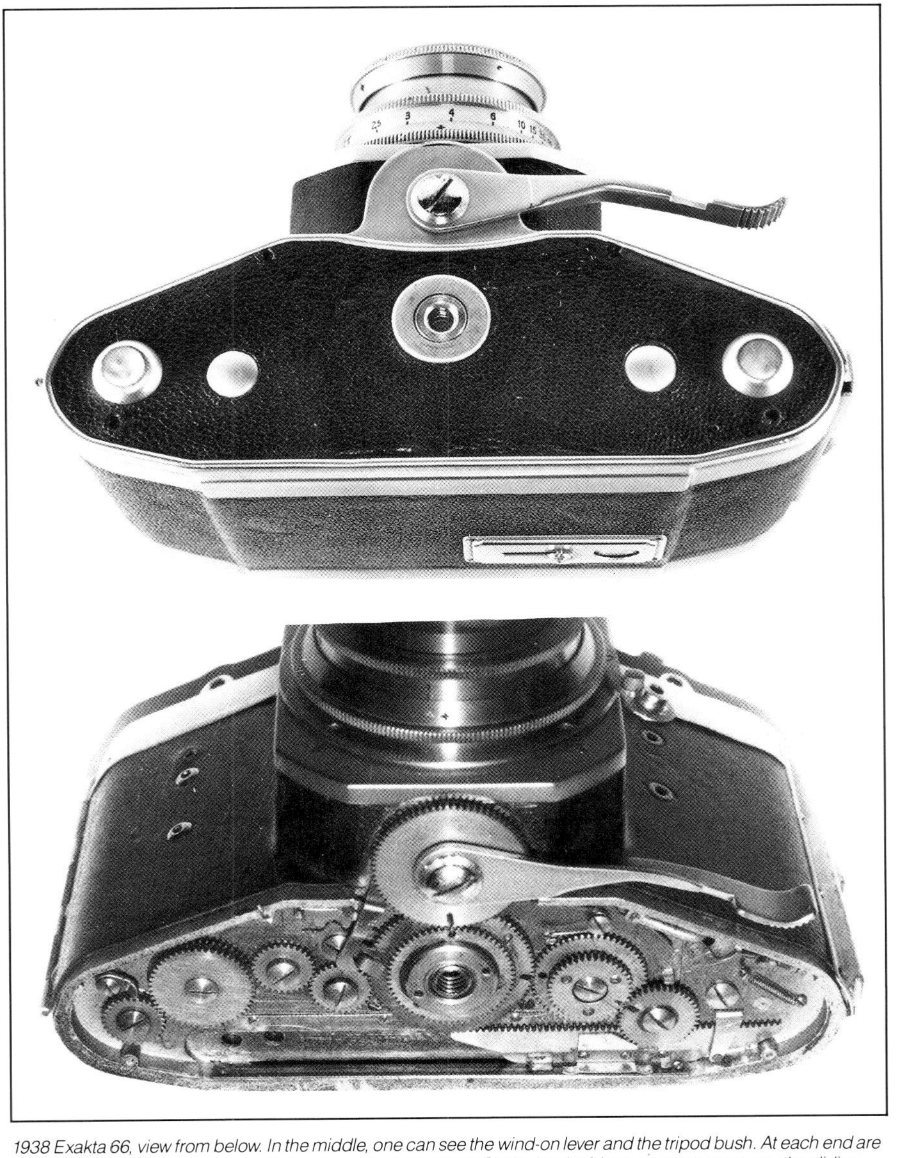

1938 Exakta 66, view from below. In the middle, one can see the wind-on lever and the tripod bush. At each end are the two feet for picture taking on a flat surface without a stand. On the back of the camera one can see the sliding cover over the red window. In the lower picture the base plate has been removed to show the wind-on and film transport mechanisms.

B. The speed range was from 12 seconds to 1/1000 plus B and Z, with delayed speeds from 6 seconds to 1/1000. The Vacublitz socket for flash bulbs was the one being used at the time by Ihagee. It had a two-pin socket with a third socket above for securing the flash gun. There was a double safety device on the shutter release that operated when the viewfinder hood was locked or when the wind-on lever was set in the neutral position. When this lever was rotated from left to right, the shutter was cocked, the film wound on, the exposure counter advanced by one frame and the mirror reset.

The camera used 120 size film spools, allowing 12 pictures of 6x6cm. A very clever device allowed the film to be positioned without any overlap, as was so often the case with this type of spool. Because of a shift problem with pictures and spaces, manufacturers had to introduce an equalisation system. In the case of the Exakta, when positioning the spool, one had to slide the paper into a clip located at the bottom left of the film gate. When the lever was advanced, this clip locked both the film and the paper against the guide rail and drove it towards the take-up spool. In order to avoid tearing the film and the paper, the film drive was controlled during motion by a friction system. When the wind-on lever was at its full stroke on the right, the shutter was cocked and the exposure counter moved one frame forward, but the shutter release remained locked. The lever then had to be brought back to the left. The shutter release was then freed and the holding clip moved backwards at the same time as the lever, thus being ready for the next frame.

After the 12th exposure the lever had to be moved until it was set on letter F (end of film) and then once more in order to roll-up the whole spool. At the end of each roll the shutter was locked. It was therefore necessary to release the mechanism by moving the small knob located in front of the fast speeds dial. All these operations take longer to describe than to perform.

The collapsible hooded viewfinder incorporated a shutter release locking pin which

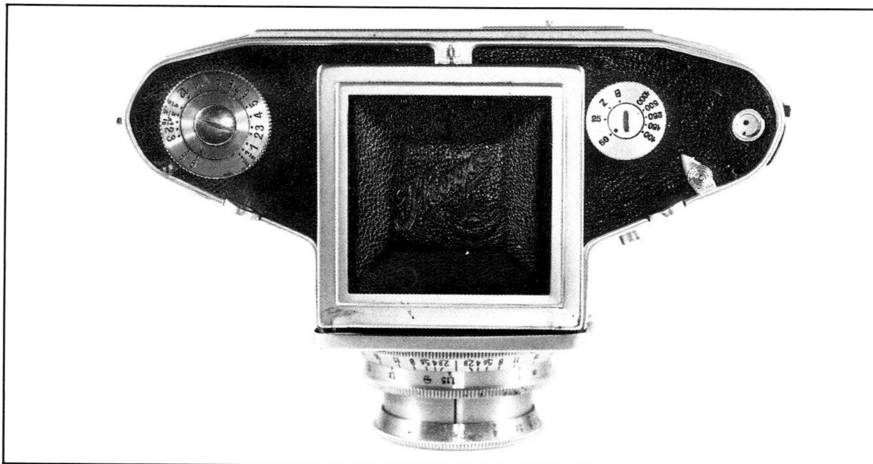

1938 Exakta 66, top view with viewing hood closed. On the left one can see the exposure counter window, the button for releasing the mechanism at the end of the spool, and the fast speeds dial with B and Z. On the right is the slow- and delayed-speeds dial.

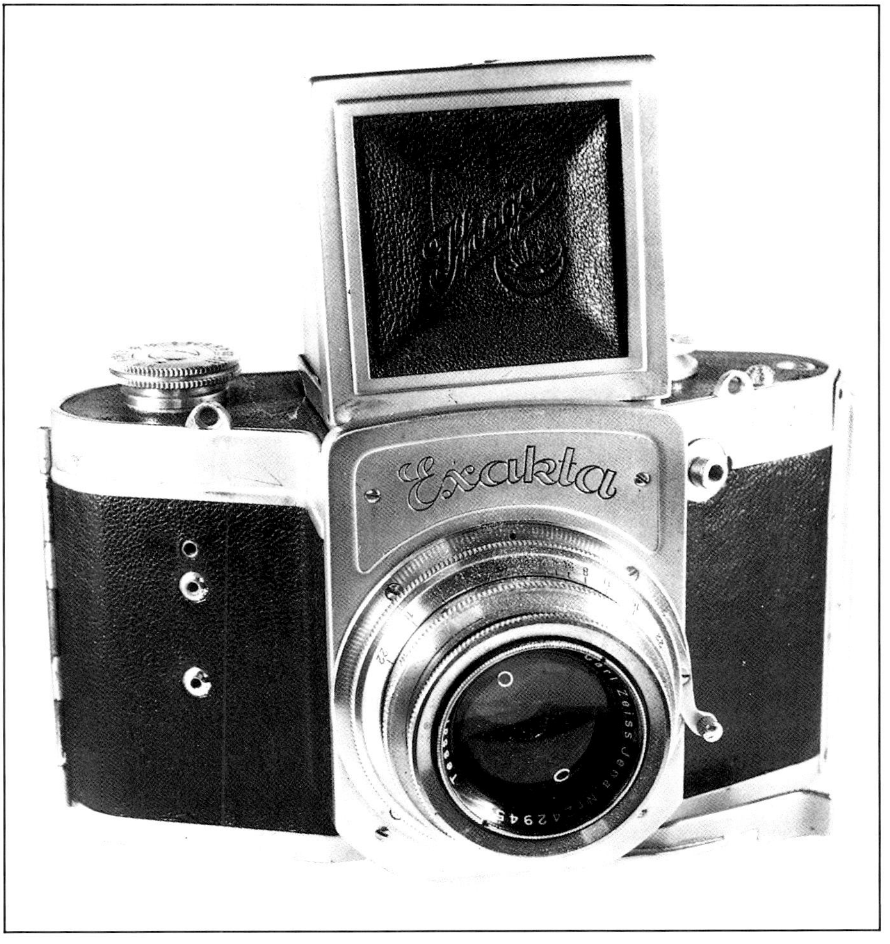

1938 Exakta 66, Viewing hood set on open position. The shoulder strap eyelets can be seen on each side. The wind-on lever is located at the bottom.

operated when it was closed. This pin was located on the upper panel (left side), the other panels numbered 1, 2 and 3 had to be folded back in that order. A detachable magnifier was provided for fine focusing. The camera was available with either a plain ground glass screen with guidelines for 4x6 horizontal format, or cross-ruled ground glass. The central part of the upper panel can be folded back to turn the hood into a frame viewfinder.

As the camera was only available for a very short period there were not many accessories. The 1939 Ihagee catalogue mentioned only two leather cases, one for the camera body equipped with its standard lens and one for the camera body equipped with a "Night" lens. The Vacublitz flash could fitted to the 6x6 camera of 1938.

EXAKTA 66 1950 ★★★★★

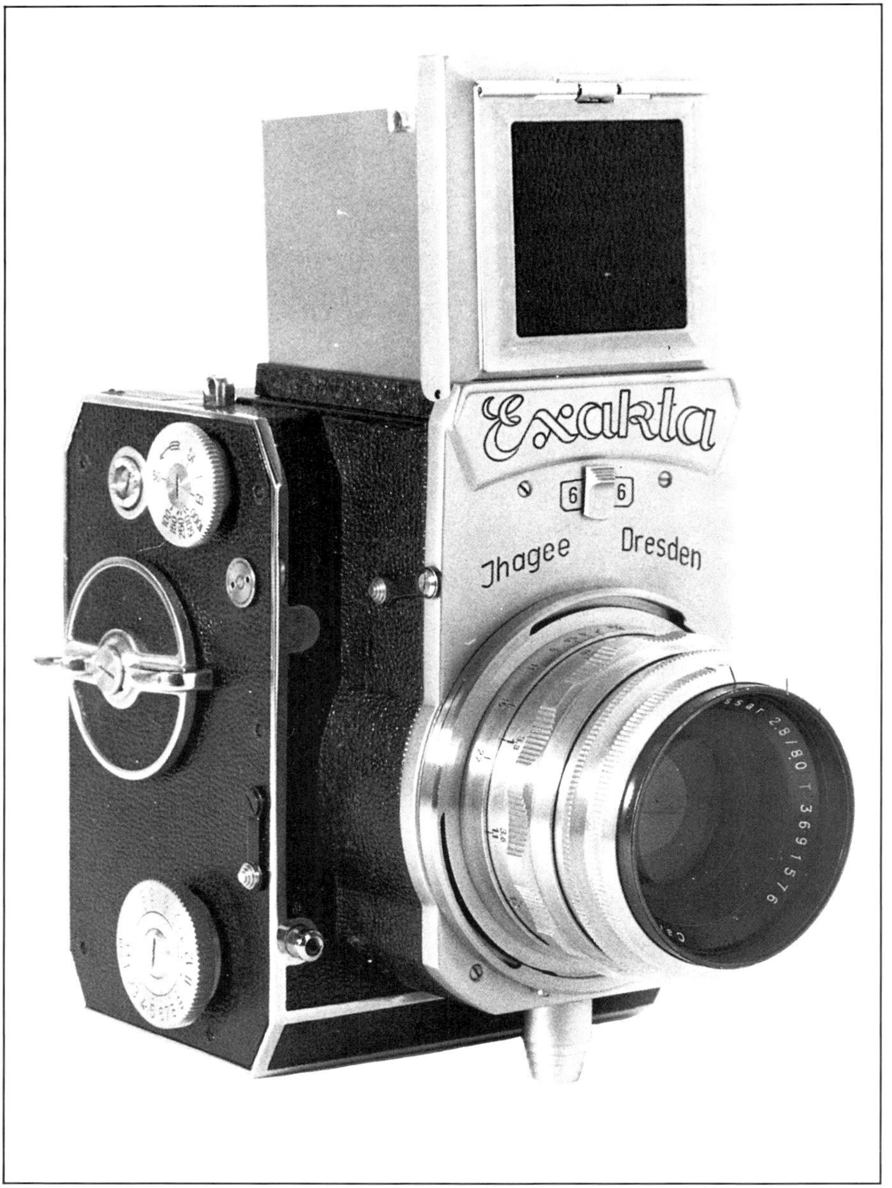

Exakta 66, No.601760, with 80mm f/2.8 Carl Zeiss Jene lens No.3691576.

Approximate range of serial numbers: 600000 to 602700.

This model, which came out in 1950, was the second 6x6cm reflex camera to be produced by Ihagee. It was completely different from the 1938 Exakta 66 and was one of the most beautiful Exakta cameras. Only one model type was made and it is much sought after by collectors.

The camera had a modular design. The lens, viewfinder and viewing optics were interchangeable. The back of the camera, which held the film, could be removed completely. Both the back and the body were of light alloy castings. The size without lens and with the viewfinder hood closed was 110x110x140mm. The camera weighed 1300g. The actual size of the picture area was 58.5x56.5mm. There was no red window.

On the right was the shutter and film drive mechanism which was operated with a key similar to those on 8mm cine cameras. This key cocked the shutter, and advanced the film and the exposure counter. Also on the left was the unlocking lever for the viewfinder hood, the viewfinder and its safety catch.

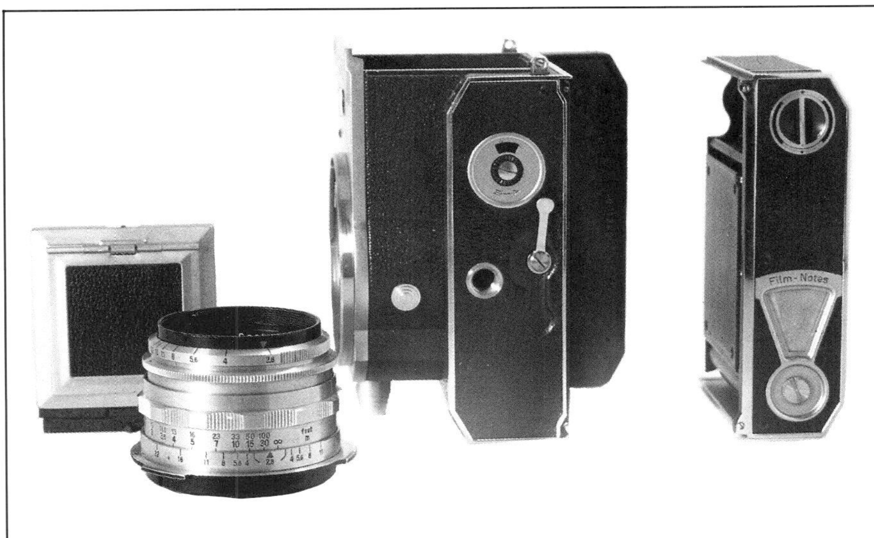

From left to right: the hooded viewfinder, the 80mm lens, the body of the camera and its back. Please note on this latter the window "Film-Notes".

On the upper part were the viewfinder and the two eyelets for the shoulder straps. On the left of the camera body, in the middle, was the locking lever for the back, a tripod bush and the synchro flash controller. The lens was fitted to the front plate, where "Exakta" and "Ihagee Dresden" were engraved on the matt chrome. Between the two inscriptions was the viewfinder unlocking catch with the number "66" engraved either side. On the bottom was a cylindrical foot which enabled the camera to stand level on a table. There was a second tripod socket in the base.

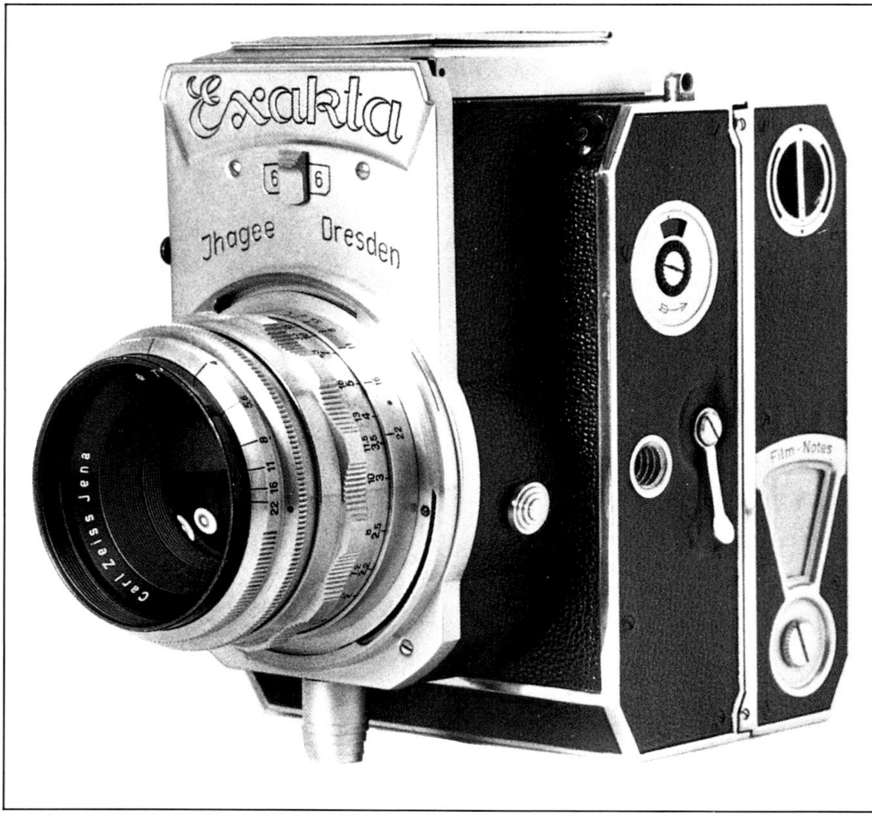

Exakta 66, left side.

At the back, instead of a red window for exposure control, was a sensor connected to a white index behind a window. Three positions were possible:

1 Empty: the index is not visible.
2 The film is positioned but the protecting paper is in contact only with the sensor. The index can be seen on the left inside the window.
3 Once the spool is advanced, the sensor presses on to the film and the index can be seen in the middle of the window. The first frame is then positioned and the counter must be brought back to "1".

On the left at the back was a window similar to a magical slate called "Film-Notes". Although the back was removeable it was not interchangeable, but it did make film loading easier.

The key was turned after each exposure. This set the shutter, lowered the mirror, advanced the film and the exposure counter. When frame 12 was reached the counter stopped at position "F" and the system was locked. Resetting to zero enabled the film

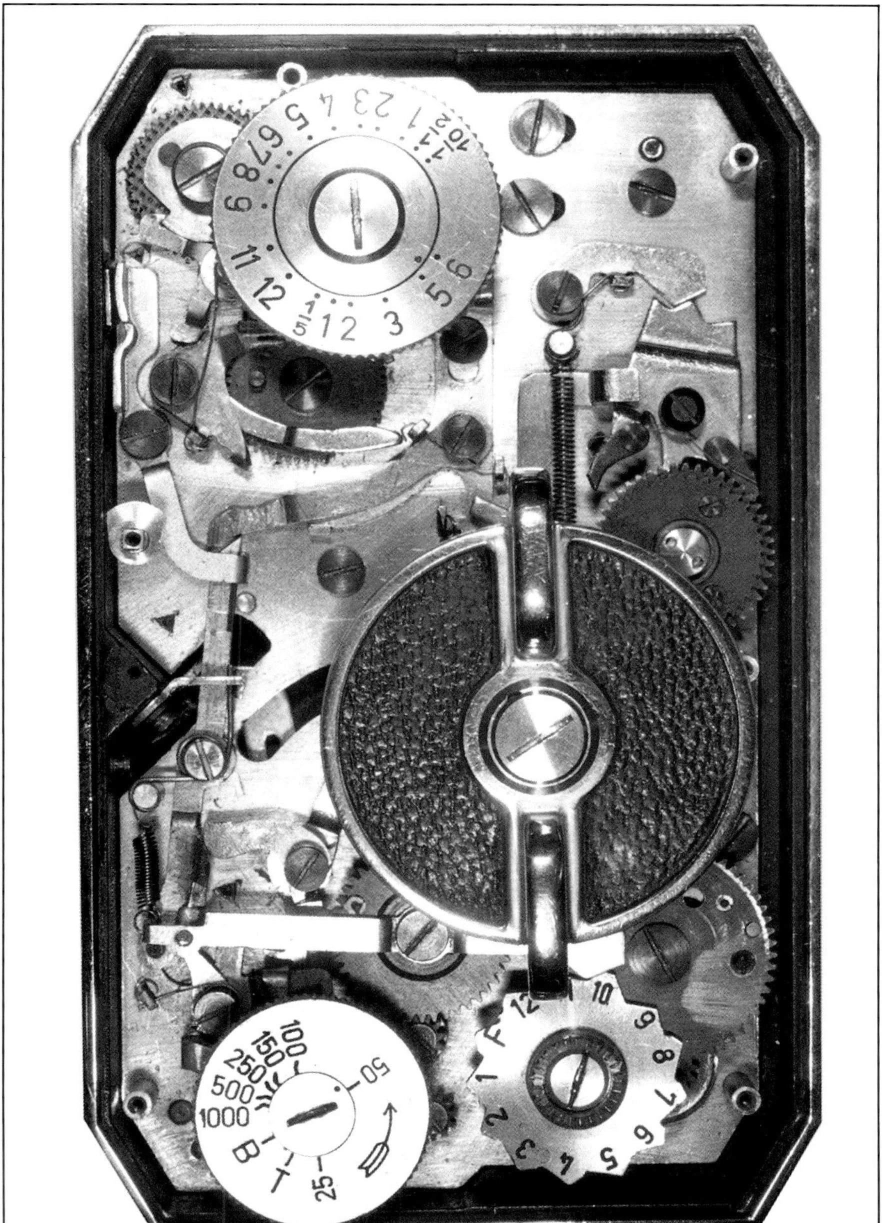

Exakta 66, right-hand side with cover removed. One can see the mechanism, the speed dials, the exposure counter and the wind-on key.

to be finally wound off for removal from the camera.

The shutter was a vertically running fabric blind type, with motion from top to bottom. It was operated by two independent knobs, one for fast speeds, B and T, and the other for slow speeds and delayed action. The speed ranges were:-

- Upper dial, 1/1000, 1/500, 1/250, 1/150, 1/100, 1/50, 1/25, plus B and T, with delayed action available.
- Lower dial, 1/10, 1/2, 1, 2, 3, 4, 5, 6, 7, 8, 9, 11 and 12 seconds, with 1/5, 1, 2, 3, 5 and 6 seconds for delayed slow speeds.

The shutter was synchronised for any type of flash through a coaxial socket located on the top of the body. The synchronisation contact delay could be adjusted from 0 to 25 milliseconds, with the value displayed through a window. This device looked like an exposure counter, but some writers have thought it was a counter for a 24x36mm magazine.

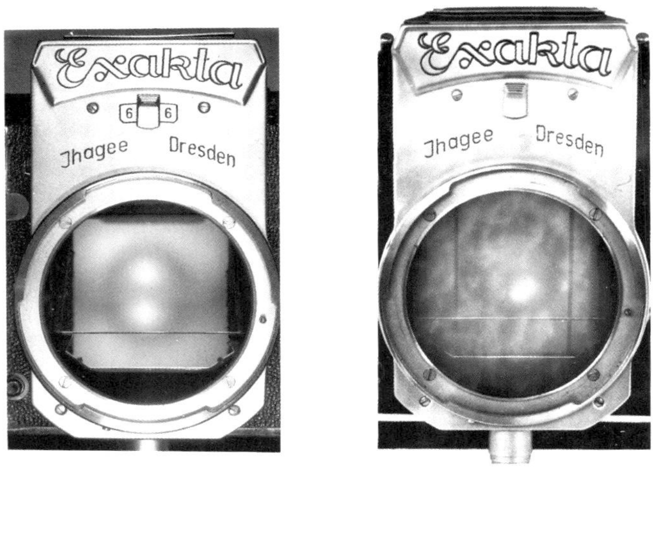

Left: Front of Exakta 66 showing large diameter bayonet with the two-component mirror in the middle; set here in the viewing position.
Right: Front plate of the rarer 1st Version with no "66" engrtaved each side of the viewfinder locking buttons.

At the time the mirror was of an uncommon design because it was made in two parts. The larger, upper component folded back against the ground glass screen. The lower component folded into the base of the viewing chamber. This device allowed the lens rear components to protrude into the viewing chamber without affecting the mirror movements. Thus short focal length lenses were possible.

The bayonet was of large diameter (60mm). The lens was positioned when two red indices were aligned and it was rotated by 30°. The system could be locked with a catch located on the left of the body at lens level. An adapter for the 1939 6x6 bayonet lenses (51 mm diameter) was made available. The standard lens was the 80mm f/2.8 Tessar equipped with a manual preselection device. The lens bayonet could be dismounted (by unscrewing two screws) to show a smaller diameter bayonet which was that of the Exakta 6x6 of 1939.

The viewfinder, together with the viewing optics, was interchangeable. To our knowledge there was only one type and that was the collapsible hood. It had three chromed panels which were numbered 1, 2 and 3 to give the closing order. It also featured a chromed hood with a black leather inset which could be used as a frame finder. The only focusing screen known was of the standard ground glass type. This focusing screen was integral with the body and not with the viewfinder, as was the case with the Exakta Varex.

There were two versions of the 1950 Exakta 66. The second version is the one described so far and was the most common. The earlier version differed in the following respects:-

- No "66" engraved on the front plate.
- Shutter release and flash sockets located at top right.
- Different slow speed knob.
- No locking lever for ground glass.

LENSES AND ACCESSORIES FOR THE EXAKTA 66

As we noted previously, the two 6x6 types did not have the same lens mount. However, the "66" lenses of 1939 could be fitted to the 1950 models with an adapter ring.

The 80mm f/2.8 Tessar of 1950 in our possession is equipped with a small diameter bayonet (1939 type) and the adapter is fixed. It can be detached by unscrewing two screws. However, we will give two separate lists for the 1939 and 1950 lenses.

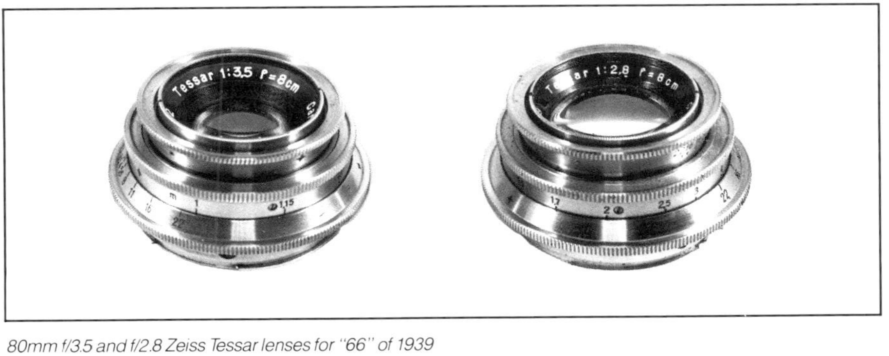

80mm f/3.5 and f/2.8 Zeiss Tessar lenses for "66" of 1939

"66" Lenses of 1939

		Focal length (cm)	*Max. Aperture f/*
	Berthiot	6.5	5.7
Tessar	Zeiss	6.5	6.3
Canter	T.T.K.	7.5	3.5
	Berthiot	7.7	3.5
Xenar	Schneider	8	2.8
Xenar	Schneider	8	3.5
Tessar	Zeiss	8	2.8
Tessar	Zeiss	8	3.5
Exaktar	Ihagee	8.5	3.5
Primotar	Meyer	8.5	3.5
	Berthiot	9	2.8
Primoplan	Meyer	10	1.9
Biotar	Zeiss	10	2
Makro-Plasmat	Meyer	10.5	2.7
Primotar	Meyer	13.5	3.5
Triotar	Meyer	13.5	4
Tele	Berthiot	15	5.5
Primotar	Meyer	18	3.5
Tele-Megor	Meyer	18	3.5
Tele-Megor	Meyer	18	5.5
Tele-Tessar	Zeiss	18	6.3
Tele-Xenar	Zeiss	24	4.5
Tele-Tessar	Zeiss	25	6.3
Tele-Megor	Meyer	30	5.5
Tele-Xenar	Zeiss	30	5.5
Tele-Xenar	Zeiss	36	5.5

Some of these lenses were illustrated in advertisements of the time, but to our knowledge they never reached the market. (e.g. Berthiot).

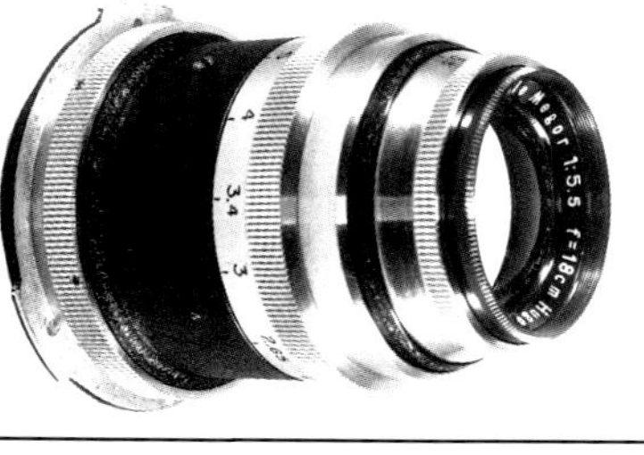

180mm f/5.5 Meyer Tele Megor for "66" mount of 1950.

"66" Lenses from 1950.

Lens	*Year Intro.*	*Focal length*	*Max. f/*
Novoflex			
Noflexar	1955	240	5.6
Noflexar	1955	500	5.6
Makro Kilar	1956	90	2.8
Pan tele			
Kilar	1956	300	4
Kilfitt			
Tele			
Kilar	1952	300	5.6
Sport Fern			
Kilar	1956	400	4
Fern Kilar	1952	400	5.6
Fern Kilar	1953	600	5.6
Zeiss			
Tessar	1950	80	2.8
Meyer			
Tele			
Magor	1950	180	5.5
Primotar	1950	180	3.5

Notes:
1. The Novoflex lenses for 6x6 format have been manufactured for many years but the adapter ring for the Exakta has not been illustrated in the catalogue since 1960. A macro bellows made by Novoflex for the 6x6 Exakta was also available.

2. This list is not exhaustive. Unfortunately, as the 6x6 of 1950 was mainly distributed in the USA, we do not have available full information on range of accessories.

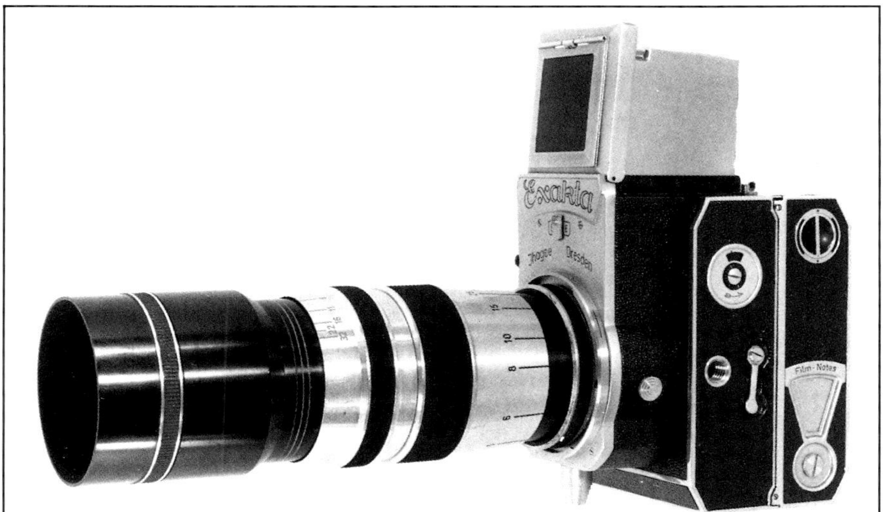

300mm f/5.6 Kilfitt Tele Kilar mounted on the Exakta 66 of 1950.

BIBLIOGRAPHY

Abel, Charles and Tyding, Kenneth; The Modern Exakta Guide and Reference Book, New York, 1951-1956.

Allinson, K.L.; 35mm Photography with an Exakta, New-York, 1952.

Allinson, K.L.; 35mm Exakta Handbook, London, 1956.

Allinson, K.L.; Exa Photography, Techniques and Practice, 1965.

Berkowitz, Georges J.; A Complete Guide to the Exakta V, New York, 1951.

Brunke, H.M.; My Beloved Exakta, New York, 1954.

Deschin, Jacob; Exakta Photography, 1959.

Döring, Wolf H.; Exakta 6x6 Buch, Halle, Saale, 1941.

Emanual, W.D.; Exakta Guide, 1st Edition, London, 1943.

Emanuel, W.D.; Exakta 35mm Guide, 1st Edition, 1956, 12th Edition, London, 1979.

Isert, Gerhart; English translations by Philip C. Smethurst, Exakta Handbook and Practical Photography with the Kine Exakta, both books pub. in 1930's.

Rober, Norlin; The Ihagee 35mm Exaktas and Exas, USA, 1977.

Tyding, Kenneth; Advanced Exakta and Exa Guide, 1960.

Wurst, Werner; Exakta Kleinbild-Fotografie, Halle, Saale, 1952-74, English edition: Exakta Manual, Fountain Press, 1960.

Wurst, Werner; Foto Exkursionen mit der Exa, Halle, Saale, 1954?, English Edition by Fountain Press.

In about 1950 the Exakta Camera Company, New York, published a magazine called "Exakta Magazine". This magazine then appeared periodically until publication ceased in the 1960's.

Other Titles Available from Hove Books

HOVE LEICA BOOKS

LEICA LENS COMPENDIUM
LEICA THE FIRST 70 YEARS
LEICA THE FIRST 60 YEARS
LEICA R COMPENDIUM
LEICA M COMPENDIUM
LEICA COLLECTORS GUIDE
MY LIFE WITH LEICA – WALTER BENSER
LEICA R8
LEICA R7
LEICA R6
LEICA R5– R3
LEICA M6 – M1 *3rd Ed*
LEICA M6 TTL
LEICA DARKROOM PRACTICE
LEICA LEN PRACTICE *2nd Ed*

HOVE LEICA POCKET BOOKS

LEICA POCKET BOOK *6th Ed*
LEICA ACCESSORY GUIDE *2nd Ed*
LEICA INTERNATIONAL PRICE GUIDE *8th Ed*

HOVE COLLECTORS BOOKS

HASSELBLAD COMPENDIUM
JAPANESE 35mm SLR CAMERAS
CLASSIC CAMERAS 1945–85
NIKON COMPENDIUM 2
NIKON RANGEFINDER CAMERAS
CANON COMPENDIUM
CANON RANGEFINDER CAMERAS 1933-68
ZEISS CAMERA COMPENDIUM 1940-72
ZEISS IKON CAMERAS 1926-39
ZEISS CONTAX REPAIR MANUAL
SPYCAMERA - THE MINOX STORY *2nd Ed*
KODAK CAMERAS FIRST 100 YEARS
EXAKTA CAMERAS 1933-78
ASAHI PENTAX REFLEX CAMERAS 1952-89
HOVE INTERNATIONAL BLUE BOOK
CINE CAMERAS

HOVE LEICA INSTRUCTION BOOKS etc

LEICA GENERAL CATALOGUE 1931
LEICA GENERAL CATALOGUE 1933
LEICA GENERAL CATALOGUE 1936
LEICA GENERAL CATALOGUE 1955/8
LEICA GENERAL CATALOGUE 1961
LEICA GENERAL CATALOGUE 1975
LEICA INSTRUCTIONS FOR MODELS 111a, 250 etc.
LEICA INSTRUCTIONS FOR MODELS 11 & 111c, f & g
LEICA INSTRUCTIONS FOR MODELS M1, 2, 3, & 4
LEICA INSTRUCTIONS FOR MODELS M5, CL, Leicaflex
LEICA INSTRUCTIONS FOR REPRODUCTION DEVICES

Hove Books Ltd.
30 The Industrial Estate, Small Dole. West Sussex. BN5 9XR. UK.
Tel: +44-(0) 1273-495757
Fax: +44-(0) 1273-494992
SEE OUR WEB SITE
www.hovebooks.com